METHODS
OF
LITERACY RESEARCH

THE METHODOLOGY CHAPTERS FROM THE

HANDBOOK
OF
READING
RESEARCH
VOLUME III

METHODS
OF
LITERACY RESEARCH

THE METHODOLOGY CHAPTERS FROM THE

HANDBOOK
OF
READING
RESEARCH
VOLUME III

Edited by

Michael L. Kamil
Stanford University

Peter B. Mosenthal
Syracuse University

P. David Pearson
Michigan State University

Rebecca Barr
National-Louis University

 LAWRENCE ERLBAUM ASSOCIATES, PUBLISHERS
2002   Mahwah, New Jersey   London

Lawrence Erlbaum Associates, Inc., Publishers
10 Industrial Avenue
Mahwah, New Jersey 07430-2262

Cover design by Kathryn Houghtaling Lacey

Library of Congress Cataloging-in-Publication Data

Methods of literacy research: the methodology chapters from the
handbook of reading research / [edited by] Michael L. Kamil ... [et al.].
        p. cm.
    Includes bibliographical references and index.
    ISBN 0-8058-3807-4 (paper)
    1. Reading. 2. Reading—Research—Methodology. I. Kamil, Michael, L.
LB1050.H278 2000
428.4′072—dc20   96-10470
                                                         CIP

Books published by Lawrence Erlbaum Associates are printed
on acid-free paper, and their bindings are chosen for strength
and durability

Printed in the United States of America
10 9 8 7 6 5 4 3 2 1

Contents

Preface

In theory there is nothing to hinder our following what we are taught; but in life there are many things to draw us aside.

Epictetus, Discourses, Chap. xxvi.

In this volume, 10 reviews of significant reading research methodologies are reprinted from *Volume III* of the *Handbook of Reading Research*. Methodology represents the organized procedures that researchers use to collect, analyze, and interpret phenomena under study. Appropriate methodology is necessary to ensure that the obtained evidence can be used to generate warranted conclusions. The centrality of methodology to reading research endeavors would suggest that this would be a crucial area of scholarship. It is, as Epictetus suggested, one way of avoiding those things that might "draw us aside."

An electronic search of the ERIC database, yields a total of 48,888 journal articles on the subjects of reading, writing, or literacy (excluding computer literacy and science literacy). Of these, 12,877 are research articles and of these, 986, or about 7.5%, are about research methodology. This appears to be a small proportion of the total, because rigorous methodology is what guarantees the trustworthiness of our research. Given that this figure includes all of the studies since the inception of the database in 1966, the number seems small.

What accounts for the lack of research on methodology? One important aspect of the explanation lies in the fact that reading researchers have adopted methodologies from other disciplines. Methods have been imported from psychology, anthropology, sociology, and even from neurology and hermeneutics. Although these methods have been adapted to the specific needs of reading researchers, they have typically not been invented by reading researchers. At times it has appeared that the methodology was less important than the results were to reading researchers. In a field where the results are often translated directly into practice, this should not be surprising.

In *Volume I* of the *Handbook of Reading Research* (1984), 3 of the 25 reviews deal specifically with methodology. Included were chapters on the Design and Analysis of Experiments, Ethnographic Approaches to Reading Research, and Directions in the Sociolinguistic Study of Reading. These represented both the established and the emergent methodological paradigms.

In *Volume II* (1991), there are no reviews that deal specifically with methodology. Rather, the new content of reading research dominated the period between *Volumes I* and *II*, and methodology took a less prominent position. In the preface to *Volume III*, the editors elaborated these differences among the volumes:

In 1893, Frederick Jackson Turner completed his momentous work, *The Significance of the Frontier in American History*. In this work, he re-directed historians' attention away from the genealogy-ridden chronicles of the Atlantic seaboard and refocused their attention on men and women taming the new western frontier. Coupled with Horace Greeley's dictum of "Go West, young man," Turner sparked imagination in what he called the "the hither edge of free land."

This "hither edge" represented what Daniel Boorstin (Boorstin & Boorstin, 1987) has called a "verge," i.e., a "place of encounter between something and something else" (p. xv). Notes Boorstin, America's history has been much more than just the verge between Turner's east and west; rather, it has been a broad succession of verges: America (has always been) a land of verges—all sorts of verges, between kinds of landscape or seascape, between stages of civilization, between ways of thought and ways of life. During our first centuries we experienced more different kinds of verges, and more extensive and more vivid verges, than any other great modern nation. The long Atlantic coast, where early colonial settlements flourished was, of course, a verge between the advanced European civilization and the stone-age culture of the American Indians, between people and wilderness . .

As cities became sprinkled around the continent, each was a new verge between the ways of the city and those of the countryside. As immigrants poured in from Ireland, Germany, and Italy, from Africa and Asia, each group created new verges between their imported ways and the imported ways of their neighbors and the new-grown ways of the New World. Each immigrant himself lived the verge encounter between another nation's ways of thinking, feeling, speaking, and living and the American ways. (xv–xvi)

It was Alexis de Tocqueville (Tocqueville , Bradley, Reeve, & Bowen, 1872) who noted that America's appreciation for verges was not shared by its European counterparts. At the time of his observations, the national pride of the English, French, German, and Italian was rooted in the grandeur of their homogeneous traditions rather than in the heterogeneous contradictions posed by proliferating verges. For these countries, national vitality was based on preserving the best of the rich past rather than pursuing the novelty of the unknown.

In contrast, America, with hardly any historical past (at least compared to that of Europe's), has always been different. Its vitality has largely been in its verges—in its new mixtures and confusions. Yet, as Alfred North Whitehead (1968) so shrewdly observed, it is one's ability to tolerate such confusion that enables progress to occur. In his words, "The progress of man (kind) depends largely on his ability to accept superficial paradoxes to see that what at first looks like a contradiction need not always remain one." (p. 354)

In designing the third *Handbook of Reading Research*, the editors were mindful of the need to preserve the continuity of the past. It is the obligation of any handbook editors to maintain the traditions of the discipline it represents. And so in this Handbook, as in *Volumes I* and *II*, the editors have included the classic topics of reading—from vocabulary and comprehension to reading instruction in the classroom. In addition, the editors instructed each contributor to provide a brief history that chronicles the legacies within each of the volume's many topics.

On the whole, however, this volume of the *Handbook of Reading Research* is not about tradition; rather, it is a book that explores the verges of reading research between the time chapters were written for *Volume II* in 1989 and the research conducted after this date. During this decade, the fortified borderlands and imperial reigns of reading research of old have given way to border crossings and new participants in the reading research of new. In this time, "we" (i.e., the common collective of reading researchers) have replaced the orthodoxy of research with the need to secure a voice for validating our own individual experiences and opinions. We, in essence, have established a new self-awareness of who we are as individuals, how we think, and what we value. Moreover, we have become more receptive to novelty and change. In this regard, we have come to embrace more the idea of "what is possible" than fixate on the idea of "what is." We have come to realize that not only can things be different, but we ourselves, as researchers and reading educators, can make that difference happen. In Northrop Frye's words (1964), we have come to realize that we "can enlarge upon the imagination" to raise new options that never before existed. In so doing, we must not only envision change, we must act to realize it.

And perhaps most importantly, we have become more community conscious. As part of creating new possibilities and exploring the unfamiliar, we have set about transforming not only ourselves but the very research community that sustains us; it is a community that, in becoming more inclusive, offers greater reassurance that difference and similarity both have their merits.

The Editors of *Volume III* identified two general themes in reading research that encompass important verges. Over the period of time between the publication of *Volumes I and II* and the publication of *Volume III*, the definition of reading was substantially broadened and the reading research agenda was dramatically expanded. The editors felt the time had come to address the plethora of new methodologies in explicit ways. As we explained in the Preface to *Volume III*:

> In this shift, the verge of reading has become one that stretches between viewing reading as the primary modality for learning to viewing reading as but one aspect of how teachers and students communicate in classrooms. To address this verge, the editors saw the need to expand reading–writing relations to include reading as part of a much broader dimension of communication including all four modalities of speaking, writing, listening, and reading....
>
> In assessing the advancements in educational research methodology writ large since *Volume II*, the editors found extensive development straddling the verge between quantitative and qualitative research. On the quantitative side, new advances have been made in such areas as hierarchical regression, path analysis, and item response theory. On the qualitative side, many new advances have been made in the areas of discourse analysis, single subject design, case study, and narrative analysis. In the editors' review of reading research over the past eight years, they saw the field incorporating many of the new advances in qualitative methodology; in contrast, they saw the field incorporating few such advances in its use of quantitative methodology. Rather than force the issue, the editors have included the qualitative aspect of the methodological verge in Volume III while leaving the quantitative perhaps for another time.

The editors have judged that the specific methodologies reviewed in *Volume III* have had great impact on reading research since the publication in 1991 of *Volume II*. However, this set of 10 reviews is not comprehensive. For example, we included no review of experimental research because we felt that there were insufficient new developments in this methodology. In addition, because we contracted for more reviews than we received (which is always the case in volumes such as this), not all methodologies we sought to include are represented. For example, we have no review of methodologies for working with large databases. We believe that work on the verge between quantitative and qualitative research will continue as reading researchers look for new ways to improve the methods by which they collect data.

There is one other significant "verge" between *Volumes I and II* of the Handbook, and *Volume III* and the present volume drawn from it. The editors and authors have all decided to forego royalties from these two volumes. Instead, the royalties will go to a fund administered by the National Reading Conference to support research in literacy

REFERENCES

Barr, R., Kamil, M., Mosenthal, P., & Pearson, P. D. (Eds.). (1991). *Handbook Of Reading Research, Volume II*. Mahwah, New Jersey: Lawrence Erlbaum Associates.

Boorstin, D. J. & Boorstin, R. F. (1987). *Hidden History (1 ed.)*. New York: Harper & Row.

Epictetus, & Dobbin, R. F. (1998). *Discourses*. Oxford: Clarendon Press; New York: Oxford University Press.

Frye, N. (1964). *The Educated Imagination*. Bloomington: Indiana University Press.

Kamil, M., Mosenthal, P., Pearson, P. D., & Barr, R. (Eds.). (2000). *Handbook Of Reading Research, Volume III*. Mahwah, New Jersey: Lawrence Erlbaum Associates.

Pearson, P. D, Barr, R., Kamil, M., & Mosenthal, P. (Eds.). (1984). *Handbook of Reading Research*. New York: Longman.

Tocqueville, A. D., Bradley, P., Reeve, H., & Bowen, F. (1945). *Democracy in America*. New York: A. A. Knopf. (Originally published 1872)

Turner, F. J. (1976). *The frontier in American history*. New York: Krieger. (Originally published in 1893.)

Whitehead, A. N. (1968). *Essays in science and philosophy*. New York: Greenwood Publishing.

CHAPTER 1

Making Sense of Classroom Worlds: Methodology in Teacher Research

James F. Baumann
University of Georgia

Ann M. Duffy-Hester
University of North Carolina at Greensboro

We had such a hard time finding methods that we thought were practical and feasible. To this day, I have not been able to master the use of a teaching journal. The idea of being videotaped gives me hives .... None of the traditional methods of collecting data were inviting to me .... I thought of what strategies I could fit into my existing classroom structure and what wouldn't drive me insane.

> —teacher researcher Debby Wood (cited in Baumann, Shockley-Bisplinghoff, & Allen, 1997, p. 138)

The 1990s have been marked by the resurgence and coming of age of teacher research (McFarland & Stansell, 1993). The recent renaissance of teacher research has resulted in the publication of numerous compendia (e.g., Bissex & Bullock, 1987; Donoahue, Van Tassell, & Patterson, 1996), full-length books (e.g., Allen, Michalove, & Shockley, 1993), and essays on classroom research (e.g., Cochran-Smith & Lytle, 1993; Goswami & Stillman, 1987). In spite of the proliferation of published teacher research studies, relatively little attention has been given to methodology processes and how they evolve and mature (Calkins, 1985). Perhaps it comes as no surprise that teacher researchers like Debby Wood and her colleagues sometimes struggle to find research methods appropriate to the unique demands of their classroom studies.

Many teacher researchers have successfully wrestled with vexing methodological issues, however, by selecting, adapting, or creating procedures that accommodate their specific research needs (Baumann et al., 1997). But what are the methodological solutions? What is the nature of methodologies teacher researchers have employed in classroom-based inquiries into literacy? We address these questions in this chapter by presenting a qualitative analysis of published literacy teacher-research studies. We begin with a discussion of theoretical issues, followed by a description of our research methods. Next, we present and discuss the categories and themes of teacher-research methodology our analysis uncovered. Finally, we address limitations and conclusions, and we consider whether teacher inquiry is a new research genre.

THEORETICAL ISSUES

Defining Teacher Research

Definitions of teacher research vary (Threat et al., 1994), but most include several common characteristics (Cochran-Smith & Lytle, 1993; Lytle & Cochran-Smith, 1994a, 1994b). Being present daily in the research and work environment, teacher researchers have an insider, or *emic*, perspective on the research process. This provides them a unique, situation-specific, participant role in an inquiry (Cochran-Smith & Lytle, 1993, p. 43). Theory and practice are interrelated and blurred in teacher research (Cochran-Smith & Lytle, 1993; Kincheloe, 1991; Lather, 1986). It is this mixture of reflection and practice, or *praxis*, in which a teacher-researcher's personal theory and theory within a field converge and affect one another. A cornerstone of teacher research is that it is *pragmatic* and *action oriented*; that is, it involves reflecting on one's teaching and practice, inquiring about it, exploring it, and then taking action to improve or alter it (Burton, 1991; Patterson & Shannon, 1993; Wells et al., 1994).

Teacher research must involve disciplined inquiry (Shulman, 1997), which means it is *intentional* and *systematic*. Teacher researchers consciously initiate and implement their inquiries and have a plan for data gathering and analysis. Teacher research embraces both inquiries steeped in conventional research traditions (e.g., qualitative, quantitative) that have well-articulated, accepted information collection and interpretation procedures and evolving research paradigms (e.g., personal narrative, formative experiment, memoir) that involve less traditional but nonetheless still regular, ordered modes of inquiry (Lytle & Cochran-Smith, 1994b). Drawing from these principles and extending Lytle and Cochran-Smith's (1994b, p. 1154) definition of teacher research, we conceive of teacher research as "reflection and action through systematic, intentional inquiry about classroom life" (Baumann et al., 1997, p. 125).

Methods Versus Methodology

In our exploration of teacher research, we distinguish between method and methodology. According to Denzin and Lincoln (1994, p. 99), epistemology involves how a researcher comes to know about the world; ontology involves a researcher's beliefs about the nature of reality; and methodology involves the means by which a researcher gains knowledge about the world. Consequently, *methodology* for teacher researchers involves their beliefs about the world of teaching, learning, children, and classroom life. *Methods*, in contrast, are the procedures and tools a researcher employs in an inquiry: the plans for gathering information, the mechanisms for reducing or synthesizing data, and the techniques for analyzing and making sense of information. Methods are determined by methodological decisions (see Dillon essay in Baumann, Dillon, Shockley, Alvermann, & Reinking, 1996).

The implication of this distinction is that our examination of methodology in teacher research involves more than simply reporting the various types of research designs, data collection procedures, and analysis techniques (i.e., methods) teacher researchers have employed. Rather, it requires that we put on a wide-angle lens to examine the general characteristics of teacher research, the process of teacher inquiry, and the nature of classroom inquiry dissemination, along with the actual methods classroom teachers use in their studies.

Literature on Methodology in Teacher Research

Teacher research has a long, rich, and varied tradition, and we refer readers to other sources to glean a full historical perspective (e.g., Cochran-Smith & Lytle, 1990; Lytle & Cochran-Smith, 1994a; McFarland & Stansell, 1993; Olson, 1990). Here we briefly trace selected works germane to methodology in teacher research.

Early in the 20th century, one finds references to the importance of teacher contributions to the knowledge base on teaching (Dewey, 1929) as well as discussions of methods appropriate for research involving teachers (Buckingham, 1926). Concurrent with the mid-century action research movement (e.g., Corey, 1953; Elliott, 1991; Stenhouse, 1973, 1975) were discussions about appropriate methodology for teacher research (Corman, 1957; Hodgkinson, 1957). More recently, authors have described various methods, tools, and procedures for engaging in teacher research (e.g., Brause & Mayher, 1991; Calhoun, 1994; Hopkins, 1993; Hubbard & Power, 1993a, 1999; Kincheloe, 1991; Mohr & Maclean, 1987; Myers, 1985; Nixon, 1981; Sagor, 1992).

Given the long-standing interest in the conduct and publication of teacher research and the more recent works describing methods and tools, it is interesting that there have been relatively few analyses of methodological perspectives employed in teacher research. Reviewers of the history or tradition of teacher research (e.g., Cochran-Smith & Lytle, 1993; Hollingsworth & Sockett, 1994; McFarland & Stansell, 1993; Olson, 1990) have commented on the methods employed and some methodological themes, but systematic analyses have been rare. Baumann et al. (1997) examined in detail the methodological perspectives employed in three specific teacher-research environments, but their cases do not provide any sense of the breadth of methodologies teacher researchers employ. The purpose of this chapter is to begin to fill this void. The following question guided our research: What is the nature of methodologies teacher researchers have employed in published classroom-based inquiries in literacy?

METHOD

Theoretical and Researcher Perspectives

This research is a qualitative study of teacher-research methodology in literacy education. Through an application of the constant comparative method to written documents (Glaser & Strauss, 1967), we analyzed 34 purposively selected teacher-research studies. Through this analysis, we generated categories and themes of teacher-research methodology that captured the essence of our sample.

We have both had experience with teacher research. Jim engaged in teacher research when taking a sabbatical from his university position to teach second-grade (Baumann & Ivey, 1997). He also worked within a teacher-research community (Baumann, Allen, & Shockley, 1994) and reflected on teacher-research methods (Baumann, 1996). Ann, a former elementary school classroom teacher and reading specialist, conducted teacher research as the instructor of a university- and field-based elementary reading education course (Duffy, 1997) and as the teacher of a summer reading program for second-grade, struggling readers (Duffy-Hester, 1999).

We believe that good teachers of literacy are theoretical as they utilize extant literacy research that informs their practice and produce new theories of teaching and learning through their teacher-research endeavors. We see teacher researchers as linking research and practice, the embodiment of reflective practitioners (Schon, 1983). We know from our own teacher research that engaging in classroom inquiry can transform an educator's views on teaching and learning.

Sampling

We selected literacy-based, teacher-research studies that were consistent with our definition of teacher research (i.e., reflection, action, and systematic intentional inquiry). We accomplished this selection through the process of *theoretical sampling*, which is "the process of data collection for generating theory whereby the analyst jointly collects, codes, and analyzes his data and decides what data to collect next and where to find them, in order to develop his theory as it emerges" (Glaser & Strauss, 1967, p. 45).

To obtain a broadly based sample of teacher-research studies, our theoretical sampling was guided by three selection criteria: (a) publication source, including journal articles, chapters in edited books, and full-length books; (b) age and grade level, including early childhood (preschool to Grade 2), elementary school (Grades 3–5), middle and junior high school (Grades 6–8), high school (Grades 9–12), and college-age students; and (c) research topic foci, including comprehension, discussion, integrated language arts, literature response, oral language, reading, spelling, writing, and whole language. We identified studies that reflected the range of diversity specified by each criterion.

As our analysis proceeded, we revisited and reevaluated our definition of teacher research, deleted studies from our list that did not seem to meet our evolving definition, and added new studies to broaden our sample. Midway through our sampling and analysis process, we created a matrix to determine whether we had adhered to our three sampling criteria of publication outlet, age/grade level, and research topic focus. We added and deleted studies as necessary so that the sample reflected our criteria and hence the broader universe of published teacher-research studies. We also shared the study sample and our criteria with a person experienced and highly published in literacy teacher research. We asked this educator to assess the sample in relation to our criteria. Based on her evaluation and suggestions, we deleted and added several studies. Table 6.1 presents the 34 teacher-research studies in our final sample.

Analysis

Our data analysis proceeded through five phases. In Phase I, *initial coding and category creation*, we independently read a subset of studies in the sample, writing researcher memos (LeCompte & Preissle, 1993) such as observer comments, methodological memos, and analytic memos. We then independently analyzed our notes to glean the emerging categories and met to discuss and create a list of common categories. In Phase II, *category refinement and theme creation*, we read additional studies, modified the existing categories, and identified emerging clusters of categories as themes. We concluded the analysis in Phase III, *data saturation*, that is, when neither of us modified or added to the 16 categories and 4 themes we had identified at this point.

In Phase IV, *establishing credibility*, we independently reread the studies and listed page numbers for which we found evidence of each category, resulting in an interrater agreement score of 88.6% across all 16 categories and 34 studies. Disagreements about a particular category were discussed and resolved in conference. In Phase V, *audit*, we provided a doctoral student trained in qualitative research methodology and knowledgeable in literacy teacher research copies of the studies, sampling and analysis procedures, data reduction and analysis documents, and a list of guiding questions (modeled after Halpern, 1983; cited in Lincoln & Guba, 1985) that evaluated the completeness, comprehensibility, utility, and linkages in our research. After reviewing six

TABLE 1.1
Teacher-Research Studies Analyzed

1. Allen, Janet. (1995). *It's never too late: Leading adolescents to lifelong literacy.* B, H, I

2. Allen, Jennifer. (1997). Exploring literature through student-led discussions. *Teacher Research: The Journal of Classroom Inquiry.* A, EL, D/LR

3. Allen, JoBeth; Michalove, Barbara; & Shockley, Betty. (1993). *Engaging children: Community and chaos in the lives of young literacy learners.* B, EC/EL, I

4. Allen, Sara. (1992). Student-sustained discussion: When students talk and the teacher listens. *Students teaching, teachers learning.* C, H, D/LR

5. Atwell, Nancie. (1987). Everyone sits at a big desk: Discovering topics for writing. *English Journal.* A, M, W

6. Avery, Carol S. (1987). Traci: A learning-disabled child in a writing-process classroom. *Seeing for ourselves: Case-study research by teachers of writing.* C, EC, W

7. Bryan, Leslie Hall. (1996). Cooperative writing groups in community college. *Journal of Adolescent & Adult Literacy.* A, C, W

8. Caulfield, Judy. (1996). Students telling stories: Inquiry into the process of learning stories. *Research in the classroom: Talk, texts, and inquiry.* C, EL/M, O

9. Christensen, Linda; & Walker, Barbara J. (1992). Researching one's own teaching in a reading education course. *Literacy research and practice: Foundations for the year 2000.* C, C, R

10. Cline, Dawn M. (1993). A year with reading workshop. *Teachers are researchers: Reflection and action.* C, M, R

11. Clyde, Jean Anne; Condon, Mark W. F.; Daniel, Kathleen; & Sommer, Mary Kenna. (1993). Learning through whole language: Exploring book selection and use with preschoolers. *Teachers are researchers: Reflection and action.* C, EC, WL

12. Commeyras, Michelle; Reinking, David; Heubach, Kathleen M.; & Pagnucco, Joan. (1993). Looking within: A study of an undergraduate reading methods course. *Examining central issues in literacy research, theory, and practice.* C, C, R

13. Cone, Joan Kernan. (1994). Appearing acts: Creating readers in a high school English class. *Harvard Educational Review.* A, H, R

14. Donoahue, Zoe. (1996). Collaboration, community, and communication: Modes of discourse for teacher research. *Research in the classroom: Talk, texts, and inquiry.* C, EL, S

15. Feldgus, Eileen Glickman. (1993). Walking to the words. *Inside/outside: Teacher research and knowledge.* C, EC, W

16. Grattan, Kristin Walden. (1997). They can do it too! Book club with first and second graders. *The book club connection: Literacy learning and classroom talk.* C, EC, D/LR

17. Grimm, Nancy. (1990). Tutoring dyslexic college students: What these students teach us about literacy development. *The writing teacher as researcher: Essays in the theory and practice of class-based research.* C, C, W

18. Harvey, Stephanie; McAuliffe, Sheila; Benson, Laura; Cameron, Wendy; Kempton, Sue; Lusche, Pat; Miller, Debbie; Schroeder, Joan; & Weaver, Julie. (1996). Teacher-researchers study the process of synthesizing in six primary classrooms. *Language Arts.* A, EC, C

19. Johnston, Patricia. (1993). Lessons from the road: What I learned through teacher research. *Inside/outside: Teacher research and knowledge.* C, M, D

(Continues)

TABLE 1.1 (Continued)

20. Maher, Ann. (1994). An inquiry into reader response. *Changing schools from within: Creating communities of inquiry.* C, EL, LR

21. Mosenthal, James. (1995). A practice-oriented approach to methods coursework in literacy teaching. *Perspectives on literacy research and practice.* C, C, I

22. Murphy, Paula. (1994). Antonio: My student, my teacher: My inquiry begins. *Teacher Research: The Journal of Classroom Inquiry.* A, M, I

23. Newton, Marianne; Nash, Doris; & Ruffin, Loleta. (1996). A whole language trilogy: The covered bridge connection. *Teachers doing research: Practical possibilities.* C, EC, WL

24. Paley, Vivian Gussin. (1997). *The girl with the brown crayon.* B, EC, LR

25. Phinney, Margaret Yatsevitch; & Ketterling, Tracy. (1997). Dialogue journals, literature, and urban Indian sixth graders. *Teacher Research: The Journal of Classroom Inquiry.* A, M, LR/W

26. Pils, Linda J. (1993). "I love you, Miss Piss." *Reading Teacher.* A, EC, W

27. Ray, Lucinda C. (1987). Reflections on classroom research. *Reclaiming the classroom: Teacher research as an agency for change.* C, H, W

28. Richards, Jane. (1987). Rx for editor in chief. *Seeing for ourselves: Case-study research by teachers of writing.* C, H, W

29. Saunders, Laura. (1995). Unleashing the voices we rarely hear: Derrick's story. *Teacher Research: The Journal of Classroom Inquiry.* A, M, LR

30. Sega, Denise. (1997). Reading and writing about our lives: Creating a collaborative curriculum in a class of high school misfits. *Teacher Research: The Journal of Classroom Inquiry.* A, H, I

31. Swift, Kathleen. (1993). Try Reading Workshop in your classroom. *Reading Teacher.* A, M, R

32. Thomas, Sally; & Oldfather, Penny. (1995). Enhancing student and teacher engagement in literacy learning: A shared inquiry approach. *Reading Teacher.* A, EL/M, I

33. Von Dras, Joan. (1990). Transitions toward an integrated curriculum. *Talking about books: Creating literate communities.* C, EL, I

34. Wood, Katie. (1993). A case study of a writer. *Teachers are researchers: Reflection and action.* C, M, W

Note. Each teacher-research study analyzed is presented in an abbreviated reference format that includes author(s), publication date, title, and publication outlet. The reference list at the end of the chapter includes complete citations for each entry in this table. We have included authors' first names in this table to fully acknowledge the identity of all teacher researchers whose work is cited. Following each entry is a three-part code. The first part identifies the type of teacher-research publication (A = journal article; B = full book; C = chapter in an edited book). The second part identifies the age or grade of research participants (EC = early childhood, including preschool, kindergarten, and Grades 1–2 children; EL = elementary children in Grades 3–5; M = middle school or junior high students in Grades 6–8; H = high school students in Grades 9–12; C = college-age students). The third part identifies the content foci for the studies (C = comprehension, D = discussion, I = integrated language arts, LR = literature response, O = oral language, R = reading, S = spelling, W = writing, WL = whole language). We acknowledge the limits and subjectivity of our classification system, particularly with respect to the content focus designations.

representative studies, the auditor concluded that the analysis procedures and inquiry path were clear, although she indicated that we had misclassified one study in the category "Teacher researchers supplement qualitative research methods with quantitative methods." To address this concern, we reviewed all 34 studies, finding evidence for this category in 3 additional studies.

RESULTS AND DISCUSSION

Our analysis of methodology in teacher research resulted in the construction of 16 categories, which clustered within four broad themes: (a) general attributes of teacher research, (b) the process of teacher inquiry, (c) teacher-research methods, and (d) writing and reporting classroom inquiry. Table 6.2 presents these themes and categories.

To facilitate reference to studies within our sample, we employ a theme/category labeling system. For example, we use 2B to identify Category B within Theme 2. We also provide a brief reference label for each category, which is shown in **boldface** type in Table 6.2. For example, **Instructive** denotes the 2B category, "Teacher researchers learn from their students," within Theme 2, "Process of Teacher Inquiry." For simplicity in citing studies within this chapter, we use a parenthetic number format that is keyed to the identifying numbers in Table 6.1. For example, (26) refers to Linda Pils's study.

Table 6.3 presents the themes and categories identified study by study. The presence of a bullet indicates that the category emerged from our analysis for a particular study. The final two columns of each row indicate the number of categories that emerged for a study, followed by the overall percentage (e.g., Study 6 possessed 12 of 16 possible categories, a 75% occurrence). The final two rows in the table present parallel data but by category (e.g., Category 1B was present in 20 of the 34 studies analyzed, a 59% occurrence).

Table 6.3 reveals several trends within the data. First, the categories had high representation across studies, with an 83% overall frequency of category occurrence. Second, there was variation by study, ranging from a 56% occurrence (Study 28) to 100%

TABLE 1.2
Themes and Categories Emerging From Analysis
of Published Teacher-Research Studies

Theme 1: General attributes of teacher research

A. **Questions from within**: Teacher research is prompted by the problems teachers face and the questions they pose within their own classrooms. (100%)

B. **Question evolution**: Research questions are modified as teachers conceptualize and implement a classroom study. (59%)

C. **Theoretically driven**: Existing theory—presented through written texts or collegial dialogue—inspires, guides, supports, or informs teachers in their own inquiries (i.e., theory → teacher research). (97%)

D. **Theoretically productive**: Engaging in teacher research leads to the creation or development of theories of teaching, learning, and schooling (i.e., teacher research→ theory). (94%)

E. **Reflective**: Teacher researchers are reflective practitioners. (100%)

Theme 2: Process of teacher inquiry

A. **Collaborative**: Teacher researchers conduct research with peers, students, families, or college faculty as coresearchers or collaborators. (91%)

B. **Instructive**: Teacher researchers learn from their students. (100%)

C. **Clarifying**: Classroom inquiry enables teachers to make sense of their classroom worlds. (94%)

D. **Unsettling**: Because classroom inquiry involves change and risk-taking, teacher researchers may feel uneasiness with innovations or changes they examine in their classrooms. (62%)

E. **Compatible or discordant**: Engaging in research and teaching are mutually reinforcing processes for some teacher researchers, whereas others experience tension between them. (26%)

(Continues)

TABLE 1.2 (Continued)

Theme 3: Teacher-research methods

A. **Pragmatic**: Teacher researchers employ methods on the basis of their practicality and efficiency for addressing research questions. (100%)

B. **Versatile**: Teacher researchers select, adapt, or create qualitative research methods for collecting and analyzing data. (100%)

C. **Complementary**: Teacher researchers supplement qualitative research methods with quantitative methods. (26%)

Theme 4: Writing and reporting classroom inquiry

A. **Narrative**: Teacher researchers employ a narrative style when reporting classroom inquiries. (94%)

B. **Illustrative**: Teacher researchers document findings by including excerpts of transcripts and interviews or reproducing student work and artifacts in research reports. (91%)

C. **Figurative**: Teacher researchers use research vignettes or metaphors to convey key points and ideas. (94%)

Note. Parenthetic percentages indicate the frequency with which a category was present across the 34 studies examined.

(Study 1). Third, there was variation by category, with frequencies ranging from 26% to 100%.

This variation is also captured, in part, in Table 6.4 (see p. 87), which presents three sets of categories clustered according to their frequency of occurrence. *Defining categories* were the most frequent features (91%–100% occurrence). *Discriminating categories* were those features that distinguished some studies from others (59%–62% occurrence). *Negative-case categories* were features of teacher research that, although low in frequency (26% occurrence), were retained because they helped define teacher research methodology through exceptions, much in the way negative-case qualitative analysis procedures (Kidder, 1981) are used to clarify and refine categories and properties. We now turn to a theme-by-theme presentation of categories with supporting data for each.

Theme 1: General Attributes of Teacher Research

Category A: Questions From Within.   *Teacher research is prompted by the problems teachers face and the questions they pose within their own classrooms.* Ann Maher (20) stated that her research on reader response "developed from my growing discomfort and dissatisfaction with the reading program in my Junior grade 4/5 classroom" (p. 81). Eileen Glickman Feldgus (15) wondered how her kindergarten students learned to use environmental print in their writing, noting that "this question haunted me" (p. 171). High school teacher Lucinda C. Ray (27) reported that she engaged in research, in part, because "I was frustrated and dissatisfied with the lack of success I had in talking with my students about their writing" (p. 219).

O'Dell (1987) argued that teachers' research questions emerge from a sense of dissonance: "Something isn't quite clear to us; something just doesn't add up" (p. 129). Bissex (1987) defined teacher researcher through questioning: "*A teacher-researcher is a questioner....*Problems become questions to investigate" (p. 4). Our data support Bissex's definition.

TABLE 1.3

Themes and Categories by Study

Study ID/Author	General Attributes					Process of TR					TR Methods			Writing TR			n	%
	1A	1B	1C	1D	1E	2A	2B	2C	2D	2E	3A	3B	3C	4A	4B	4C		
1. Allen, Janet	•	•	•	•	•	•	•	•	•	•	•	•	•	•	•	•	16	100
2. Allen, Jennifer	•	•	•	•	•	•	•	•	•	•	•	•	•		•	•	15	94
3. Allen, JoBeth, et al.	•	•	•	•	•	•	•	•	•		•	•			•		12	75
4. Allen, Sara	•	•	•	•	•	•	•	•	•	•	•	•		•	•	•	15	94
5. Atwell, Nancie	•	•	•	•	•	•	•	•	•		•	•			•		12	75
6. Avery, Carol. S	•	•	•	•	•	•	•	•	•		•	•			•		12	75
7. Bryan, Leslie Hall	•	•	•	•	•	•	•	•	•		•	•			•		12	75
8. Caulfield, Judy	•	•	•	•	•	•	•	•	•	•	•	•	•		•	•	15	94
9. Christensen & Walker	•	•	•	•	•	•	•	•	•		•	•		•	•	•	14	88
10. Cline, Dawn M.	•	•	•	•	•	•	•	•	•		•	•		•	•	•	14	88
11. Clyde, Jean Anne, et al.	•	•	•	•	•	•	•	•	•		•	•		•	•	•	14	88
12. Commeyras, Michelle, et al.	•	•	•	•	•	•	•	•	•		•	•			•		12	75
13. Cone, Joan Kernan	•	•	•	•	•	•	•	•	•	•	•	•		•	•	•	15	94
14. Donoahue, Zoe	•	•	•	•	•	•	•	•	•		•	•			•		12	75
15. Feldgus, Eileen Glickman	•	•	•	•	•	•	•	•	•		•	•		•	•	•	13	81
16. Grattan, Kristin Walden	•	•	•	•	•	•	•	•	•		•	•		•	•	•	13	81
17. Grimm, Nancy	•	•	•	•	•	•	•	•	•		•	•		•	•	•	13	81
18. Harvey, Stephanie, et al.	•	•	•	•	•	•	•	•	•		•	•		•	•	•	13	81

(Continues)

TABLE 1.3 (Continued)

Study ID/Author	General Attributes					Process of TR					TR Methods			Writing TR			n	%
	1A	1B	1C	1D	1E	2A	2B	2C	2D	2E	3A	3B	3C	4A	4B	4C		
19. Johnston, Patricia	•	•	•	•	•	•	•	•	•	•	•	•		•	•	•	15	94
20. Maher, Ann	•	•	•	•	•	•	•	•			•	•		•	•	•	13	81
21. Mosenthal, James	•	•	•	•	•	•	•				•	•		•	•	•	12	75
22. Murphy, Paula	•	•	•	•	•	•	•	•			•	•		•	•	•	13	81
23. Newton, Marianne, et al.	•	•	•		•	•	•		•		•	•	•	•	•	•	13	81
24. Paley, Vivian Gussin	•	•	•	•	•	•	•			•	•	•		•	•	•	13	81
25. Phinney & Ketterling	•	•	•	•	•	•	•	•	•	•	•	•		•	•	•	15	94
26. Pils, Linda J.	•	•	•	•	•	•	•	•			•	•		•	•	•	13	81
27. Ray, Lucinda C.	•	•	•	•	•	•	•	•	•		•	•	•	•	•		14	88
28. Richards, Jane	•		•	•	•		•				•	•		•	•		9	56
29. Saunders, Laura	•	•	•	•	•	•	•	•	•	•	•	•		•	•	•	15	94
30. Sega, Denise	•		•	•	•	•	•				•	•		•	•	•	11	69
31. Swift, Kathleen	•	•	•	•	•	•	•	•	•		•	•	•	•	•		14	88
32. Thomas & Oldfather	•		•	•	•	•	•	•	•	•	•	•		•	•	•	14	88
33. Von Dras, Joan	•		•	•	•	•	•	•			•	•		•	•	•	12	75
34. Wood, Katie	•	•	•	•	•	•	•	•	•		•	•	•		•	•	14	88
n	34	20	33	32	34	31	34	32	21	9	34	34	9	32	31	32	452	
%	100	59	97	94	100	91	100	94	62	26	100	100	26	94	91	94		83

TABLE 1.4

**Teacher Research Categories Clustered
by Overall Frequency Across Studies**

Cluster 1: Defining categories (category present in 91%–100% of all studies)	1A	**Questions from within:** Teacher research is prompted by the problems teachers face and the questions they pose within their own classrooms.
	1C	**Theoretically driven:** Existing theory—presented through written texts or collegial dialogue—inspires, guides, supports, or informs teachers in their own inquiries (i.e., theory → teacher research).
	1D	**Theoretically productive:** Engaging in teacher research leads to the creation or development of theories of teaching, learning, and schooling (i.e., teacher research → theory).
	1E	**Reflective:** Teacher researchers are reflective practitioners.
	2A	**Collaborative:** Teacher researchers conduct research with peers, students, families, or college faculty as coresearchers or collaborators.
	2B	**Instructive:** Teacher researchers learn from their students.
	2C	**Clarifying:** Classroom inquiry enables teachers to make sense of their classroom worlds.
	3A	**Pragmatic:** Teacher researchers employ methods on the basis of their practicality and efficiency for addressing research questions.
	3B	**Versatile:** Teacher researchers select, adapt, or create qualitative research methods for collecting and analyzing data.
	4A	**Narrative:** Teacher researchers employ a narrative style when reporting classroom inquiries.
	4B	**Illustrative:** Teacher researchers document findings by including excerpts of transcripts and interviews or reproducing student work and artifacts in research reports.
	4C	**Figurative:** Teacher researchers use research vignettes or metaphors to convey key points and ideas.
Cluster 2: Discriminating categories (category present in 59%–62% of all studies)	1B	**Question evolution:** Research questions are modified as teachers conceptualize and implement a classroom study.
	2D	**Unsettling:** Because classroom inquiry involves change and risk-taking, teacher researchers may feel uneasiness with innovations or changes they examine in their classrooms.
Cluster 3: Negative-case categories (category present in 26% of all studies)	2E	**Compatible or discordant:** Engaging in research and teaching are mutually reinforcing processes for some teacher researchers, whereas others experience tension between them.
	3C	**Complementary:** Teacher researchers supplement qualitative research methods with quantitative methods.

Category B: Question Evolution.   Research questions are modified as teachers conceptualize and implement a classroom study. Kathleen Swift's (31) inquiry about the impact Reading Workshop had on the attitudes of her sixth graders led her to new questions: "What was happening to students' reading skills as a result of Reading Workshop? I wondered how well Reading Workshop strengthened and built comprehension. What effect did it have on the learning disabled students and below-grade-level readers?" (p. 367). University teacher researchers Linda Christiansen and Barbara J. Walker (9) likewise reported that "taking a closer look at one's teaching has led both to restructuring courses and providing questions for further research" (p. 63). Lucinda C. Ray's (27) four initial research questions grew along with her inquiry: "I learned some answers to these questions.... I learned to ask some new questions which I hadn't anticipated" (p. 222).

Although research question evolution is common (Baumann, Allen, & Shockley, 1994), Hubbard and Power (1993b) argued that "many teachers have to do some wandering to get to their wonderings" (p. 21). Our findings support this process.

Category C: Theoretically Driven.   *Existing theory—presented through written texts or collegial dialogue—inspires, guides, supports, or informs teachers in their own inquiries (i.e., theory → teacher research).* Some teacher researchers demonstrate their familiarity and use of existing theory through literature reviews. Marianne Newton, Doris Nash, and Loleta Ruffin (23) found that by reading the professional literature, they were able to make "natural *connections* between the research others had done and what we were trying to do with the children in our classrooms" (p. 83–84). Theoretical grounding also came in the form of personal contacts. Sara Allen (4) reported how her department chair challenged her to engage in classroom inquiry, and Nancie Atwell (5) related how a research consultant brought "authority as a teacher and researcher [and] a wealth of knowledge" (p. 179) to their research team.

Teacher research is not atheoretical. Teacher researchers confer with colleagues, take courses and attend workshops on research, and read professional materials (Cochran-Smith & Lytle, 1993). We found this linkage of extant theory to classroom inquiry an almost universal characteristic of teacher research.

Category D: Theoretically Productive.   *Engaging in teacher research leads to the creation or development of theories of teaching, learning, and schooling (i.e., teacher research → theory).* Carol S. Avery's (6) case study of a learning-disabled, first-grade child led to modification of her teaching philosophy and practices, and Joan Kernan Cone's (13) research led her to "know high school reading instruction in a way that would dramatically change the way I teach" (p. 87). Others reported that teacher research affirmed their theories, such as Eileen Glickman Feldgus (15), who found that her study of kindergartners strengthened several of her "personal beliefs" and "convictions" about emergent readers and writers (p. 177).

Teacher research involves a recursive relationship between theory and practice. Ann Keffer described how this notion of praxis played out for her daily: "Classroom research is not something one gets through with. Instead, it is a different approach to teaching in which theory informs practice and *practice informs theory* continually and immediately right in the classroom" (cited in Baumann et al., 1997, p. 139).

Category E: Reflective.   *Teacher researchers are reflective practitioners.* Reflection was evident in all studies examined. Laura Saunders (29) described introspection in relation to her case study of an eighth-grade student: "As I reflect upon my decision making where Derek was concerned …" (p. 56). Kristin Walden Grattan (16) wrote about her research with primary-grade children: "As I reflect on my journey of exploring and modifying Book Club to meet my classroom needs, I realize that it was a rather bumpy road" (p. 279). Leslie Hall Bryan (7), in the midst of her research with developmental studies college students, mused: "At this point I reflected on the process as a whole and the direction I wanted to go for the last weeks of the term" (p. 191). Lucinda C. Ray (27) stated that "reflection … describes the impact of the study on me as a researcher and learner" (p. 222).

All who have analyzed the teacher-research process (Goswami & Stillman, 1987) or the development of teacher-research communities (Lytle & Cochran-Smith, 1992) acknowledge the centrality of reflective practice (Schon, 1983). Our data further reinforce this conclusion.

Theme 2: Process of Teacher Inquiry

Category A: Collaborative.   *Teacher researchers conduct research with peers, students, families, or college faculty as coresearchers or collaborators.* Zoe Donoahue (14) described an inquiry that involved "several communities—the teacher group, a university-based group to which I belonged, and the classroom community" (p. 91), and school/university research teams are common configurations (3, 8, 18). Sometimes parents became involved in the research, as when Carol S. Avery (6) asked Traci's mother to help collect case study data at home. In other instances, elementary (2), middle school (19), and high school (30) students collaborated with their teachers. For example, Sally Thomas and Penny Oldfather (32) invited students to help them learn about motivation for literacy across their upper elementary and secondary school years.

Goswami and Stillman (1987) reported that teacher researchers "collaborate with their students to answer questions important to both, drawing on community resources in new and unexpected ways" (p. ii). Our data affirm the prevalence and power of teachers collaborating with students and others in the teacher-research process.

Category B: Instructive.   *Teacher researchers learn from their students.* Carol S. Avery (6) commented how her teaching evolved by learning from her students: "They are such wonderful teachers!" (p. 60). Jane Richards (28) received help from her high school students when trying to modify how she taught spelling and punctuation, and Ann Maher (20) reported that her research on reader response began to seriously unfold when she began "listening to the children" (p. 85).

Denise Sega (30) had a banner across the front of her high school classroom that read, "WE CAN ALL LEARN FROM EACH OTHER" (p. 111). She reported that once she realized she could learn from and with her students, everyone's learning, including her own, reached new heights: "I asked them, they told me, I listened, and we learned" (p. 110). Sega's experience revealed that teacher researchers learn from and along with their students.

Category C: Clarifying.   *Classroom inquiry enables teachers to make sense of their classroom worlds.* Teacher research provides a focusing lens for viewing the instructional environment. Nancy Grimm's (17) research on a tutorial program for dyslexic college students taught her to question previously unquestioned developmental models of literacy, leading to instructional innovations. Paula Murphy's (22) exploration of Antonio's reading development led her to greater sensitivity and knowledge about what it might be like to be a struggling, low-income, minority adolescent reader. The analysis Michelle Commeyras and colleagues (12) conducted on preservice literacy teacher education programs promoted growth in their own teaching: "Undertaking this study has had a positive influence on teaching in our department" (p. 304).

Britton (1987) argued that every lesson a teacher teaches involves inquiry, resulting in "some further discovery" (p. 15). It is through these new discoveries that teacher researchers learn to understand their classroom worlds and how to improve them as learning environments.

Category D: Unsettling.   *Because classroom inquiry involves change and risk-taking, teacher researchers may feel uneasiness with innovations or changes they examine in their classrooms.* Marianne Newton and colleagues (23) referred to their application of whole-language practices in their classrooms as "an unsettling exploration into our own philosophies of education," but they soon "discovered that our hesitancies and uncertainties were a natural part of our learning" (p. 83). Sara Allen (4) anticipated uneasiness in her research on engaging her senior students with English literature, explaining that "I knew I might be in for some chaos." But Allen proceeded anyway, clarifying that "I was willing to risk that [the chaos]. I was desperate" (p. 82).

The exploration of dialogue journals between Margaret Yatsevitch Phinney's university students and Tracy Ketterling's sixth-grade students (25) yielded successes and "some things that *didn't* work" (p. 24), leading them to "recognize that teaching and learning are imperfect activities" (p. 40). Thus, unsettling as classroom inquiry may be, teacher researchers accept the uncertainty and learn from it.

Category E: Compatible or Discordant.   *Engaging in research and teaching are mutually reinforcing processes for some teacher researchers, whereas others experience tension between them.* Jennifer Allen (2) noted how she "shifted back and forth between the roles of researcher and teacher" (p. 124), but she also related how she eventually "balanced the roles of researcher and teacher" (p. 138). Some teacher researchers described how inquiry became an inseparable part of what it meant to teach students (e.g., see Shockley essay in Baumann et al., 1996); others reported a bit of discord. Patricia Johnston (19) commented, "I found that the doing and the being of teacher research are at once second nature to me and somehow touching on foreign soil" (p. 178), and Linda Pils (26) talked about how research involved "both an inward and outward struggle" (p. 648).

O'Dell (1987) argued that teacher research "arises from a sense of dissonance or conflict or uncertainty" (p. 129). Laura Saunders (29) commented that "the tension between conducting classroom inquiry and the daily demands of a classroom teacher transformed my ability to teach and learn" (p. 57). Thus, the tension can be beneficial by clarifying methodological, ethical, and pragmatic issues for teacher researchers (Baumann, 1996).

Theme 3: Teacher-Research Methods

Category A: Pragmatic   *Teacher researchers employ methods on the basis of their practicality and efficiency for addressing research questions.* University-based researcher James Mosenthal (21) studied the nature and adequacy of the learning processes of one of his students by examining a variety of data sources, which allowed him to reconstruct a "history of the experience" (p. 361). Margaret Yatsevitch Phinney and Tracy Ketterling (25) selected methods that enabled them "to keep track of the elements that affected the project positively and negatively" (p. 26). Katie Wood (34) explained that she included excerpts from interviews with Jo, the participant in her case study, "because her [Jo's] responses are so thought provoking and have a voice of their own" (pp. 106–107).

Shulman (1997) argued that "good research is a matter not of finding the one best method but of carefully framing that question most important to the investigator and the field and then identifying a disciplined way in which to inquire into it" (p. 4). Our data suggest that teacher researchers chose methods that were practical and efficient in answering their research questions in a disciplined manner.

Category B: Versatile.   *Teacher researchers select, adapt, or create qualitative research methods for collecting and analyzing data.* Qualitative procedures of many variations constituted the methods of choice within the teacher-research studies we examined. JoBeth Allen, Barbara Michalove, and Betty Shockley (3), in their collaborative investigation of the effects of a whole-language curriculum on students who struggled with literacy development, identified methods used by other literacy researchers (Almy & Genishi, 1979; Hansen, 1989) and adapted them to suit their unique needs. Sara Allen (4) reported that she "developed and refined" (p. 83) qualitative data collection procedures. Well into her study, Judy Caulfield (8) revamped her analysis of students' storytellings, moving away from counting false starts to looking at students' storytelling attempts as forms of rehearsal and elaboration.

Nocerino (1993) argued that "it is flexibility that encourages the exploration, development, and refinement of meaningful research" (p. 91). We found that teacher researchers employed flexible, selective, and adaptive qualitative research methods in their studies.

Category C: Complementary. *Teacher researchers supplement qualitative research methods with quantitative methods.* Some teacher researchers used quantitative data to support qualitative data. Judy Caulfield (8) counted the number of false starts students made in storytelling. Michelle Commeyras and colleagues (12) used inferential statistics to analyze questionnaires. Dawn M. Cline (10) analyzed students' grades, grade-point averages, and SAT scores. Other researchers analyzed student test scores (23, 31), used percentages and pie charts to present interview data (1), or computed frequencies when analyzing conference data (27).

Qualitative researchers Miles and Huberman (1994) commented that "we have to face the fact that numbers and words are *both* needed if we are to understand the world" (p. 40). Clearly, some of the teacher researchers in our sample reached the same conclusion.

Theme 4: Writing and Reporting Classroom Inquiry

Category A: Narrative. *Teacher researchers employ a narrative style when reporting classroom inquiries.* Paula Murphy (22) told the story of one of her students in a compensatory reading education class by describing her learning about "Antonio's world" (p. 79). Vivian Paley (24) characterized her writing about Reeny, a child in her class who falls in love with books, as a "literary tale," commenting that "it is Reeny's story that is told in these pages" (p. viii). Stephanie Harvey, Sheila McAuliffe, Laura Benson, Wendy Cameron, Sue Kempton, Pat Lusche, Debbie Miller, Joan Schroeder, and Julie Weaver (18) used separate narratives to retain their individual voices while describing their collaborative study.

A narrative style is used by many who write about teaching and classrooms (Carter, 1993; Connelly & Clandinin, 1990; Krall, 1988). Erickson (1986) asserted that "within the details of the story, selected carefully, is contained a statement of a theory of organization and meaning of the events described" (p. 150). Narratives allow teacher researchers to convey both the details of their research and the context and meaning of these events.

Category B: Illustrative. *Teacher researchers document findings by including excerpts of transcripts and interviews or reproducing student work and artifacts in research reports.* Joan Von Dras (33) used student work to document how children were able to connect with and respond to literature. Sally Thomas and Penny Oldfather (32) illustrated students' engagement with literacy learning by reproducing one child's drawing showing "My 10 Favorite Books" and various dialogue journal exchanges between Sally and her students. Linda Pils (26) integrated excerpts of the writing of Gary, one of her first-grade students, along with her own journal to document Gary's growth.

Booth, Colomb, and Williams (1995) recommend that researchers "offer readers evidence that *they* will consider reliable in support of a claim that *they* will judge specific and contestable" (p. 126). Through the inclusion of many and varied illustrative data clips, teacher researchers enable their audiences to judge and interpret their research.

Category C: Figurative.   *Teacher researchers use research vignettes or metaphors to convey key points and ideas.* Paula Murphy (22) used a vignette to describe how she met Antonio, the student whose learning she chronicled, and Laura Saunders (29) used an excerpt from Derrick's autobiography to introduce her inquiry involving dialogue journals. Jean Anne Clyde, Mark W. F. Condon, Kathleen Daniel, and Mary Kenna Sommer (11) used an opening vignette that described how deaf, preschool children and their teachers used oral and written texts during dramatic play. Patricia Johnston (19) described teacher research metaphorically as "embarking on a journey toward making sense of classroom practice," relating how "this adventure through uncharted territory revealed much about student response" (p. 178). Marianne Newton, Doris Nash, and Loleta Ruffin (23) used the metaphor of a covered bridge to describe their exploration of whole language, explaining their initial uneasiness ("old bridges can feel shaky," p. 83) and how they supported one another in their research ("it was not an easy decision to cross this bridge together," p. 85).

Dey (1993) asserted that "using metaphors can enrich an account by conveying connotations which elaborate on and illuminate our basic meaning" (p. 245). Teachers often use such rhetorical devices to express and interpret what they learn from their inquiries.

LIMITATIONS

Our study is limited in several ways. First, our inquiry is limited to the sample of teacher-research studies we analyzed. Although we selected a diverse set of research reports that we believe reflect the full range of published teacher inquiry, we cannot claim transferability to the complete body of teacher research. Second, the results are limited by the information the authors provided in their reports. We identified categories only when an author provided explicit or highly implied evidence of their presence. We acknowledge that researchers may not have chosen to provide certain content because it was not relevant to their research presentation, thus resulting in possible underrepresentation of some categories. Third, our inquiry is limited by the qualitative research paradigm we employed, including the personal perspectives we brought to it (Alvermann, O'Brien, & Dillon, 1996). Thus, we leave it to readers to assess the dependability and credibility of our results and conclusions, or to offer alternate explanations for them.

CONCLUSIONS

We present the overall findings from our study through the medium of *substantive theory*, which describes "everyday-world situations" that have "a specificity and hence usefulness to practice" (Merriam, 1998, p. 17). This notion of everyday practice is philosophically and practically suited for an overall framework of methodology in teacher research.

Our findings confirm that methodology in teacher research reflects both commonality and diversity. The defining categories (see Table 6.4) reflect several common methodological traits of teacher research. The internal locus of questions (1A) and the theoretical nature of classroom research—both driving an inquiry (1C) and subsequent classroom instruction (1D)—characterize the methodology teacher researchers employ. Our data support most definitions of teacher research, which typically involve the reflective nature of classroom inquiry (1E), how the research process helps teachers make sense of their classroom worlds (2C), and how teachers learn from and with their students while engaging in research (2B). We found research collaborations (2A) a common occurrence. There are also commonalities in the methods teacher researchers employ. Teachers select pragmatic, useful methods for collecting and analyzing data (3A), and they are creative in selecting, adapting, or inventing qualitative methods that suit their research questions (3B). We found that teacher-research reports typically possessed several substantive and stylistic qualities, including a storytelling form (4A); the inclusion of many illustrative elements such as transcripts, journal entries, students' work reproductions, and other artifacts (4B); and the use of figurative devices such as metaphor and vignettes (4C).

But teacher research is not a homologous form of inquiry; it also is diverse in process, method, and reporting, as documented by our discriminating and negative-case categories. Although questions germinating from the teacher's world may be the sine qua non of teacher research, we found less than universal evidence that such questions underwent change throughout the course of a study (1B). Similarly, some, but not all, teacher researchers indicated uneasiness with the risk and change involved with classroom exploration (2D). In a few cases, teachers addressed the issue of compatibility between the responsibility they had for teaching students and their choice to engage in classroom research: Some indicated that there was a mutually reinforcing relationship between teaching and researching whereas others indicated that there was tension between them at times (2E). Even though qualitative data were the norm in teacher research, some teachers also used quantitative data to supplement qualitative findings (3C).

Unlike other, long-standing research traditions (Jaeger, 1997), many of which involve fairly formalized, routinized procedures, teacher research has an almost paradoxical combination of theme and individuality. The themes involve the attributes, processes, methods, and dissemination structures we extracted from the corpus of studies examined. But because of the reflective, action-oriented nature of inquiry into classroom life that defines teacher research, it simultaneously exudes a character that defies definition. Therefore, rather than there being a single portrait of teacher research, we suggest that teacher research is represented by a family album that includes many members who possess ancestry resemblance but are also readily distinguishable from one another.

A NEW GENRE?

Teacher research has been characterized "as its own genre" (Cochran-Smith & Lytle, 1993, p. 10), as a "new research paradigm" (Atwell, 1993, p. viii), and as "a unique genre of research" (Patterson & Shannon, 1993, p. 7). Cochran-Smith and Lytle (1993) argued that teacher research possesses "some quite distinctive features" (p. 10) when compared to research conducted by academics. We believe that our data support the "new genre" and "distinctive features" characterization of teacher research.

One distinctive feature is the evolutionary nature of methodology in teacher research. We found teacher researchers choosing, discarding, revisiting, and revising extant methodological paradigms and specific methods in their quest to find practical, versatile research perspectives and tools, a process not commonly reported in conventional research on teaching. Another distinctive feature involves audience, purpose, and publication outlet. Although traditional literacy research typically appears in professional periodicals that serve academic audiences, publication outlets for teacher research are usually different. Most teacher-research reports appear in applied serials or books, outlets that reach teacher-research consumers: other classroom teachers and school personnel.

Finally, classroom inquiry is unique, we believe, in the roles and responsibilities faced by a teacher researcher. Although teacher researchers have drawn from quantitative methods to conduct classroom experiments both historically (Olson, 1990) and contemporarily (Santa & Santa, 1995), our analysis indicates that teacher researchers tend to employ qualitative methods. But does that plant teacher research squarely within the qualitative methodology tradition? We think not. Teacher researchers, like qualitative researchers, are immersed in the research environment, but there are important distinctions. Qualitative researchers are first and foremost *researchers*, with participation being a planned means to achieve insight into the social setting under study. In contrast, teacher researchers are first and foremost *teachers*, who are responsible for the learning and well-being of the students assigned to them. Teacher research is not an ethnographic field study in which the researcher lives in the community; a teacher researcher not only lives in the community but works in and has responsibility for it. Erickson (1986) characterized a teacher researcher's role as "not that of the participant observer who comes from the outside world to visit, but that of an unusually observant participant who deliberates inside the scene of action" (p. 157). The insider role of teacher researcher brings with it a unique combination: the power associated with first-person insight, the limitation of participant perspective, and perhaps a bit of tension involved with trying to simultaneously teach and study one's teaching environment. It is this unique combination of qualities, we believe, that gives teacher research its individuality and status as a new research genre.

In his introduction to the second edition of *Complementary Methods for Research in Education* (Jaeger, 1997), Shulman (1997) described the promise of "the creation of forms of 'teacher research,'" predicting that the teacher research movement "will grow sufficiently in strength to provide another new paradigm for educational research" (pp. 19–20). We agree that teachers are in the best position to explore their own practice and to make sense of the classroom worlds "because they are full-time inhabitants of those settings rather than episodic visitors" (p. 21). We disagree with Shulman, however, about the tense. Rather than anticipating that teacher research "will grow" to provide a new paradigm, we believe that teacher research has already achieved a new educational research genre status. As such, we look forward not only to the use of *teacher research* without quotation marks in the future, but also to the inclusion of a chapter on teacher research methodology in the third edition of *Complementary Methods*.

ACKNOWLEDGMENTS

We thank JoBeth Allen and Ruth Shagoury Hubbard for their review of our sample of teacher-research studies and their useful suggestions for how to make it more representative of the diversity within published teacher research. We thank Cheri Triplett for her detailed, thoughtful, and critical evaluation of our analysis procedures and emerging themes and categories.

REFERENCES

Allen, J. (1995). *It's never too late: Leading adolescents to lifelong literacy.* Portsmouth, NH: Heinemann.
Allen, J. (1997). Exploring literature through student-led discussions. *Teacher Research: The Journal of Classroom Inquiry, 4*(2), 124–139.
Allen, J., Michalove, B., & Shockley, B. (1993). *Engaging children: Community and chaos in the lives of young literacy learners.* Portsmouth, NH: Heinemann.
Allen, S. (1992). Student-sustained discussion: When students talk and the teacher listens. In N. A. Branscombe, D. Goswami, & J. Schwartz (Eds.), *Students teaching, teachers learning* (pp. 81–92). Portsmouth, NH: Boynton/Cook.
Almy, M., & Genishi, C. (1979). *Ways of studying children.* New York: Teachers College Press.
Alvermann, D. E., O'Brien, D. G., & Dillon, D. R. (1996). On writing qualitative research. *Reading Research Quarterly, 31,* 114–120.

Atwell, N. (1987). Everyone sits at a big desk: Discovering topics for writing. In D. Goswami & P. R. Stillman (Eds.), *Reclaiming the classroom: Teacher research as an agency for change* (pp. 178–187). Upper Montclair, NJ: Boynton/Cook.

Atwell, N. (1993). Forward. In Patterson, L., Santa, C. M., Short, K. G., & Smith, K. (Eds.), *Teachers are researchers: Reflection and action* (pp. vii–xii). Newark, DE: International Reading Association.

Avery, C. S. (1987). Traci: A learning-disabled child in a writing-process classroom. In G. L. Bissex & R. H. Bullock (Eds.), *Seeing for ourselves: Case-study research by teachers of writing* (pp. 59–75). Portsmouth, NH: Heinemann.

Baumann, J. F. (1996). Conflict or compatibility in classroom inquiry? One teacher's struggle to balance teaching and research. *Educational Researcher, 25*(7), 29–36.

Baumann, J. F., Allen, J., & Shockley, B. (1994). Questions teachers ask: A report from the National Reading Research Center School Research Consortium. In D. J. Leu & C. K. Kinzer (Eds.), *Multidimensional aspects of literacy research, theory, and practice*, 43rd Yearbook of the National Reading Conference (pp. 474–484). Chicago: National Reading Conference.

Baumann, J. F., Dillon, D. R., Shockley, B. B., Alvermann, D. A., & Reinking, D. (1996). Perspectives for literacy research. In L. Baker, P. P. Afflerbach, & D. Reinking (Eds.), *Developing engaged readers in school and home communities* (pp. 217–245). Mahwah, NJ: Lawrence Erlbaum Associates.

Baumann, J. F., & Ivey, G. (1997). Delicate balances: Striving for curricular and instructional equilibrium in a second-grade, literature/strategy-based classroom. *Reading Research Quarterly, 32*(3), 244–275.

Baumann, J. F., Shockley-Bisplinghoff, B., & Allen, J. (1997). Methodology in teacher research: Three cases. In J. Flood, S. B. Heath, & D. Lapp (Eds.), *Handbook of research on teaching literacy through the communicative and visual arts* (pp. 121–143). New York: Macmillan.

Bissex, G. L. (1987). What is a teacher-researcher? In G. L. Bissex & R. H. Bullock (Eds.), *Seeing for ourselves: Case-study research by teachers of writing* (pp. 3–5). Portsmouth, NH: Heinemann.

Bissex, G. L., & Bullock, R. H. (Eds.). (1987). *Seeing for ourselves: Case-study research by teachers of writing.* Portsmouth, NH: Heinemann.

Booth, W. C., Colomb, G. G., & Williams, J. M. (1995). *The craft of research.* Chicago: University of Chicago Press.

Brause, R. S., & Mayher, J. S. (Eds.). (1991). *Search and re-search: What the inquiring teacher needs to know.* London: Falmer.

Britton, J. (1987). A quiet form of research. In D. Goswami & P. R. Stillman (Eds.), *Reclaiming the classroom: Teacher research as an agency for change* (pp. 13–19). Upper Montclair, NJ: Boynton/Cook.

Bryan, L. H. (1996). Cooperative writing groups in community college. *Journal of Adolescent & Adult Literacy, 40,* 188–193.

Buckingham, B. R. (1926). *Research for teachers.* New York: Silver, Burdett.

Burton, F. R. (1991). Teacher-researcher projects: An elementary school teacher's perspective. In J. Flood, J. M. Jensen, D. Lapp, & J. R. Squire (Eds.), *Handbook of research on teaching the English language arts* (pp. 226–230). New York: Macmillan.

Calhoun, E. F. (1994). *How to use action research in the self-renewing school.* Alexandria, VA: Association for Supervision and Curriculum Development.

Calkins, L. M. (1985). Forming research communities among naturalistic researchers. In B. W. McClelland & T. R. Donovan (Eds.), *Perspectives on research and scholarship in composition* (pp. 125–144). New York: Modern Language Association.

Carter, K. (1993). The place of story in the study of teaching and teacher education. *Educational Researcher, 22*(1), 5–12.

Caulfield, J. (1996). Students telling stories: Inquiry into the process of learning stories. In Z. Donoahue, M. A. Van Tassell, & L. Patterson (Eds.), *Research in the classroom: Talk, texts, and inquiry* (pp. 51–64). Newark, DE: International Reading Association.

Christensen, L., & Walker, B. J. (1992). Researching one's own teaching in a reading education course. In N. D. Padak, T. V. Raskinski, & J. Logan (Eds.), *Literacy research and practice: Foundations for the year 2000*, 14th Yearbook of the College Reading Association (pp. 57–64). Kent, OH: College Reading Association.

Cline, D. M. (1993). A year with reading workshop. In L. Patterson, C. M. Santa, K. G. Short, & K. Smith (Eds.), *Teachers are researchers: Reflection and action* (pp. 115–121). Newark, DE: International Reading Association.

Clyde, J. A., Condon, M. W. F., Daniel, K., & Sommer, M. K. (1993). Learning through whole language: Exploring book selection and use with preschoolers. In L. Patterson, C. M. Santa, K. G. Short, & K. Smith (Eds.), *Teachers are researchers: Reflection and action* (pp. 42–50). Newark, DE: International Reading Association.

Cochran-Smith, M., & Lytle, S. L. (1990). Research on teaching and teacher research: The issues that divide us. *Educational Researcher, 19*(2), 2–11.

Cochran-Smith, M., & Lytle, S. L. (Eds.). (1993). *Inside/outside: Teacher research and knowledge.* New York: Teachers College Press.

Commeyras, M., Reinking, D., Heubach, K. M., & Pagnucco, J. (1993). Looking within: A study of an undergraduate reading methods course. In D. J. Leu & C. K. Kinzer (Eds.), *Examining central issues in literacy research, theory, and practice*, 42nd Yearbook of the National Reading Conference (pp. 297–304). Chicago: National Reading Conference.

Cone, J. K. (1994). Appearing acts: Creating readers in a high school English class. *Harvard Educational Review, 64*(4), 450–473.

Connelly, F. M., & Clandinin, D. J. (1990). Stories of experience and narrative inquiry. *Educational Researcher, 19*(5), 2–14.

Corey, S. M. (1953). *Action research to improve school practices.* New York: Teachers College Bureau of Publications, Columbia University.

Corman, B. R. (1957). Action research: A teaching or a research method? *Review of Educational Research, 27,* 545–547.

Denzin, N. K., & Lincoln, Y. S. (1994). Part II: Major paradigms and perspectives. In N. K. Denzin & Y. S. Lincoln (Eds.), *Handbook of qualitative research* (pp. 99–104). Thousand Oaks, CA: Sage.

Dewey, J. (1929). *The sources of a science of education.* New York: Liverright.

Dey, I. (1993). *Qualitative data analysis: A user-friendly guide for social scientists.* New York: Routledge.

Donoahue, Z. (1996). Collaboration, community, and communication: Modes of discourse for teacher research. In Z. Donoahue, M. A. Van Tassell, & L. Patterson (Eds.), *Research in the classroom: Talk, texts, and inquiry* (pp. 91–107). Newark, DE: International Reading Association.

Donoahue, Z., Van Tassell, M. A., & Patterson, L. (Eds.). (1996). *Research in the classroom: Talk, texts, and inquiry.* Newark, DE: International Reading Association.

Duffy, A. (1997, December). *Outstanding elementary school preservice teachers' perceptions of, learnings about, and work with struggling readers.* Paper presented at the 47th Annual Meeting of the National Reading Conference, Scottsdale, AZ.

Duffy-Hester, A. M. (1999). *Effects of a balanced literacy program on the reading growth of elementary school struggling readers.* Unpublished doctoral dissertation, University of Georgia.

Elliott, J. (1991). *Action research for educational change.* Milton Keynes, England: Open University Press.

Erickson, F. (1986). Qualitative methods in research on teaching. In M. C. Wittrock (Ed.), *Handbook of research on teaching* (3rd ed., pp. 119–161). New York: Macmillan.

Feldgus, E. G. (1993). Walking to the words. In M. Cochran-Smith & S. Lytle (Eds.), *Inside/outside: Teacher research and knowledge* (pp. 170–177). New York: Teachers College Press.

Glaser, B. G., & Strauss, A. L. (1967). *The discovery of grounded theory: Strategies for qualitative research.* Hawthorne, NY: Aldine de Gruyter.

Goswami, D., & Stillman, P. (Eds.). (1987). *Reclaiming the classroom: Teacher research as an agency for change.* Upper Montclair, NJ: Boynton/Cook.

Grattan, K. W. (1997). They can do it too! Book club with first and second graders. In S. I. McMahon & T. E. Raphael (Eds.), *The book club connection: Literacy learning and classroom talk* (pp. 267–283). New York: Teachers College Press.

Grimm, N. (1990). Tutoring dyslexic college students: What these students teach us about literacy development. In D. A. Daiker & M. Morenberg (Eds.), *The writing teacher as researcher: Essays in the theory and practice of class-based research* (pp. 336–342). Portsmouth, NH: Boynton/Cook.

Halpern, E. S. (1983). *Auditing naturalistic inquiries: The development and application of a model.* Unpublished doctoral dissertation, Indiana University.

Hansen, J. (1989). Anna evaluates herself. In J. Allen & J. Mason (Eds.), *Risk makers, risk takers, risk breakers* (pp. 19–29). Portsmouth, NH: Heinemann.

Harvey, S., McAuliffe, S., Benson, L., Cameron, W., Kempton, S., Lusche, P., Miller, D., Schroeder, J., & Weaver, J. (1996). Teacher-researchers study the process of synthesizing in six primary classrooms. *Language Arts, 73,* 564–574.

Hodgkinson, H. L. (1957). Action research: A critique. *Journal of Educational Sociology, 31*(4), 137–153.

Hollingsworth, S., & Sockett, H. (Eds.). (1994). *Teacher research and educational reform,* 93rd Yearbook of the National Society for the Study of Education, Part 1. Chicago: University of Chicago Press.

Hopkins, D. (1993). *A teacher's guide to classroom research* (2nd ed.). Buckingham, England: Open University Press.

Hubbard, R. S., & Power, B. M. (1993a). *The art of classroom inquiry: A handbook for teacher-researchers.* Portsmouth, NH: Heinemann.

Hubbard, R. S., & Power, B. M. (1993b). Finding and framing a research question. In L. Patterson, C. M. Santa, K. G. Short, & K. Smith (Eds.), *Teachers are researchers: Reflection and action* (pp. 19–25). Newark, DE: International Reading Association.

Hubbard, R. S., & Power, B. M. (1999). *Living the questions: A guide for teacher-researchers.* York, ME: Stenhouse.

Jaeger, R. M. (Ed.). (1997). *Complementary methods for research in education* (2nd ed.). Washington, DC: American Educational Research Association.

Johnston, P. (1993). Lessons from the road: What I learned through teacher research. In M. Cochran-Smith & S. Lytle (Eds.), *Inside/outside: Teacher research and knowledge* (pp. 178–184). New York: Teachers College Press.

Kidder, L. H. (1981). Qualitative research and quasi-experimental frameworks. In M. B. Brewer & R. E. Collins (Eds.), *Scientific inquiry and the social sciences* (pp. 226–256). San Francisco: Jossey-Bass.

Kincheloe, J. L. (1991). *Teachers as researchers: Qualitative inquiry as a path to empowerment.* London: Falmer.

Krall, F. R. (1988). From the inside out—personal history as educational research. *Educational Theory, 38,* 467–479.

Lather, P. (1986). Research as praxis. *Harvard Educational Review, 56,* 257–277.

LeCompte, M. D., & Preissle, J. (1993). *Ethnography and qualitative design in educational research* (2nd ed.). New York: Academic Press.

Lincoln, Y. S., & Guba, E. G. (1985). *Naturalistic inquiry.* Newbury Park, CA: Sage.

Lytle, S., & Cochran-Smith, M. (1992). Teacher research as a way of knowing. *Harvard Educational Review, 62*(4).

Lytle, S. L., & Cochran-Smith, M. (1994a). Inquiry, knowledge, and practice. In S. Hollingsworth & H. Sockett (Eds.), *Teacher research and educational reform,* 93rd Yearbook of the National Society for the Study of Education, Part 1 (pp. 22–51). Chicago: University of Chicago Press.

Lytle, S. L., & Cochran-Smith, M. (1994b). Teacher research in English. In A. C. Purves (Ed.), *Encyclopedia of English studies and language arts* (pp. 1153–1155). New York: Scholastic.

Maher, A. (1994). An inquiry into reader response. In G. Wells, L. Bernard, M. A. Gianotti, C. Keating, C. Konjevic, M. Kowal, A. Maher, C. Mayer, T. Moscoe, E. Orzechowska, A. Smieja, & L. Swartz (Eds.), *Changing schools from within: Creating communities of inquiry* (pp. 81–97). Portsmouth, NH: Heinemann.

McFarland, K. P., & Stansell, J. C. (1993). Historical perspectives. In L. Patterson, C. M. Santa, K. G. Short, & K. Smith (Eds.), *Teachers are researchers: Reflection and action* (pp. 12–18). Newark, DE: International Reading Association.

Merriam, S. B. (1998). *Qualitative research and case study applications in education.* San Francisco: Jossey-Bass.

Miles, M. B., & Huberman, A. M. (1994). *An expanded sourcebook: Qualitative data analysis* (2nd ed.). Thousand Oaks, CA: Sage.

Mohr, M., & Maclean, M. (1987). *Working together: A guide for teacher-researchers.* Urbana, IL: National Council of Teachers of English.

Mosenthal, J. (1995). A practice-oriented approach to methods coursework in literacy teaching. In K. A. Hinchman, D. J. Leu, & C. K. Kinzer (Eds.), *Perspectives on literacy research and practice,* 44th Yearbook of the National Reading Conference (pp. 358–367). Chicago: National Reading Conference.

Murphy, P. (1994). Antonio: My student, my teacher: My inquiry begins. *Teacher Research: The Journal of Classroom Inquiry, 1*(2), 75–88.

Myers, M. (1985). *The teacher-researcher: How to study writing in the classroom.* Urbana, IL: National Council of Teachers of English.

Newton, M., Nash, D., & Ruffin, L. (1996). A whole language trilogy: The covered bridge connection. In G. Burnaford, J. Fischer, & D. Hobson (Eds.), *Teachers doing research: Practical possibilities* (pp. 82–90). Mahwah, NJ: Lawrence Erlbaum Associates.

Nixon, J. (1981). *A teacher's guide to action research.* London: Grant McIntyre.

Nocerino, M. A. (1993). A look at the process. In L. Patterson, C. M. Santa, K. G. Short, & K. Smith (Eds.), *Teachers are researchers: Reflection and action* (pp. 86–91). Newark, DE: International Reading Association.

O'Dell, L. (1987). Planning classroom research. In D. Goswami & P. R. Stillman (Eds.), *Reclaiming the classroom: Teacher research as an agency for change* (pp. 128–160). Upper Montclair, NJ: Boynton/Cook.

Olson, M. W. (1990). The teacher as researcher: A historical perspective. In M. W. Olson (Ed.), *Opening the door to classroom research* (pp. 1–20). Newark, DE: International Reading Association.

Paley, V. G. (1997). *The girl with the brown crayon.* Cambridge, MA: Harvard University Press.

Patterson, L., & Shannon, P. (1993). Reflection, inquiry, action. In L. Patterson, C. M. Santa, K. G. Short, & K. Smith (Eds.), *Teachers are researchers: Reflection and action* (pp. 7–11). Newark, DE: International Reading Association.

Phinney, M. Y., & Ketterling, T. (1997). Dialogue journals, literature, and urban Indian sixth graders. *Teacher Research: The Journal of Classroom Inquiry, 4*(2), 22–41.

Pils, L. J. (1993). "I love you, Miss Piss." *Reading Teacher, 46,* 648–653.

Ray, L. C. (1987). Reflections on classroom research. In D. Goswami & P. R. Stillman (Eds.), *Reclaiming the classroom: Teacher research as an agency for change* (pp. 219–242). Upper Montclair, NJ: Boynton/Cook.

Richards, J. (1987). Rx for editor in chief. In G. L. Bissex & R. H. Bullock (Eds.), *Seeing for ourselves: Case-study research by teachers of writing* (pp. 139–142). Portsmouth, NH: Heinemann.

Sagor, R. (1992). *How to conduct collaborative action research.* Alexandria, VA: Association for Supervision and Curriculum Development.

Santa, C. M., & Santa, J. L. (1995). Teacher as researcher. *JRB: A Journal of Literacy, 27,* 439–451.

Saunders, L. (1995). Unleashing the voices we rarely hear: Derrick's story. *Teacher Research: The Journal of Classroom Inquiry, 3*(1), 55–68.

Schon, D. A. (1983). *The reflective practitioner: How professionals think in action.* New York: Basic Books.

Sega, D. (1997). Reading and writing about our lives: Creating a collaborative curriculum in a class of high school misfits. *Teacher Research: The Journal of Classroom Inquiry, 4*(2), 101–111.

Shulman, L. S. (1997). Disciplines of inquiry in education: A new overview. In R. M. Jaeger (Ed.), *Complementary methods for research in education* (2nd ed., pp. 3–29). Washington, DC: American Educational Research Association.

Stenhouse, L. (1973). The humanistic curriculum project. In H. Butcher & H. Pont (Eds.), *Educational research in Britain 3* (pp. 149–167). London: University of London Press.

Stenhouse, L. (1975). *An introduction to curriculum research and development.* London: Heinemann.

Swift, K. (1993). Try Reading Workshop in your classroom. *Reading Teacher, 46,* 366–371.

Thomas, S., & Oldfather, P. (1995). Enhancing student and teacher engagement in literacy learning: A shared inquiry approach. *Reading Teacher, 49,* 192–202.

Threatt, S., Buchanan, J., Morgan, B., Strieb, L. Y., Sugarman, J., Swenson, J., Teel, K., & Tomlinson, J. (1994). Teachers' voices in the conversation about teacher research. In S. Hollingsworth & H. Sockett (Eds.), *Teacher research and educational reform*, 93rd Yearbook of the National Society for the Study of Education, Part 1 (pp. 222–244). Chicago: University of Chicago Press.

Von Dras, J. (1990). Transitions toward an integrated curriculum. In K. G. Short & K. M. Pierce (Eds.), *Talking about books: Creating literate communities* (pp. 121–133). Portsmouth, NH: Heinemann.

Wells, G., Bernard, L., Gianotti, M. A., Keating, C., Konjevic, C., Kowal, M., Maher, A., Mayer, C., Moscoe, T., Orzechowska, E., Smieja, A., & Swartz, L. (Eds.). (1994). *Changing schools from within: Creating communities of inquiry*. Toronto: Oise Press.

Wood, K. (1993). A case study of a writer. In L. Patterson, C. M. Santa, K. G. Short, & K. Smith (Eds.), *Teachers are researchers: Reflection and action* (pp. 106–114). Newark, DE: International Reading Association.

CHAPTER 2

Designing Programmatic Interventions

Therese D. Pigott
Loyola University, Chicago

Rebecca Barr
National-Louis University, Chicago

The purpose of this chapter is to think carefully about how literacy scholars can conduct useful evaluation studies of literacy interventions. Literacy interventions represent an important class of studies where theory, practice, and policy intersect. The history of evaluation research highlights many issues salient to the study of programmatic interventions. The tensions between the use of evaluation findings to inform local practice versus higher level policy, the difficulties in comparing different approaches to alleviate a problem, and the conflict between the purposes of basic research and evaluation research have been in existence since the first attempts at intervention studies.

Recognizing the struggles inherent in evaluation research emphasizes both the importance and the difficulty in designing and implementing research on programmatic interventions. As shown in this chapter, studies of literacy interventions differ in the extent to which they pursue implications for practice, theory development and policy; most often, interest in practice and policy prevails over that in theory. We argue that evaluations of programmatic interventions can, in fact, contribute to the three areas of theory, practice, and policy through careful design and a grounding in both literacy theory and classroom practice, a view not held by all concerned with evaluation (see Wolf, 1990).

This chapter provides a historical overview of evaluation research and its transformation during the past decade to include interpretive and formative modes of research. Throughout, studies by literacy researchers are discussed that have as their goal the assessment of programmatic interventions. The development of three approaches is considered: (a) experimental or quasi-experimental studies to compare the effectiveness of developed programs, (b) qualitative documentation to understand how a program works, and (c) formative modes of evaluation to enhance the design and development of programs. In the final section of the chapter, we draw conclusions and discuss ways in which literacy researchers can design studies of programmatic interventions with theoretical, practical, and policy implications.

TRADITIONAL PROGRAM EVALUATIONS

Much of the early writing on evaluation began with Smith and Tyler's (1942) Eight Year Study of curriculum changes in secondary schools. Smith and Tyler located the importance of this work in practice, seeking to gather information that would help teachers understand their influence on student behavior. Smith and Tyler did not mention policymakers as major stakeholders in the process of developing and improving programs, and were not concerned with the theoretical implications that might derive from assessing the relative merits of several options to alleviate a given problem.

With the expansion of programs to aid the poor during the Great Depression and the simultaneous development of new statistical techniques, interest in evaluation increased. The advent of federally funded evaluation studies in the 1960s brought a change in both the design and audience of evaluations. Where Smith and Tyler (1942) were concerned with providing empirical data for teachers to improve student achievement, the focus of large-scale evaluations centered on providing quantitative data for policymakers to make decisions about program effectiveness. Experimental design, influenced by Campbell and Stanley (1963), was the guiding principle for evaluation research. The methods Campbell and Stanley advocated were based on the random assignment of participants to a "treatment" and a "control" group in order to make causal inferences about the effects of an intervention. When random assignment was not feasible (a common occurrence), Campbell and Stanley suggested a number of quasi-experiments where a nonrandomly assigned "treatment" group is compared to a nonrandomly assigned control group such as the teacher's class from a previous year or a comparable class from a nearby school. A second type of quasi-experiment—an interrupted time-series design—compares an individual or a class during intervention with performance on multiple measures before and after the intervention. Discontinuities in the pattern of responses before and after an intervention are evidence for the treatment's effect. In this manner, a class or individual serves as its own control.

The results of experimental or quasi-experimental evaluation research provided policymakers with evidence about whether a program causes particular outcomes. The goal of many evaluation studies such as First Grade Reading and Head Start was to make value judgments about the relative merit of several different approaches to alleviate a social problem. Cronbach (1963) wrote about the usefulness of evaluations for making decisions about programs, especially about the large national projects from the 1960s, stressing the need to look at a wide range of possible consequences of programs, both intended and unintended by the program designers.

Program evaluations in the reading research literature since the 1900s have also been driven by the question: Which method is best? Based on the research approaches of psychologists and others following analytic science traditions, literacy researchers have tended to use quasi-experimental designs to establish the causal impact of programs on student outcomes (Pressley & Harris, 1994). In the reading research literature, traditional evaluation studies fall into two main groups: (a) smaller scale local studies comparing one or several experimental programs motivated by considerations of practice and sometimes theory, and (b) large-scale assessments of programs serving policy and accountability functions.

Small-Scale Intervention Studies

Studies conducted in the first half of the century, often by doctoral students, tended to be small-scale comparisons of an innovative method with a traditional approach in several matched classrooms. Chall (1967/1983/1995), for example, summarized that portion of the early literature that pertains to beginning reading methods. Although programmatic comparisons have long been the mainstay of literacy research, they were reinvigorated by research on reading processes in the 1970s and early 1980s. Once knowledge and strategies characterizing proficient reading were identified, attempts were made to see whether less proficient students could be taught this knowledge and learn to use these strategies. Although research of this sort focuses on many aspects of literacy, two areas in particular have received concentrated attention: (a) phonemic awareness and beginning reading methods (see the chapters by Blachman and Hiebert & Taylor in this volume) and (b) metacognitive and comprehension strategy research (see the chapter by Pressley in this volume). The goal of these studies was to determine the optimal methods to foster the literacy development of individuals with a focus on classroom practice.

This research differs from large-scale interventions (to be discussed next) in scope and sometimes in duration. Typically a series of instructional activities is developed to elaborate, but not replace, ongoing instruction. The duration of these activities may vary from a few days to a semester or a year. More recent studies have shifted in focus to longer term and more comprehensive content-specific strategy programs in such areas as literacy, social studies, history, science, and math (e.g., Bereiter & Bird, 1985; Gaskins, Anderson, Pressley, Cunicelli, & Sallow, 1993; Guthrie et al., 1996; Morrow, Pressley, Smith, & Smith, 1997; Paris & Oka, 1986; Pressley et al., 1992; Siegel & Fonzi, 1995). We are making a distinction between the use of experimental methods in evaluation of interventions and experimental research in general. Intervention studies have as their express purpose the evaluation of a program for improving instruction. The broader field of experimental research in education and the social sciences includes intervention studies, but also may include experiments focused on questions not related to a classroom or instructional intervention.

Many validity concerns characterize these smaller scale studies. Lysynchuk, Pressley, d'Ailly, Smith, and Cake (1989) examined 38 studies of comprehension strategy instruction in elementary schools that had been published in selective educational research journals. They found a variety of internal validity flaws including "(a) not assigning subjects randomly to treatment and control conditions, (b) not exposing experimental and control subjects to the same training materials, (c) not providing information about the amount of time spent on dependent variable tasks, (d) not including checks on the success of the manipulation and process measures, (e) not using the appropriate units of analysis, and (f) not assessing either long-term effects or the generalization of the strategies to other tasks and materials" (p. 458). Unfortunately, as they noted, some studies with major flaws limiting the conclusions that can be drawn have already influenced theory and practice (see Ridgeway, Dunston, & Qian, 1993, for similar findings for research conducted in secondary schools).

Until recently, it has been common practice not to observe the experimental and control instruction; thus it has not been possible to know whether the theoretically based ideal program has been realized and the extent to which its manifestation varies across classes for different pupils and situational conditions. As Lysynchuk and colleagues (1989) found, another common design error of small-scale studies has been to treat the individual student as the unit of analysis, rather than the class (or school or district). Yet, when the class is used as the unit of analysis, with only two or three classes involved in each condition, there is insufficient power to detect a reliable difference between treatment and control conditions.

Some smaller scale case studies by literacy researchers use variations on traditional experimental designs, such as the interrupted time-series and control series designs (Campbell, 1963; 1969). Yaden (1995) described what he referred to as "reversal designs" involving a time series including a period in which baseline data are taken, a period of intervention during which the same response data are taken, followed by a period in which the intervention is withdrawn. Smolkin, Yaden, Brown, and Hofius (1992), for example, used time series measures during parent–child read-alouds to assess the effect of such features of texts as genre, visual design choices, and discourse. Rose and Beattie (1986) used a base period followed by an intervention to assess the effects of teacher-directed versus taped previewing on oral reading. Single-subject experimental research involving an individual child, a group, or a class is becoming more common as a useful means to assess the effects of literacy programs (Neuman & McCormick, 1995).

Large-Scale Evaluation Studies in the Reading Literature

The 1960s also saw an emphasis on large-scale summative evaluations of literacy programs. Prompted by the Russian launching of Sputnik (Pearson, 1997) and perhaps by concerns pertaining to the relatively low literacy achievement of minority groups (Willis & Harris, 1997), federal funding for the First Grade Reading Studies was provided to address, once and for all, the best way to teach beginning reading (Bond & Dykstra, 1967; Dykstra, 1968). The large number of classrooms representing each method promised enough statistical power to detect differences between methods even when the classroom served as the unit of analysis. A common set of tests of pupil prereading ability permitted assessment of the comparability of samples across project sites and methods before and after the intervention.

Despite the attention to experimental design issues, comparisons between basal and nonbasal approaches to reading produced mixed results. The experimental group outperformed the comparison group on only some of the outcome measures, and these results varied across sites (Bond & Dykstra, 1967). The failure to discern differences in effectiveness among methods may have been due to the large variation found in learning outcomes within methods. This variation suggests that treatment implementation may have been inconsistent and/or that situational factors may have had a strong influence on the way methods developed locally. Because instruction was not observed, these possibilities could not be confirmed. In addition, the theoretical implications of the evaluation were limited because the measures used, although common across sites, were not tied conceptually to the unique characteristics of the programs.

Similarly, in the 1970s, evaluations of the Follow Through interventions in primary grades designed to provide support for at-risk children (Stallings, 1975; Stebbins, St. Pierre, Proper, Anderson, & Cerva, 1977) addressed the problem of how to compare curricula that differed widely in philosophies and goals. The comparisons involved multiple measures and multiple outcomes, not all of which were shared by each program. Observational evidence describing what the treatment was and who the children were revealed that the instruction children experienced was not uniform across all sites. Variability occurred both in the implementation of the study design and in the programs themselves, lessening the confidence of researchers in the potential of large-scale evaluation to influence and create policy.

Large-scale evaluations such as the First Grade Reading Studies and Follow Through also suffered from a number of threats to internal validity due to the selection of students from the low end of a test-score distribution. These threats include statistical regression to the mean, subject selection bias, and mortality issues. Recent reviews of the evaluations of Reading Recovery (Hiebert, 1994; Shanahan & Barr, 1995) identified such concerns as limiting confidence in conclusions that can be drawn about program effectiveness. Large-scale evaluations of federally funded programs for at-risk students, such as the Chapter and Title programs, suffer from similar threats to internal validity.

QUALITATIVE DOCUMENTATION OF PROGRAMS

The equivocal results of evaluations based on a quasi-experimental model led many to call for considering descriptions of programs and the perceptions of participants as part of evaluations. Weiss (1972) argued that decisions about a given program rarely focus on a summative judgment, such as a choice between a program and no program. Often, what is of interest to policymakers, teachers, and other stakeholders centers on what aspects of particular programs are related to the program's intended and unintended consequences (what Weiss calls a "process model"). Cook and Reichardt (1979) edited a monograph advocating the joining of qualitative and quantitative forms of evaluation. Even earlier, from a sociological perspective, Hyman, Wright, and Hopkins (1962) argued for the importance of including evidence that described the nature of programs, participant perspectives, and unanticipated outcomes. Understanding what aspects of a program are optimal and what are less than desirable requires intimate knowledge of the students, teachers, and classroom processes from both the evaluator and participants' perspectives.

Since the mid 1980s, the frustration with the lack of use of evaluation studies by policymakers has paralleled that in the broader field of educational research (see, e.g., Peterson, 1998), leading to discussions about the nature of social reality, and ultimately to discussions about the most appropriate methodology for examining a program or intervention. Stake (1975) was one of the first evaluators to question the exclusive use of strategies focusing on the identification of input-output relationships in evaluation research. Influenced by Stake's perspective, researchers such as Guba and Lincoln (1989) rejected the premises underlying experimental and quasi-experimental studies altogether, arguing that there is no single social reality to be discovered by empirical research, but instead that individuals in a situation construct their own meanings and interpretations of a given context. Thus, researchers using interpretive data collection methods see the goal of research to understand and document a given situation or context. Although evaluators such as Patton (1990), Eisner (1991), and Pitman and Maxwell (1992) agree with Guba and Lincoln's emphasis on gathering participants' perceptions and observations as the primary method for data collection, each takes a slightly different approach to evaluating programs that reflects various concerns about the field of evaluation and social science research.

In literacy research, qualitative evaluation methods have been used in two ways: (a) to provide a description of the nature of the experimental instruction in the context of traditional evaluation studies, and (b) to represent interpretively the perceptions and experiences of participants concerning the program. For both, a guiding question may be "How does the program work?" but the assumptions underlying the two approaches differ.

Experimental Program Documentation

Literacy researchers, recognizing the limitations of skeletal descriptions of instruction, have begun to observe program implementation and solicit the perceptions of program participants (see, e.g., Alvermann, O'Brien, & Dillon, 1990; Beck, McKeown, Sandora, Kucan, & Worthy, 1996; Gaskins et al., 1993; Goldenberg, 1992; Guzzetti & Williams, 1996; Pressley et al., 1992; Saunders, O'Brien, Lennon, & McLean, 1998). Although the basic evaluation goal continues to focus on determining whether a program accounts for learning outcomes, the inclusion of more comprehensive descriptions of programs empowers researchers to understand why certain results have occurred. Robinson (1998), in her discussion of research methods for bridging the research-practice gap, argued that the understanding of practice requires the acknowledgment that classroom practices are context dependent.

In their comparison of skills-based or whole language classroom programs, for example, Dahl and Freppon (1995) examined how inner-city children in the United States made sense of their beginning reading and writing instruction. Data were gathered through field notes, audio recordings of reading and writing episodes, student papers, and the pre/post written language measures. In addition, Dahl and Freppon identified important instructional differences based on their ethnographic observation.

Teaching approaches were characterized in terms of learning opportunities in the areas of phonics, writing, and response to literature. These descriptions suggested that both sets of teachers taught in these areas, but did so in different ways. In the area of phonics, for example, skills-based teachers addressed letter–sound relations in skill lessons, by showing students how to sound out words, and having students sound out words as they read aloud. Whole-language teachers also demonstrated sounding out procedures, but during whole group instruction with big books, and provided practice on letter–sound relations during reading and writing. In addition to validating adherence to a theoretically based method, such observations enable researchers to understand how students learn, and to assess how other conditions may affect the outcomes.

Interpretive Approaches to Evaluation Research

As discussed earlier, some qualitative researchers argue that the preoccupation of evaluation researchers with linear and causal relations misrepresents the complexity of the interaction that occurs between instruction programs and student development. As an alternative, interpretive researchers such as Guba and Lincoln (1989) and Eisner (1991) argued for seeing evaluation as a value-laden activity that is inherently social and political. Studies of response to literature, with origins in the theoretical and empirical work of scholars from the reader response tradition within literacy theory, tend to reflect evaluation models that are interpretive in form (see, e.g., Brock, 1997; Hickman, 1983; Marshall, 1987; McMahon, 1997).

To illustrate, Eeds and Wells (1989) in their study of "grand conversations" sought to describe patterns of classroom discussion and how teachers and students responded to text and to each other. They compared what actually occurred in groups with an idealized model that they referred to as "grand conversation." By this, they meant the construction and disclosure of "deeper meaning, enriching understanding for all participants" (p. 5). Focus in this form of evaluation research is on the relation between "intents or goals," as implicit in the notion of "grand conversations," and what was experienced by participants in groups as described through journal responses and observation. The intentions become the standard against which judgments are made about the success and appropriateness of the group activities. This approach entails a description of programs as seen through the eyes of participants, and allows for differences to emerge in goals (those of program developers vs. those of teachers or students), as well as in constructions of program interaction (those of observers and those of participants).

FORMATIVE APPROACHES TO PROGRAM EVALUATION

A final shift in thinking about evaluation research has occurred recently. Instead of conceptualizing evaluation as an experimental or an interpretive portrayal of an established program, researchers have argued that it is more useful to use evaluation in a formative way to enhance program effectiveness as it is being developed. This approach comes to education via the design sciences developed by technological researchers. In considering the many technologies introduced into classrooms, Collins (1991) noted that remarkably little systematic knowledge has accumulated to guide the design of future innovations. He described the importance of developing "a methodology for carrying out design experiments, to study the different ways of using technology in classrooms and schools" (p. 17). Similarly, Newman (1990, 1991) argued for the usefulness of what he referred to as formative experiments. These new approaches are more akin to the design sciences of aeronautics and artificial intelligence than the analytic sciences of physics and psychology. That is, they seek to focus on what teaching and learning is going on as students interact in the context of a new program, rather than the more traditional question of whether certain programs are better or worse for certain types of learners or for certain types of content.

In a design experiment or a formative experiment, a researcher might, for example, identify two comparably effective teachers with differences in style of teaching (activity centers vs. whole-class instruction) who wish to teach a selected unit developed by the researchers. Assuming the teachers teach multiple classes, each would be asked to use the specially developed unit with half their classes and their own curriculum with the other half. Evaluation of the experiment might include pre- and posttests of student understanding, structured interviews with students, class observations, teacher daily notes, and follow-up after a year or two to determine student retention of learning and teacher practice. Such an approach holds the promise for addressing issues of practice and theory, as well as policy.

Although not yet a common evaluation approach in the field of literacy, several researchers have conducted evaluation research of this sort. Brown (1992) stated, "As a design scientist in my field, I attempt to engineer innovative educational environments and simultaneously conduct experimental studies of those innovations" (p. 141). Based on Newman's (1990) description of formative experiments, Reinking and colleagues (Reinking & Pickle; 1993; Reinking & Watkins, 1997) implemented a time-series evaluation through which they assessed ways in which multimedia book reviews could be enhanced to increase the independent reading of fourth graders. Instead of the conventional book review, Reinking and his collaborators developed a multimedia book review designed, because of its novelty, to enhance student involvement in reading. They collected baseline data on students' reading prior to the intervention, as well as measures of students attitudes toward reading, field observations, focus-group interviews, parent questionnaires, and teacher logs. Given this evidence, they discovered that the intervention had unanticipated effects on students' writing. One was that poor readers in one class avoided creating the multimedia book reviews, which they attributed to the public nature of the database. The solution they tried was to encourage all students to consider entering reviews of easy books for lower grade children to read. Although the implications of formative experiments and design experiments for practice are clear and immediate, their consequence for theory and policy will be easier to assess once more studies using this approach have been conducted and reported.

IMPLICATIONS FOR THEORY, PRACTICE, POLICY, AND RESEARCH

Debates about the use of experimental designs, interpretive data analysis, and formative approaches to evaluation continue. How can we design evaluation studies to be useful to multiple audiences at the local and policy levels, and how can evaluation studies provide information that can be useful to practice, policy, and theory? At the local, practice level, usefulness implies that the evaluation provides information about the program, its implementation, and its effectiveness for a specific classroom or a particular school with particular children. At the policy level, usefulness encompasses information about the program that can influence decision making, such as information about the benefits and costs of a program and its potential for alleviating a social problem. At the level of theoretical development, however, expectations have been more limited about whether evaluation studies could contribute to knowledge about teaching and learning. Because of the emphasis on usefulness to local and policy stakeholders, many evaluations have been atheoretical, unconcerned with how the information gathered in the evaluation of a particular program may help educational researchers think about issues of classroom learning and teaching.

The expense and importance of conducting evaluation research require attention to the design of evaluations that can contribute to theory, practice, and policy. Although it may be difficult to serve all three purposes, inattention to many of these issues has left the field in a crisis of credibility. Evaluation studies provide an important opportunity to work at the intersection of practice, theory, and policy because the research is inherently concerned with how an intervention "works" in a given context. These ideas are not new; August and Hakuta (1997), in a review of studies on educating language-minority children, called for similar measures to strengthen the research literature on this issue and to develop the potential for research to have a larger influence on public policy. As shown in the previous examples, a number of issues must be addressed in an evaluation in order to contribute to theory, practice, and policy.

First, the intervention and evaluation should both be grounded in theory. The intervention should have some demonstrated connection to literacy theory, which will in turn influence decisions about the design of the evaluation itself. For example, the data to be collected, whether involving tests and scales or observations and interviews, should be selected while keeping the nature of the intervention(s) in mind. One lesson from the early large-scale assessment studies is the danger of using measures that are not sensitive to the particular goals of the program.

Second, the question of "what works" is an important one for studying programmatic interventions, but needs to be modified. As Venezky (personal communication, 1997) wrote, the question should be "for whom does it work, and why?" The translation from theory to practice is not linear—information about the implementation of the intervention, how it works in a given setting, and whether teachers and students experience differential effects of the program (including unintended and potentially harmful effects) allows a deeper understanding not only of practice but also of how theory might be improved as a result of practice. The large-scale evaluation studies provide an example of the importance of understanding implementation issues. Knowing *if* the program works is not enough. How the program works, under what conditions, and for what particular students and teachers provides the information needed to contribute to theory, practice and policy.

Third, the study must be well designed, with attention to alternative explanations for results, and possible confounding factors. Campbell and Stanley (1963) and Cook and Campbell (1979) detailed these threats in experimental and quasi-experimental studies. Descriptive studies are not immune to these issues. Multiple sources of information allow a fuller description of the programmatic innovation, and decrease the risk of the evaluation missing other perspectives on the program. Although the goal of these studies may not be to generalize to a wide group, attention to competing views of the program increases the likelihood of assessing important outcomes and addressing implementation issues.

The development of evaluation research methods that can provide theoretically based knowledge to inform both practice and policy will continue. Recently, writing about evaluation and the relationship between research, policy, and practice focused on the importance of collaborations of participants at differing levels of the educational system. Patton (1997) summarized his theory of utilization-focused evaluation by emphasizing that evaluations should be driven by the intended use of the results for the intended users. As Hargreaves (1996) wrote, "Policy is therefore best secured … through communities of people within and across schools who create policies, talk about them, process them, inquire into them, and reformulate them, bearing in mind the circumstances and the children they know best" (p. 115). For evaluation research to contribute to educational research, policy, and practice, we need both carefully designed studies and collaborative participation from all those who care about research, policy, and practice.

REFERENCES

Alvermann, D. E., O'Brien, D. G., & Dillon, D. R. (1990). What teachers do when they say they're having discussions of content area reading assignments: A qualitative analysis. *Reading Research Quarterly, 25,* 296–322.

August, D., & Hakuta, K. (1997). Program evaluation. In D. August & K. Hakuta (Eds.), *Educating language minority children* (pp. 55–71). National Research Council Institute of Medicine. Washington, DC: National Academy Press.

Beck, I. L., McKeown, M. G., Sandora, C., Kucan, L., & Worthy, J. (1996). Questioning the author: A yearlong classroom implementation to engage students with text. *Elementary School Journal, 96,* 385–414.

Bereiter, C., & Bird, M. (1985). Use of thinking aloud in identification and teaching of reading comprehension strategies. *Cognition and Instruction, 2,* 131–156.

Bond, G. L., & Dykstra, R. (1967). The Cooperative Research Program in first-grade reading instruction. *Reading Research Quarterly, 2,* 5–142.

Brock, C. (1997). Exploring the use of Book Club with second-language learners in mainstream classrooms. In S. I. McMahon, & T. E. Raphael (Eds.), *The Book Club connection: Literacy learning and classroom talk* (pp. 141–158). New York: Teachers College Press.

Brown, A. L. (1992). Design experiments: Theoretical and methodological challenges in creating complex interventions in classroom settings. *Journal of the Learning Sciences, 2,* 141–178.

Campbell, D. T. (1963). From description to experimentation: Interpreting trends as quasi-experiments. In C. W. Harris (Ed.), *Problems in measuring change* (pp. 212–242). Madison: University of Wisconsin Press.

Campbell, D. T. (1969). Reforms as experiments. *American Psychologist, 24,* 409–429.

Campbell, D. T., & Stanley, J. C. (1963). *Experimental and quasi-experimental designs for research.* Chicago: Rand McNally.

Chall, J. S. (1995). *Learning to read: The areas debate.* New York: McGraw-Hill. (Original work published 1968 and 1983)

Collins, A. (1991). Toward a design science of education. In E. Scanlon & T. O'Shea (Eds.), *New directions in educational technology* (pp. 15–22). New York: Springer-Verlag.

Cook, T. D., & Campbell, D. T. (1979). *Ouasi-experimentation: Design and analysis issues for field settings.* Chicago: Rand McNally.

Cook, T. D., & Reichardt, C. S. (Eds.). (1979). *Qualitative and quantitative methods in evaluation research.* Beverly Hills, CA: Sage.

Cronbach, L. J. (1963). Course improvement through evaluation. *Teachers College Record, 64,* 672–684.

Dahl, K. L., & Freppon, P. A. (1995). A comparison of inner-city children's interpretations of reading and writing instruction in the early grades in skills-based and whole language classrooms. *Reading Research Quarterly, 30,* 50–74.

Dykstra, R. (1968). Summary of the second grade phase of the Cooperative Research Program in primary reading instruction. *Reading Research Quarterly, 4,* 49–70.

Eeds, M., & Wells, D. (1989). Grand conversations: An explanation of meaning construction in literature study groups. *Research in the Teaching of English, 23,* 4–29.

Eisner, E. W. (1991). *The enlightened eve: Qualitative inquiry and the enhancement of educational practice.* New York: Macmillan.

Gaskins, I. W., Anderson, R. C., Pressley, M., Cunicelli, E. A., & Sallow, E. (1993). Six teachers' dialogue during cognitive process instruction. *Elementary School Journal, 93,* 277–304.

Goldenberg, C. (1992). Instructional conversations: Promoting comprehension through discussion. *Reading Teacher, 46,* 316–326.

Guba, E. G., & Lincoln, Y. S. (1989). *Fourth generation evaluation.* Newbury Park, CA: Sage.

Guthrie, J. T., Van Meter, P., McCann, A. D., Wigfield, A., Bennett, L., Poundstone, C .C., Rice, M. E., Faibisch, F. M., Hunt, B., & Mitchell, A. M. (1996). Growth of literacy engagement: Changes in motivations and strategies during concept-oriented reading instruction. *Reading Research Quarterly, 31,* 306–332.

Guzzetti, B. J., & Williams, W. O. (1996). Gender, text, and discussion: Examining intellectual safety in the science classroom. *Journal of Research in Science Teaching, 22,* 5–20.

Hargreaves, A. (1996). Transforming knowledge: Blurring the boundaries between research, policy, and practice. *Educational Evaluation and Policy Analysis, 18,* 105–122.

Hickman, J. (1983). Everything considered: Response to literature in an elementary school setting. *Journal of Research and Development in Education, 16,* 8–13.

Hiebert, E. H. (1994). Reading Recovery in the United States: What difference does it make to an age cohort? *Educational Researcher, 23*(9), 15–25.

Hyman, H. H., Wright, C. R., & Hopkins, T. K. (1962). *Applications of methods of evaluation: Four studies of the encampment for citizenship.* Berkeley: University of California Press.

Lysynchuk, L. M., Pressley, M., d'Ailly, H., Smith, M., & Cake, H. (1989). A methodological analysis of experimental studies of comprehension strategy instruction. *Reading Research Quarterly, 24,* 458–470.

Marshall, J. D. (1987). The effects of writing on students' understanding of literary texts. *Research in the Teaching of English, 21,* 30–63.

McMahon, S. I. (1997). Reading in the Book Club program. In S. I. McMahon & T. E. Raphael (Eds.), *The Book Club connection* (pp. 47–68). New York: Teachers College Press.

Morrow, L. M., Pressley, M., Smith, J. K., & Smith, M. (1997). The effect of a literature-based program integrated into literacy and science instruction with children from diverse backgrounds. *Reading Research Quarterly, 32,* 55–76.

Neuman, S. B., & McCormick, S. (Eds.). (1995). Single-subject experimental research: *Applications for literacy.* Newark, DE: International Reading Association.

Newman, D. (1990). Opportunities for research on the organizational impact of school computers. *Educational Researcher, 19,* 8–13.

Newman, D. (1991). Formative experiments on the convolution of technology and the educational environment. In E. Scanlon & T. O'Shea (Eds.), *New directions in educational technology* (pp. 15–22). New York: Springer-Verlag.

Paris, S. G., & Oka, E. R. (1986). Children's reading strategies, metacognition, and motivation. *Developmental Review, 6,* 25–56.

Patton, M. Q. (1990). *Qualitative evaluation and research methods* (2nd ed.). London: Sage.

Patton, M. Q. (1997). *Utilization-focused evaluation* (3rd ed.). Thousand Oaks, CA: Sage.

Pearson, P. D. (1997). The First-Grade Studies: A personal reflection. *Reading Research Quarterly, 32,* 428–432.

Peterson, P. L. (1998). Why do educational research? Rethinking our roles and identified, our texts and contexts. *Educational Researcher, 27*(3), 4–10.

Pitman, M. A., & Maxwell, J. A. (1992). Qualitative approaches to evaluation: Models and methods. In M. D. LeCompte, W. L. Millroy, & J. Preissle (Eds.), *The handbook of qualitative research in education* (pp. 729–770). New York: Academic Press.

Pressley, M., El-Dinary, P. B., Gaskins, I., Schuder, T., Bergman, J., Almasi, J., & Brown, R. (1992). Beyond direct explanation: Transactional instruction of reading comprehension strategies. *Elementary School Journal, 92,* 511–554.

Pressley, M., & Harris, K. R. (1994). Increasing the quality of educational intervention research. *Educational Psychology Review, 6,* 191–208.

Reinking, D., & Pickle, J. M. (1993). Using a formative experiment to study how computers affect reading and writing in classrooms. In D. J. Leu & C. K. Kinzer (Eds.), *Examining central issues in literacy research, theory, and practice* (pp. 263–270). Chicago, IL: National Reading Conference.

Reinking, D., & Watkins, J. (1997). *Balancing change and understanding in literacy research through formative experiments.* Paper presented at the meeting of the National Reading Conference, Scottsdale, AZ.

Ridgeway, V. G., Dunston, P. J., & Qian, G. (1993). A methodological analysis of teaching and learning strategy research at the secondary school level. *Reading Research Quarterly, 28,* 335–349.

Robinson, V. M. J. (1998). Methodology and the research-practice gap. *Educational Researcher, 27,* 17–26.

Rose, T. L., & Beattie, J. R. (1986). Relative effects of teacher-directed and taped previewing on oral reading. *Learning Disabilities Quarterly, 9,* 193–199.

Saunders, W., O'Brien, G., Lennon, D., & McLean, J. (1998). Making the transition to English literacy successful: Effective strategies for studying literature with transition students. In R. Gersten & R. Jimenez (Eds.), *Effective strategies for teaching language minority students* (pp. 99–132). Belmont, CA: Wadsworth.

Siegel, M., & Fonzi, J. M. (1995). The practice of reading in an inquiry-oriented mathematics class. *Reading Research Quarterly, 30,* 632–673.

Shanahan, T., & Barr, R. (1995). Reading Recovery: An independent evaluation of the effects of an early instructional intervention for at risk learners. *Reading Research Quarterly, 30,* 958–996.

Smith, E. R., & Tyler, R. W. (1942). *Appraising and recording student progress.* New York: Harper & Row.

Smolkin, L. B., Yaden, D. B., Brown, L., & Hofius, B. (1992). The effects of genre, visual design choices, and discourse structure on preschoolers' responses to picture books during parent-child read-alouds. In C. K. Kinzer & D. J. Leu (Eds.), *Literacy research, theory and practice: Views from many perspectives* (pp. 291–301). Chicago: National Reading Conference.

Stake, R. E. (Ed.). (1975). *Evaluating the arts in education: A responsive approach.* Columbus, OH: Merrill.

Stallings, J. (1975). Implementation and child effects of teaching practices in Follow Through classrooms. *Monographs of the Society for Research in Child Development, 40.*

Stebbins, L. B., St. Pierre, R. G., Proper, E. G., Anderson, R. B., & Cerva, T. R. (1977). *Education as experimentation: A planned variation model. Vol. IV-A. An evaluation of Follow Through.* Cambridge, MA: Abt Associates.

Weiss, C. H. (1972). *Evaluation research: Methods for assessing program effectiveness.* Englewood Cliffs, NJ: Prentice Hall.

Willis, A. I., & Harris, V. J. (1997). Expanding the boundaries: A reaction to the First-Grade Studies. *Reading Research Quarterly, 32,* 439–445.

Wolf, R. M. (1990). *Evaluation in education: Foundations of competency assessment and program review* (3rd ed.). New York: Praeger.

Yaden, D. B. (1995). Reversal designs. In S. B. Neuman & S. McCormick (Eds.), *Single subject experimental research: Applications for literacy* (pp. 32–46). Newark, DE: International Reading Association.

CHAPTER 3

Undertaking Historical Research in Literacy

E. Jennifer Monaghan
Brooklyn College of the City University of New York

Douglas K. Hartman
University of Pittsburgh

VALUES OF STUDYING THE HISTORY OF LITERACY

The value of history has its own history. Called *historiodicy*, this justification of the study of the past has been an essential practice of historians for almost 3,000 years (Marrou, 1966). Their work has been shouted down, burned up, declared evil, proclaimed prophetic, forgotten, and ignored. It is this marginalization of historical work, especially as it relates to the literacy community, that moves us to sketch briefly several reasons why studying the history of literacy is of value (Moore, Monaghan, & Hartman, 1997).

The most time-honored rationale for knowing and doing history is that we can learn from the past. The challenge, however, is in knowing which lessons to draw on and how best to make use of them. Making straightforward, one-on-one applications of the past to the present can distort the unique dimensions of each event and lead to erroneous conclusions. Even judiciously constructed lessons are no guarantee of what to do or decide in the present. Thomas Jefferson, for example, wrote that the lessons of history were better for preventing a repeat of past follies than for divining wise future directions (cited in Gagnon, 1989, p. 113). So the pedagogical value of historical research on literacy is that it provides us with possible rather than probable understandings, and the ability to take precautions rather than control possible futures.

There are other reasons for undertaking historical work. One is that history provides yet another layer of context for understanding events by locating them in specific times and places. Understanding a particular reading method, for instance, requires more than simply knowing about it: It must be located in the milieu of its times. Moreover, historical research helps us to identify who we are as a community. History is a vital sign of any community's maturity, vitality, and growing self-awareness, and it provides the basis for a collective sense of direction and purpose. By creating a set of connections

33

between past and present, we see ourselves as part of a drama larger than our own particular interests, areas of study, or organizational affiliations. As members of the reading community, in particular—a community that has neglected its own past—we need to gain a clearer picture of who we are by examining where we have been.

Historical research also promotes interdisciplinarity. To answer the questions that matter in our past brings us in contact with a wider circle of colleagues and their work, from librarians to antiquarians. In addition, studying history is intellectually enriching and challenging. The most thought-provoking history asks the "why" questions. Why did progressive education fail? Why did the *McGuffey Readers* become the most popular school readers of the 19th century? Why were women in colonial America taught to read, but less often to write? And why is the book shaped as it is? Answering questions like these forces us to theorize, search for and weigh evidence, make inferences, and draw conclusions. All social scientists do this, of course, but the work of history is especially adept at asking and answering questions that are not amenable to experimental, observational, or case study approaches. Finally, historical research is fun. What other discipline allows one to snoop into the concerns of others and label the product serious scholarly work?

Perhaps the biggest disadvantage associated with literacy history is that its messages for the present are equivocal. Indeed, this may have been why it has taken a profession wedded to presentism so long to embrace it.

A SHORT HISTORY OF HISTORIOGRAPHY

Not only do the values of history have a history, but the methods of doing history have one as well. Called *historiography*, this self-conscious practice of thinking about the development of historical scholarship traces the ways in which history has been undertaken back to the oldest known artifacts of human activity. The historical practices of early human beings were very different from those of today. By their oral telling of myths, legends, and fables, humans attempted to explain the unpredictable happenings of the world as products of supernatural causes. And their written records recounted long lists of deeds done in warfare, sometimes chronologically, but mostly in registers of isolated pieces of information that offered no interpretation or analysis (Butterfield, 1981).

Historical work took on some measure of analytic detachment with the Jews of ancient Israel. Their reports in the books of the Old Testament displayed a capacity for assembling information from many sources with an eye toward accurate appraisals, but their accounts were still primarily the product of religious experience rather than any kind of analytic inquiry (Momigliano, 1990).

The first move toward an analytic approach that looked into the facts and determined their accuracy was undertaken by the Greeks. Herodotus and Thucydides, for example, departed from the practice of explaining human events as the outcome of divine will and interpreted the human affairs of governance and warfare as the product of human wills. They did so by checking information against participant and eyewitness reports, consulting archived documents, and thinking carefully about the motivations and causations for actions and events. And when they wrote, they wrote to instruct others, anticipating parallel future circumstances that could be avoided or taken. The underlying assumption in all their work was that history repeated itself through endless cycles (Grant, 1970).

The Romans, influenced by the Greeks, further developed practices for writing biography and memoir. But the emerging Christian view of history that was taking hold within the Roman empire melded the religious and analytic historical practices of the past. Early on, Christians compiled the Gospels in such a way that their beliefs, grounded in what they held were actual occurrences, could be defended against challenges and used to display the continuities of the New Testament with the Old. Later they developed universalist histories that located all human activity under the hand of God from Creation, in Genesis, to Armageddon, in Revelation. These were followed by ecclesiastical histories that detailed the rise of Christianity throughout the Mediterranean world after the Roman Emperor Constantine converted in the fourth century (Gay & Cavanaugh, 1972).

But St. Augustine's *The City of God* provided the most influential statement of the Christian interpretation of history. He rejected outright the Greek idea of cyclical history movements and reframed history as a progression along a line with a clear beginning, middle, and end—from Creation, through this world, to the eternal world, as God worked out his will through history (Barker, 1982).

Augustine's method of using analytic tools within this religious framework was followed closely by medieval historians for 10 centuries. They faithfully informed readers of their information sources, but relied unquestioningly on information from earlier accounts, rarely using original sources to check and cross-check the accuracy of historical statements or the truthfulness of earlier assertions. To question the accuracy and motives of earlier historical accounts would be to question God's providence itself (Dahmus, 1982).

Historical methods in the modern age developed gradually from the 14th through the 19th centuries. The fundamental change entailed a shift away from supernatural explanations of history toward secular approaches (Breisach, 1983/1994). By the early 20th century, academic history had become completely secularized, and the history of the United States was viewed as a steady march toward perfection (American "triumphalism").

But, ironically, at a time when verification of sources was easier than it had ever been, the validity of historical knowledge itself came under public attack. Public confidence in history as the purveyor of "truth" yielded to skepticism, as younger historians presented conflicting versions of reality: Was Christopher Columbus the heroic seafarer of the older history or the purveyor of genocide of the new? Historians became aware of how their own predilections, and even language itself, influenced their scholarship.

Since the late 1950s, historians have moved through a succession of reconceptualizations of their craft. First came the new social history of the 1960s and 1970s, which made quantitative research the norm and the lives of the marginalized its target. Then followed, in the 1970s and 1980s, investigations of the intersections among history, language, and thought. These are associated with the work of Michel Foucault (1972), who insisted on the importance of discoursing about discourse, and with that of Jacques Derrida (1967/1976, 1978), who challenged the authority of text by positing that each reader reads (deconstructs) text differently. Both writers, in making language itself an object of study, cast doubt on language's ability to represent reality. Finally, the "postmodernism" of the 1990s elevated culture to a level of importance once held by the supernatural.

In response to these transformations of the field, Joyce Appleby urged, as do we, that historians of the new histories should continue to be "cultural translators," interpreting our past for consumers of history while new questions lead to new answers "through the mediating filter of culture" (Appleby, 1998, pp. 11, 12; cf. Appleby, Hunt, & Jacob, 1994).

AN ANALYSIS OF PAST METHODOLOGIES
IN RESEARCHING THE HISTORY OF LITERACY

The historiography of literacy has been influenced by these shifting currents. Disciplines other than the reading professional community have approached the history of literacy in a variety of ways. The first, and oldest, of these have been histories of schooling, which discussed literacy within the larger framework of formal education and as a feature of American triumphalism (e.g., Cubberley, 1919/1934). The work, however, of Bernard Bailyn (1960) and Lawrence Cremin (1970, 1980, 1988) moved educational historians away from considering formal schooling as the chief agency of education toward including other educating agencies, such as churches, the community, and the family. (An ironic consequence has been a reduced interest on the part of educational historians in the role of schooling in literacy acquisition.)

A few decades later another group, generally known as "literacy historians," began to pursue a second, and different, approach, by applying the quantitative methodologies of the social historians to the topic of literacy. In order to discuss the relationship between literacy and society, they estimated the number of literates by comparing the proportion of those who could sign their names to a document with those who could only make a mark. The signature was hailed as a proxy for literacy: a uniform and quantifiable measure that was constant over time. This was more plausible during those centuries in which reading was taught at an earlier age than writing, so that reading acquisition could be inferred from signing ability. (For examples of discussions based mainly on signature counts, see Cressy, 1980, for 16th- and 17th-century England, and Lockridge, 1974, for colonial New England.)

The signature/mark approach, however, had its problems. Quite apart from the fact that, up to the 19th century, it seriously underestimated the number of those who could read even though they could not write (E. J. Monaghan, 1989), it only identified the minimally literate without showing how or why literates used their literacy. Nonetheless, the discovery of steadily increasing signature literacy up to the present time stimulated debates about the role played by literacy in different cultures. (For an overview, see Venezky, 1991.) Some historians have integrated signature counts into a variety of other sources in order to comment on popular culture (e.g., Vincent, 1989).

A third major approach has been to quantify not who was literate but what was read. The French historians of the "Annales school" provided the socioeconomic framework for the founders of the "histoire de livre" or history of the book, seeking, in Robert Darnton's words, to "discover the literary experience of ordinary readers" (1989, p. 28). Their number includes scholars such as Lucien Febvre and Henri-Jean Martin (1958/1976) and Roger Chartier (1994) in France, and Robert Darnton (1989) and David Hall (1996) in the United States. Book historians have examined what people read (numbers and kinds of books), paying particular interest to "low-culture" reading interests. This "history of the book" approach has now broadened its scope and fostered the investigation of all the links among books and their readers, from the creative act of the author, through the physical process of editing, publishing, and selling, to the book's reception by its reader. It has also sparked a series of publications on the history of the book in different countries (e.g., Amory & Hall, 2000).

The fourth and most recent trend, however, which represents a further evolution of the history of the book scholarship, has been an emphasis on a history of audiences (Rose, 1992). Studies of books alone rely for their generalizations on presumed or inferred effects upon readers, but historians now search for readers/writers who have reported on the meanings of their literacy. This approach is therefore dependent on qualitative data found in primary sources such as diaries, autobiographies, and letters. For instance, Barbara Sicherman (1989) used family letters and published memoirs to evaluate the role played by reading in the lives of the daughters of an upper-middle-class family at Fort Wayne, Indiana, in the late 19th century. This last approach, which ideally combines qualitative with quantitative data, may prove to be the prevalent one for some time to come for historians of the book.

LITERACY HISTORY AND THE READING RESEARCH COMMUNITY

There is now a large body of work on the history of reading and literacy, but most of it has been undertaken by scholars who are outside the reading research community. (For examples, see works cited in Moore, Monaghan, & Hartman, 1997.) In contrast to the historical approaches used by scholars from the social sciences and literature arenas, those in the reading professional community have used fewer and more limited approaches. The few reading researchers who have approached the history of literacy have traditionally done so through an examination of the textbooks used to teach reading (e.g.. Hoffman & Roser, 1987; Reeder, 1900; Robinson, Faraone, Hittleman, & Unruh, 1990; Smith, 1965).

The best known study of this kind remains that of Nila Banton Smith. Her study began as a published dissertation and received successive updates (1934, 1965, 1986). Although of value even today, Smith's work is inevitably a creature of its time. Her discussions of the contents of American reading instructional textbooks are innocent of any consideration of how literacy instruction has been mediated by gender, class, or race—themes that preoccupy contemporary historians.

Courses in the history of literacy created by reading professionals within schools of education have been influenced by the history of the book scholarship (e.g., Cranney & Miller, 1987), but this scholarship has yet to make a major impact on researchers in the reading professional community, in spite of Richard Venezky's call for a new history of reading instruction (1987b). In fact, little interest has been shown by most of the reading community in doing historical research, whatever the approach.

There are, however, a few important exceptions. Bernardo Gallegos's work (1992) on the links between literacy and society in early New Mexico used both qualitative and quantitative data—such as a letter by a friar describing how he taught the Indians and signature evidence from military enlistment papers. Allan Luke integrated content analysis into his history of the Canadian "Dick and Jane" experience (1988). Other studies have also demonstrated a broader scope of approach, especially in terms of sources and topics. They include biographical studies of well-known reading experts such as William S. Gray (Mavrogenes, 1985; H. M. Robinson, 1985) or Laura Zirbes (Moore, 1986); studies of the history of a particular reading methodology (Balmuth, 1982) or content area (Moore, Readence, & Rickelman, 1983); oral histories of teachers and students (Clegg, 1997), and studies of what literacy has meant to certain communities of readers (Weber, 1993). Moreover, Venezky's (1987a) review of the history of American readers sets them in a broad historical context.

UNDERTAKING HISTORICAL RESEARCH IN LITERACY

Notwithstanding these contributions, the history of literacy remains wide open to research by the reading community. Before we review these different approaches to the topic in more detail, it may be useful to clarify some terminology regarding sources.

Primary, Secondary, and Original Sources

It is important to distinguish between *primary* and *secondary* sources. Primary sources are documents or artifacts generated by the persons actually involved in, or contemporary to, the events under investigation. In this sense, a curriculum guide to reading instruction and a diary discussion of what the diarist's children are reading are both primary sources. Secondary sources are the products of those who try to make sense of primary sources—historians. But a source may be primary or secondary, depending on what the researcher is looking for. Smith's *American Reading Instruction* (1965), for instance, is obviously a secondary source: She wrote her history basing her generalizations mainly on the study of a large number of textbooks that she had personally examined. Her book could also, however, be used as a primary source: It would be an indispensable source if Smith herself and her views on reading instruction were the object of investigation.

The distinction also needs to be made between *primary* and *original* sources. It is by no means always necessary, and all too often it is not possible, to deal only with original sources. Printed copies of original sources, provided they have been undertaken with scrupulous care (such as the published letters of the Founding Fathers), are usually an acceptable substitute for their handwritten originals. Again, it depends on the researcher's purpose. If the researcher wishes to study the spelling of the founding fathers, a reproduction will do, but if the penmanship of the Founding Fathers is the object of study, no printed substitute will suffice. In either case, primary sources are the bedrock of historical research.

Historiographers generally use both primary and secondary sources. Although it is certainly possible to produce useful and important historical work based only on secondary sources (Balmuth, 1982, for instance, used mainly secondary sources), much of the excitement of historical work lies in entering the world of the past through primary sources, including those used by other historians before. Historical advances are made not only by using sources seldom used by others but by looking at familiar material in new ways—ways made possible because the world view of the researcher has changed from that of earlier historians. In the last four decades, for instance, we have come to appreciate the importance of gender, race, and class as constructs that have influenced literacy instruction.

Four Approaches to the Past

The four approaches to the past detailed next all use primary sources as their chief database. We have identified them as qualitative and quantitative approaches, content analysis, and oral history.

The first approach may be termed *qualitative*. This is what most laypersons think of as "history": the search for a story inferred from a range of written or printed evidence. The resultant written/published history is organized chronologically and presented as a factual tale: a tale of a person who created reading textbooks, such as a biography of William Holmes McGuffey (Sullivan, 1994) or of Lindley Murray and his family (C. Monaghan, 1998). The sources of qualitative history are various, ranging from manuscripts such as account books, school records, marginalia, letters, diaries, and memoirs to imprints such as textbooks, children's books, journals, and other books of the time period under consideration. In qualitative history, the researcher inevitably draws inferences from what is all too often an incomplete body of data and makes generalizations on the basis of relatively few pieces of evidence.

The second approach is *quantitative*. Here, rather than relying on "history by quotation," as the former approach has been pejoratively called, researchers deliberately look for evidence that lends itself to being counted and that is therefore presumed to have superior validity and generalizability. In literacy studies, as we noted earlier, a prime example of the quantitative approach has been the tabulation of signatures and marks to estimate the extent of literacy. Other researchers have sought to estimate the popularity of a particular textbook by tabulating the numbers printed, based on the author's copyright records (e.g., E. J. Monaghan, 1983). These studies seek to answer the question, among others, of "How many?" The assumption is that broader questions (e.g., the relationship between literacy and industrialization, or between textbooks and their influence on children) can then be addressed more authoritatively.

Armed with numbers, historians can perform statistical analyses to establish correlations, as did Soltow and Stevens (1981), between schooling and literacy.

A third approach is *content analysis*. Here the text itself is the object of scrutiny. This approach takes as its data published works (in the case of literacy history, these might be readers, penmanship manuals, or examples of children's literature) and subjects them to a careful analysis that usually includes both quantitative and qualitative aspects. Smith (1965), for example, paid attention to such quantitative features as the size of a given textbook, the proportion of illustration to text, and the number of pages devoted to different content categories. In contrast, Lindberg (1976) used a qualitative approach to draw implications from the changing contents of the *McGuffey Eclectic Readers* in successive editions and comment on topics such as their attitude to slavery or their shift in theological viewpoint. Content analysis has been particularly useful in investigating constructs such as race (e.g., Larrick, 1965; MacCann, 1998) or gender (Women on Words and Images, 1972).

All three of these approaches—qualitative, quantitative, and content—use written or printed text as their database. (For examples of all three approaches, see Kaestle, Damon-Moore, Stedman, Tinsley, & Trollinger, 1991.) In contrast, the fourth approach, *oral history*, turns instead to living memory. Oral historians ask questions of those who are willing to talk about the past. For instance, oral historians interested in literacy look for those who can remember their early schooling or teaching (e.g., Clegg, 1997). These four approaches are not, of course, mutually exclusive. (Most content analyses, for instance, involve tabulation.) Indeed, historians avail themselves of as many of these as their question, topic, and time period permit. Arlene Barry (1992) and Thecla Spiker (1997) both used all four approaches in their dissertations.

The integrative use of approaches is made possible because the nature of historical research cuts across all genres of approaches, all of which begin with the identification of a topic and the framing of a question.

Identifying the Topic/Framing the Question.   As in experimental research, the investigator has a question or problem that he or she wishes to answer or solve. (The classic beginner's mistake is to ask too large a question.) The complexity of the question and the breadth of the investigation are guided by the anticipated historiographical outcome—the written report.

Questions will be proportionate in scope to the anticipated length of the answer. One study asked what prominent variations of the phonics/whole-word debate in the late 1960s appeared in contemporary readers, but restricted its time frame to 5 years (Iversen, 1997). The result was a master's thesis. Another, probing deeper, asked what had led to the creation, development, and discontinuance of an entire textbook series, the *Cathedral Basic Readers*, over a half century (Spiker, 1997). Yet another asked how the inhabitants of a small, rural, midwestern community used printed information over a 30-year period (Pawley, 1996). Both these became doctoral dissertations. Other studies probed the professional life of a progressive reading educator, Laura Zirbes (Moore, 1986); the literacy of a small group of Wampanoag Indians (E. J. Monaghan, 1990); the family literacy of a particular 18th-century Boston family (E. J. Monaghan, 1991); and the meaning reading held for American farm wives at the turn of the 20th century (Weber, 1993). These, focusing intently on a limited topic, were all published in scholarly journals.

Identifying Undergirding Theories.   Just as social science researchers do, historians proceed from a theoretical position, whether this is articulated or not. Smith (1965), for instance, was heavily influenced by the measurement movement of her time: She provided considerable detail on the size of the textbooks she studied, the number of their pages, how many pages were devoted to which topic, and so forth. Today, literacy historians are much more likely to be explicit about their theoretical positions, and invoke, say, modernization theory, or their stances on gender, race, and class, as the theories undergirding their approach.

A related issue is researcher stance. All of us are located within the particular perspectives of our own time and setting, and it might appear that if we are explicit about where we come from, this will militate against the possibility of observer bias. However, what we are looking for dictates what we will find. Some studies clearly have a particular perspective that may slant the conclusions drawn and even restrict the data considered worthy of study. Some authors pursue particular goals—heroic ones such as using history "to provide a sense of legitimacy for those who seek a different kind of literacy" (Shannon, 1990, p. x), or, at the other end of the political spectrum, political ones such as promoting a conservative agenda (e.g., Blumenthal, 1973). Any predetermined agenda runs the risk of slanting the evidence to its own needs. What emerges may be "the truth," but it is less likely to be close to "the whole truth," even if there were such a thing, because it may not do justice to opposing points of view.

Identifying and Locating Potential Sources.   Although, for simplicity of exposition, we have discussed the issue of the researcher's question/problem first, there are in fact strictly practical decisions that affect the choice of topic from the outset—namely, where are the sources to be found? If most of the relevant sources are half a continent away, the practical difficulties of expense and time will preclude a particular topic, however appealing it is to the researcher. Most historical research takes place in the manuscript and rare book rooms of public, private, and university libraries or at state and town historical societies, so the researcher has to have the time and money to get there. Considerations like these may guide the researcher to one approach rather than another: A content analysis of a textbook owned by the author, housed in a local library, or amenable to photocopying, for instance, may be more feasible than attempting a biography of an author whose letters and records are housed on the other side of the country. (See http://www.historyliteracy.org/research/archives/index.html for archives relating to the history of literacy.)

As researchers debate the merits of potential topics, they need to make an initial mental survey of all the possible relevant primary sources. In terms of manuscripts, are there any letters, diaries, or journals written by the target person or related to the target topic? What about school records at the local, town, or state level? What exists in printed form? Have any of the manuscripts been published? Are there schoolbooks, children's books, contemporary educational journals, contemporary books? Where are they, and how can access be obtained? Are there still people alive who would remember the event or the person or the book or the approach being investigated?

Fortunately, problems of access to the written/printed word are diminishing as time passes. Access to materials housed in distant libraries is being increasingly provided by interlibrary loans, photocopies, and microfilms. A collection of 844 primers and other introductory reading materials is available in microfiche form (*American Primers*, 1990; Venezky, 1990), and textbooks are being put on microfilm at Harvard University. And now there is the Internet, where the World Wide Web has already given access to works not restricted by copyright protection. The obverse of this coin is that immediate access to the original manuscripts is also diminishing—and with it some of the pleasure of the research. There is no emotional substitute for reading the original letter, with its faded ink on a yellowed page, removed from the hand that penned it only by the passage of time.

The ease of finding sources once again depends on the topic. The names of persons are by far the easiest to research: They are always indexed by libraries, particularly if a person is well known. A search for material on, say, William Holmes McGuffey will produce a wealth of entries. Subjects such as "adult reading" are far harder to research, for they may not be listed under the rubric one expects—or they may not be catalogued at all. This is where a reference librarian is indispensable in guiding the novice to the relevant Library of Congress subject headings or to key words to be used in the search. Nowadays, posting a request for help on an Internet listserv (such as the History of Reading Special Interest Group of the International Reading Association's HoRSIG or the Society for the History of Authorship, Reading and Publishing's SHARP-L) can recruit informed others in your search for relevant sources. In addition, a comprehensive bibliography of historical sources in American reading education for the 1900–1970 period is under preparation (R. D. Robinson, in press).

Once the topic has been pinned down, what is equivalent to the literature review of experimental research should begin. Dissertations are a key resource here, along with articles and books. Secondary sources will normally provide clues that will lead back to more primary sources.

Much is made, in some of the few "how-to" pages on historical research that are occasionally included in textbooks on undertaking educational research, of establishing the authenticity of the sources, refusing to accept any but triangulated sources, and so on. In fact, although the question of authenticity is certainly important, and forgeries do turn up from time to time, in general the authentication of sources has already been undertaken by experts at the libraries where the documents are housed. And in most cases, triangulation is neither possible nor desirable.

Collecting and Recording the Data.   Now, armed with a wish list of what you want to explore, precise information on where it is, and your professional identification for easy library admission, comes the time for data collection. Although the old method was to record the relevant material in pencil (because all manuscript/rare book rooms prohibit the use of pens), usually by copying selected passages for later analysis, the advances in computerization of libraries—and the computer skills of scholars—over the past few years are making this obsolete. Many libraries are equipped with electric outlets for laptop computers. (It is prudent to call ahead and bring old-fashioned equipment in case all the outlets are in use.) Data collected electronically has the great advantage of only needing to be entered once. Note-taking, filing, and organizing are all made easier by the aid of the word processor. Scanning an original text into your own computer with a hand scanner may be the next technological leap.

Material taken down by hand, of course, will have to be entered into a computer at a later date. If you prefer the hand route, or if the absence of electrical outlets mandates it, think carefully about the surface on which you plan to record data. Many historians used to use large 5 by 7 inch note cards, which helped organize data by topic. One major drawback of these was that, at the same time, the chronology and sequence of the data were lost. An approach that preserves both of these is to record everything in a notebook or on numbered sheets of paper, and then index it all topically (most efficiently done on a word processor) at your workplace. It is also helpful to record the date and place of a given piece of research at the top of each page of notes.

Here are some more practical hints. First, it can be helpful, and especially so if your topic is obscure, to alert the librarian ahead of time to your research interests, so that the librarian can be thinking about sources for you, as well as confirm whether you can use your laptop. Second, always bring with you to the library all the equipment that you need on the spot. Libraries of historical societies, in particular, may be sited in neighborhoods that have few computer supply or stationery stores nearby. Manuscript rooms will provide you with the occasional pencil (and a pencil sharpener is always on site), but not paper.

Third, treat every entry as if this is the last time you will ever set eyes on it. Although it is relatively easy to backtrack one's bibliographical omissions for books, it is much harder to figure out what collection a manuscript came from. In fact, even with the manuscript in front of you, you may not be able to tell. Record all the identifying material on something that will not be surrendered to the librarian *before* you hand in your request slip. Fourth, pay lavishly for photocopying and—the latest technology, which allows for the reproduction of pages from books too fragile to be subjected to the rigors of xeroxing—computer scanning. Better yet, see if you can borrow the text itself through interlibrary loan, or purchase a contemporary reproduction. Nothing is more helpful than having the text in your possession at your own workspace.

The collection of oral histories deserves a chapter to itself. Here we can only note that there are particular challenges, as well as joys, for the researcher who relies on the memories of the living as his or her sources. Memories are fallible, and cross-verification often difficult to obtain. The resultant data, however, may be of such intrinsic interest or charm that researchers often publish their reminiscences with little interpretation (e.g., Terkel, 1970), so providing, in essence, primary sources for further study.

Oral history takes much more time than one would think. The next technological breakthrough, already underway, will be the translation of speech directly into print; until this is perfected, however, painstaking transcription by hand from the audiotape is the only method available. For detailed information, including legal caveats, we suggest joining the Oral History Association (see the Research Resources of the web page of the History of Reading Special Interest Group of the International Reading Association, 1999, for professional associations relevant to historians of literacy). There are also tips and bibliographies on oral history that have been prepared by reading researchers (e.g., King & Stahl, 1991; Stahl, Hynd, & Henk, 1986; Stahl, King, Dillon, & Walker, 1994).

Interpreting the Data.   Once the work of data collection is completed—or, more accurately, you have called a halt to it—the work of analysis begins. Sources should not be taken at face value.

Two kinds of analysis are necessary. The first is an analysis of internal aspects of the data. This is the point at which one detects bias within the sources themselves. Given the self-serving nature of our species, autobiographies and diaries need particular scrutiny. Oral histories, too, pose unusual problems of verification, because the data provided are removed at a distance of time of perhaps as much as a half century from the period under investigation, and are filtered through the fallible and limited human memory.

The second kind of analysis is external to the sources themselves: It is the work of interpretation and organization. Historical research can be considered a kind of anthropology of the past. The historian looks for patterns and themes, and compares, combines, and selects material that will support generalizations and answer the questions or problems that motivated the study. No matter what questions the study began with, others will inevitably arise from the data itself. If the initial focus of the study changes with any newfound information, it is well worth the effort to pursue the new direction.

Communicating Interpretations/Writing the Results.   What historians discover as they pore over their data commits them to one kind of organization over another. Organization can be a function of the source's chronology, as is the case in a biography; or it may be both chronological and conceptual, with the topics that emerged later in time also appearing later in the book; or it could be largely topical. Given that so much history is a study of causes and effects, and that cause always animates effect, the chronological element will undergird the telling of the history.

Once the organization is in place and writing begun, the social science researcher must confront issues of documentation. The purpose of documentation is to allow readers of the history to scrutinize, if they choose, the actual sources, in order to satisfy themselves that a particular source has been invoked in a way that accurately reflects its content. Reading researchers are comfortable and familiar with the American Psychological Association (APA) style (used, in fact, throughout this volume), which simply cites author and date within the body of the text and provides the complete reference at the end. As an adequate reference system in the writing of history, however, APA has several severe disadvantages. APA does have a mechanism for direct quotation, but if the historian has paraphrased instead of quoting, the standard APA procedure is simply to refer to the entire book. In these cases the reader has to search through the whole book to find the few relevant pages. There is also no short way, in APA, to cite manuscripts. And over and above these technical objections, there are aesthetic and cognitive ones: Within-text citations encumber the text greatly. Some paragraphs in a historical text or even individual sentences are based not on one source but on many; citing them in APA style produces a visual clutter that distracts greatly from the meaning and stylistic integrity of the writing.

This explains why historians document their assertions by using numbered notes, which appear as superscripts in the body of the text and are fully referenced in footnotes or endnotes. *The Chicago Manual of Style* (1993), now in its 14th edition, or some variation of it is by far the most popular style sheet for historical work. Footnotes are out of favor these days; instead, endnotes appear at the end of the work.

Nonetheless, the APA habit is so strong that the great majority of theses and dissertations sponsored by schools of education have used the APA style. We recommend that dissertation chairs advocate historical referencing for historical writing and support their students in doing battle with the establishment on its behalf.

Publication.   The final objective of historical research is, as in behavioral research, publication. Although historical research is still a fledgling enterprise among reading researchers, several studies that began as theses or dissertations within the reading community have reached the pages of literacy journals or appeared in book form. For example, Barry's article (1994) on high school remedial reading programs and Gallegos' book (1992) on literacy and society in early New Mexico both stem from doctoral dissertations. Books on the history of reading are often published by university presses (Association of American University Presses, 1999). There is unquestionably a market out there for historical work.

FINAL WORD

The time for historical research in reading to take its rightful place with other methodologies is, in our opinion, long overdue. There is a need to site reading history within the larger contexts of its times. But it is not easy to become a good historian overnight. Those who wish to pursue this genre of research should consider sitting in on a course on historical methods given at their own institution and joining appropriate historical societies. We particularly recommend the History of Reading Special Interest Group of the International Reading Association, which supports a web page, www.historyliteracy.org, that offers many research resources.

REFERENCES

Amory, H., & Hall, D. D. (Eds.). (2000). *A history of the book in America. Vol. 1: The colonial book in the Atlantic world.* Cambridge: Cambridge University Press & American Antiquarian Society.

American Primers. (1990). (Microform.) Frederick, MD: University Publications of America.

Appleby, J. (1998). The power of history. *American Historical Review, 103,* 1–14.

Appleby, J., Hunt, L., & Jacob, M. (1994). *Telling the truth about history.* New York: Norton.

Association of American University Presses. (1999). *Association of American University Presses: Directory, 1999–2000.* New York: Author.

Bailyn, B. (1960). *Education in the forming of American society: Needs and opportunities.* Chapel Hill, NC: Institute of Early American History and Culture.

Balmuth, M. (1982). *The roots of phonics: A historical introduction.* New York: McGraw-Hill.

Barker, J. (1982). *The superhistorians: Makers of our past.* New York: Charles Scribner.

Barry, A. (1992). *The evolution of high school remedial reading programs in the United States.* Unpublished doctoral dissertation, University of Wisconsin, Madison.

Barry, A. L. (1994). The staffing of high school remedial reading programs in the United States since 1920. *Journal of Reading, 38,* 14–22.

Blumenthal, S. L. (1973). *The new illiterates—And how you can keep your children from becoming one.* New Rochelle, NY: Arlington House.

Breisach, E. (1994). *Historiography: Ancient, medieval, and modern,* (2nd ed.). Chicago: University of Chicago. (Original work published 1983)

Butterfield, H. (1981). *The origins of history.* New York: Basic Books.

Chartier, R. (1994). *The order of books: Readers, authors and libraries in Europe between the fourteenth and eighteenth centuries* (L. G. Cochrane, Trans.). Stanford, CA: Stanford University Press.

Chicago Manual of Style (14th ed.). (1993). Chicago: University of Chicago Press.

Clegg, L. B. (1997). *The empty schoolhouse: Memories of one-room Texas schools.* College Station: Texas A & M University Press.

Cranney, A. G., & Miller, J. [A]. (1987). History of reading: Status and sources of a growing field. *Journal of Reading, 30,* 388–398.

Cremin, L. A. (1970). *American education: The colonial experience, 1607–1783.* New York: Harper & Row.

Cremin, L. A. (1980). *American education: The national experience, 1783–1876.* New York: Harper & Row.

Cremin, L. A. (1988). *American education: The metropolitan experience, 1876–1980.* New York: Harper & Row.

Cressy, D. (1980). *Literacy and the social order: Reading and writing in Tudor and Stewart England.* New York: Cambridge University Press.

Cubberley, E. P. (1934). *Public education in the United States: A study and interpretation of American educational history* (Rev. ed.). Boston: Houghton Mifflin. (Original work published 1919)

Dahmus, J. H. (1982). *Seven medieval historians: An interpretation and a bibliography.* Chicago: Nelson Hall.

Darnton, R. (1989). What is the history of books? In C. N. Davidson (Ed.), *Reading in America: Literature and social history* (pp. 27–52). Baltimore, MD: Johns Hopkins University Press.

Derrida, J. (1976). *Of grammatology* (G. C. Spivak, Trans.). Baltimore, MD: Johns Hopkins University Press. (Original work published 1967)

Derrida, J. (1978). *Writing and difference* (A. Bass, Trans.). Chicago: University of Chicago Press.

Febvre, L. P. V., & Martin, H. -J. (1976). *The coming of the book: The impact of printing 1450–1800.* London: N.L.B. (Original work published 1958)

Foucault, M. (1972). *The archaeology of knowledge* (A. M. S. Smith, Trans.). New York: Pantheon.

Gagnon, R. (1989). *Historical literacy: The case for history in American education.* New York: Collier Macmillan.

Gallegos, B. P. (1992). *Literacy, education, and society in New Mexico, 1693–1821.* Albuquerque: University of New Mexico Press.

Gay, P., & Cavanaugh, G. J. (1972). *Historians at work: From Herodotus to Froissart* (Vol. 1). New York: Harper & Row.

Grant, M. (1970). *The ancient historians.* New York: Charles Scribner.

Hall, D. D. (1996). *Cultures of print: Essays in the history of the book.* Amherst: University of Massachusetts Press.

History of Reading Special Interest Group of the International Reading Association. (1999). *History of Literacy* [Online]. Available: http://www.historyliteracy.org.

Hoffman, J. V., & Roser, N. (Eds.). (1987). The basal reader in American reading instruction [Special issue]. *Elementary School Journal, 87*(3).

Iversen, S. J. (1997). *Initial reading instruction in United States' schools: An exploratory examination of the history of the debate between whole-word and phonic methods, 1965 through 1969.* Unpublished Master's thesis, Ohio State University.

Kaestle, C. F., Damon-Moore, H., Stedman, L. C., Tinsley, K., & Trollinger, W. V., Jr. (1991). *Literacy in the United States: Readers and reading since 1880.* New Haven, CT: Yale University Press.

King, J. R., & Stahl, N. A. (1991). Oral history as a critical pedagogy: Some cautionary issues. In B. L. Hayes & K. Camperell (Eds.), *Yearbook of the American Reading Forum, 11,* 219–226.

Larrick, N. (1965, September 11). The all-white world of children's books. *Saturday Review,* pp. 63–65, 84–85.

Lindberg, S. W. (1976). *The annotated McGuffey: Selections from the McGuffey Eclectic Readers, 1836–1920.* New York: Van Nostrand Reinhold.

Lockridge, K. A. (1974). *Literacy in colonial New England: An enquiry into the social context of literacy in the early modern West.* New York: Norton.

Luke, A. (1988). *Literacy, textbooks and ideology: Postwar literacy and the mythology of Dick and Jane.* New York: Falmer.

MacCann, D. (1998). *White supremacy in children's literature: Characterizations of African Americans, 1830–1900.* New York: Garland.

Marrou, H. I. (1966). *The meaning of history* (R. J. Olsen, Trans.). Baltimore, MD: Helicon.

Mavrogenes, N. A. (1985). William S. Gray: The person. In J. A. Stevenson (Ed.), *William S. Gray: Teacher, scholar, leader* (pp. 1–23). Newark, DE: International Reading Association.

Momigliano, A. (1990). *The classical foundations of modern historiography.* Berkeley, CA: University of California Press.

Monaghan, C. (1998). *The Murrays of Murray Hill.* Brooklyn, NY: Urban History Press.

Monaghan, E. J. (1983). *A common heritage: Noah Webster's blue-back speller.* Hamden, CT: Archon Books.

Monaghan, E. J. (1989). Literacy instruction and gender in colonial New England. In C. N. Davidson (Ed.), *Reading in America: Literature and social history* (pp. 53–80). Baltimore, MD: Johns Hopkins University Press.

Monaghan, E. J. (1990). "She loved to read in good Books": Literacy and the Indians of Martha's Vineyard, 1643–1725. *History of Education Quarterly, 30,* 493–521.

Monaghan, E. J. (1991). Family literacy in early 18th-century Boston: Cotton Mather and his children. *Reading Research Quarterly, 26,* 342–370.

Moore, D. W. (1986). Laura Zirbes and progressive reading instruction. *Elementary School Journal, 86,* 663–672.

Moore, D. W., Monaghan, E. J., & Hartman, D. K. (1997). Values of literacy history. *Reading Research Quarterly, 32,* 90–102.

Moore, D. W., Readence, J. E., & Rickelman, R. J. (1983). An historical exploration of content area reading instruction. *Reading Research Quarterly, 18,* 419–438.

Pawley, C. (1996). *Reading on the middle border: The culture of print in Osage, Iowa, 1870–1900.* Unpublished doctoral dissertation, University of Wisconsin.

Reeder, R. R. (1900). *The historical development of school readers and of method in teaching reading.* New York: Macmillan.

Robinson, H. M. (1985). William S. Gray: The scholar. In J. A. Stevenson (Ed.), *William S. Gray: Teacher, scholar, leader* (pp. 24–36). Newark, DE: International Reading Association.

Robinson, H. A., Faraone, V., Hittleman, D. R., & Unruh, E. (1990). *Reading comprehension instruction, 1783–1987: A review of trends and research.* Newark, DE: International Reading Association.

Robinson, R. D. (in press). *Historical sources in U.S. reading education: 1900–1970.* Newark, DE: International Reading Association.

Rose, J. (1992). Rereading the English common reader: A preface to a history of audiences. *Journal of the History of Ideas, 51,* 47–70.

Shannon, P. (1990). *The struggle to continue: Progressive reading instruction in the United States.* Portsmouth, NH: Heinemann.

Sicherman, B. (1989). Sense and sensibility: A case study of women's reading in late-Victorian America. In C. N. Davidson (Ed.), *Reading in America: Literature and social history* (pp. 201–225). Baltimore, MD: Johns Hopkins University Press.

Smith, N. B. (1934). *American reading instruction: Its development and its significance in gaining a perspective on current practices in reading.* New York: Silver, Burdett.

Smith, N. B. (1965). *American reading instruction.* Newark, DE: International Reading Association.

Smith, N. B. (1986). *American reading instruction* (Prologue by L. Courtney, FSC, and epilogue by H. A. Robinson). Newark, DE: International Reading Association.

Soltow, L., & Stevens, E. (1981). *The rise of literacy and the common school in the United States: A socioeconomic analysis to 1870.* Chicago: University of Chicago Press.

Spiker, T. M. W. (1997). *Dick and Jane go to church: A history of the Cathedral Basic Readers.* Unpublished doctoral dissertation, University of Pittsburgh.

Stahl, N. A., Hynd, C. R., & Henk, W. A. (1986). Avenues for chronicling and researching the history of college reading and study skills instruction. *Journal of Reading, 29,* 334–341.

Stahl, N. A., King, J. R., Dillon, D., & Walker, J. R. (1994). The roots of reading: Preserving the heritage of a profession through oral history projects. In E. G. Sturtevant & W. M. Linek (Eds.), *Pathways for literacy: Learners teach and teachers learn. The sixteenth yearbook of the College Reading Association* (pp. 15–24). Commerce, TX: College Reading Association.

Sullivan, D. P. (1994). *William Holmes McGuffey: Schoolmaster to the nation.* Rutherford, NJ: Fairleigh Dickinson University Press.

Terkel, S. (1970). *Hard times: An oral history of the Great Depression.* New York: Pantheon.

Venezky, R. L. (1987a). A history of the American reading textbook. *Elementary School Journal, 87,* 247–265.

Venezky, R. L. (1987b). Steps toward a modern history of reading instruction. In E. Z. Rothkopf (Ed.), *Review of research in education* (Vol. 13, pp. 129–167). Washington, DC: American Educational Association.

Venezky, R. L. (1990). *American primers: Guide to the microfiche collection; Introductory essay.* Frederick, MD: University Publications of America.

Venezky, R. L. (1991). The development of literacy in the industrialized nations of the West. In R. Barr, M. L. Kamil, P. B. Mosenthal, & P. D. Pearson (Eds.). *Handbook of reading research* (Vol. II, pp. 46–67). New York: Longman.

Vincent, D. (1989). *Literacy and popular culture: England, 1750–1914.* New York: Cambridge University Press.

Weber, R. (1993). Even in the midst of work: Reading among turn-of-the-century farmers' wives. *Reading Research Quarterly, 28,* 293–302.

Women on Words and Images. (1972). *Dick and Jane as victims: Sex stereotyping in children's readers.* Princeton, NJ: Author.

CHAPTER 4

Narrative Approaches

Donna E. Alvermann
University of Georgia

> *The telling of stories can be a profound form of scholarship moving serious study close to the frontiers of art.*
>
> — Joseph Featherstone (1989, p. 377)

Presently researchers in the social sciences are engaged in the telling of stories[1] that span a range of narrative approaches (e.g., autobiography, autoethnographies, biography, personal narratives, life histories, oral histories, memoirs, and literary journalism). A growing number of these researchers (e.g., Lawrence-Lightfoot & Davis, 1997; Richardson, 1993, 1997) are writing their storied narratives in ways that combine empirical and aesthetic descriptions of the human condition, thus pushing at "the frontiers of art" to which Featherstone earlier alluded. Still others (e.g., Denzin, 1997; hooks, 1991) are critiquing the notion that one should ever rightfully assume the authority to tell other people's stories. This chapter is about these researchers and their work, as well as the work of other researchers who use narrative approaches to study literacy. It is also about issues that currently encompass narrative inquiry as a way of knowing and writing, and the implications of such issues for research and practice in the field of literacy education.

Thematically speaking, the issues discussed in this chapter cluster around what is commonly referred to as the *postmodern* or *poststructural critique* of narrative inquiry. This critique is concerned primarily with three major issues—those dealing with subjectivity, truth claims, and representation. Although the term *postmodern* is troublesome in some circles, Marcus's (1994) assessment of the situation is that theorists in the social sciences have absorbed much of postmodernism's preoccupation with these

---

[1]Following Polkinghorne (1995), I use the term *story* in the sense of a storied narrative that combines a succession of events that are alleged to have occurred. Polkinghorne's definition of a storied narrative is "the linguistic form that preserves the complexity of human action with its interrelationship of temporal sequence, human motivation, chance happenings, and changing interpersonal and environmental contexts" (p. 7).

three issues without necessarily laying claim to its label.[2] For example, present interest in subjectivity and the turn toward self-critical reflexivity mark a departure from earlier times when it was simply assumed that researchers would strive to maintain a distance between the knower (narrator) and the known (narrated). Similarly, researchers are having to rethink what it means to be concerned about truth claims when aspects of the global are now encompassed by the local—when "the scientist and the artist are both claiming that *in the particular resides the general*" (Lawrence-Lightfoot, 1997, p. 14). Finally, the current interest in re-presenting others' representations marks a departure from a time when researchers could count on the fact that discovering new truths was valued over gaining critical insights into existing interpretations.

Before examining these issues in greater depth and the implications they hold for literacy research and practice, I first situate narrative inquiry historically. After that, I provide several examples of how literacy researchers are using this form of inquiry to understand their own lives and the lives of others whom they study both in and out of school.

NARRATIVE INQUIRY: FROM PAST TO PRESENT

What counts as narrative inquiry varies widely across researchers and those who critique their work. Although there are traces of various forms of narrative mixing with philosophy as early as the 18th century (Lawrence-Lightfoot & Davis, 1997), narrative inquiry as a method of analysis is thought to have taken hold during the 20th century with the Russian formalists' study of fairy tales and Levi-Strauss's analysis of myths (Manning & Cullum-Swan, 1994). More recent work, often referred to as the "new narrative research" (Casey, 1995, p. 211), focuses specifically on lives and lived experience. In this chapter, I use the term *narrative inquiry* to refer to a variety of research practices ranging from those that tell a story of how individuals understand their actions through oral and written accounts of historical episodes (Riessman, 1993) to those that explore certain methodological aspects of storytelling (Richardson, 1997).

Narrative inquiry's recent emphasis on how people understand themselves and their experiences began in the mid 1970s, according to Bruner (1986), when "the social sciences had moved away from their traditional positivist stance towards a more interpretive posture" (p. 8). The move toward a teller's point of view has not been limited to storytelling in the strict linguistic sense of the term. For example, some narratives have neither protagonists nor culminating events, but instead depict snapshots of past events that are linked thematically. Others depict the interconnectedness and meaning of seemingly random activities that social groups perform as part of daily living (Polkinghorne, 1988; Riessman, 1993).

There has been a tendency of late among education researchers to elevate narrative inquiry, especially that dealing with teachers' thinking and collaborative research, to new heights—to what some would say is a privileged way of knowing. This practice continues to draw criticism from both teacher educators (e.g., Carter, 1993; de la Luna & Kamberelis, 1997) and research methodologists (e.g., Constas, 1998; Emihovich, 1995). Presently the more general critique of narrative inquiry, however, has focused on issues made increasingly visible by the postmodern turn and its preoccupation with the loss of innocence in academic writing. For example, researchers working from a postmodernist narrative perspective are becoming more critically reflexive in locating their own subjectivities in the stories they write. Richardson (1997) captured the gist of this critique in her questioning of the academy's adherence to outdated canons of writing practices:

---

[2]Although internal critiques of research traditions typically associated with the natural sciences had already begun in literature, history, sociology, anthropology, philosophy, and law before the advent of postmodernity in the early 1980s, Marcus (1994) argued that it took postmodernism's intersection with those developing critiques to both radicalize and consolidate them.

We are restrained and limited by the kinds of cultural stories available to us. Academics are given the "story line" that the "I" should be suppressed in their writing, that they should accept homogenization and adopt the all-knowing, all-powerful voice of the academy. But contemporary philosophical thought raises problems that exceed and undermine the academic story line. We are always present in our texts, no matter how we try to suppress ourselves. (p. 2)

Similar critiques related to the twin crises of legitimation (truth claims) and representation abound (Britzman, 1995; Denzin, 1994, 1997; Lather & Smithies, 1997; Lenzo, 1995; Tierney & Lincoln, 1997). In one form or another, these same issues occupy the very center of researchers' thinking in a variety of disciplines that use narrative inquiry as a way of understanding life and lived experiences (Cortazzi, 1993). However, in keeping with this handbook's focus, the examples of narrative approaches that I include in the next chapter section are limited to those involving literacy research. In an effort to avoid overlapping with other chapters in the handbook that focus on teacher research, case studies, and ethnographic approaches, I have omitted literacy teachers' memoirs (e.g., Hankins, 1998), first- and second-hand accounts of teachers' classroom literacy experiences (Cochran-Smith & Lytle, 1993; Lalik, Dellinger, & Druggish, 1996), and ethnographic accounts of literacy teaching and learning (Allen, Michalove, & Shockley, 1993; Dyson, 1997; Fishman, 1988; Heath, 1983). The examples that are included illustrate how literacy researchers are presently using narrative inquiry to understand their own lives and the lived experiences of others.

UNDERSTANDING LIVES AND LIVED EXPERIENCE THROUGH STORYTELLING

We must lay in waiting for ourselves.
Throughout our lives.
Abandoning the pretense that we know.
— William F. Pinar (1976a, p. viii)

This quotation from Pinar's introduction to a book he coauthored with Madeleine Grumet (Pinar & Grumet, 1976) on curriculum reform aptly illustrates a central need in the stories we tell about ourselves—namely, the need to be vigilant in recovering the forgotten or suppressed memories that are the autobiographical antecedents of our professional lives. Kathryn Au, whose research focuses on how students of diverse backgrounds become literate while maintaining a connection to their cultural identities, recalled the following childhood memory in a chapter she wrote for Neumann and Peterson's (1997) edited volume on the life histories of notable women researchers in education. In Au's (1997) words:

Until I was a teenager, I spent all of my summer vacations at the house in Paia [the location of a Hawaiian sugar plantation on which Au's maternal grandfather, Hew Sing Cha, worked as a cook and baker]. After dinner, Grandmother Hew and the adult relatives often 'talked story,' reminiscing and gossiping in a mixture of Hakka and English. My grandmother was a skillful storyteller with an excellent memory, and others in the circle often turned to her with questions. As a child I did not participate in these discussions, but I developed an appreciation for uses of language and literacy that did not necessarily involve English or a printed text. (p. 74)

In a later section that dealt with her development as a researcher, Au (1997) told of an incident that led her to hypothesize a connection between Hawaiian children's lively interactive styles in reading circle and the talk-story style of communicating that she had observed while seated among her adult relatives in her Grandmother Hew's house. Au wrote:

> My attitudes toward schooling and literacy were shaped by the experiences of family members.... As a Chinese American with an interest in my own cultural heritage, I have explored avenues of bringing students to high levels of literacy through forms of classroom instruction respectful of their cultures.
>
> One conclusion to be drawn from my research on talk-story-like reading lessons is that effective instruction may take more than one form. Definitions of effective teaching need to be broad enough to take into account a range of practices beyond those typically seen in mainstream settings. Another conclusion growing from my research is that students of diverse backgrounds can become excellent readers and writers when they receive well-conceived, culturally responsive instruction. (pp. 87–88)

Biography is another form of narrative inquiry. In a dissertation titled *Jane's Story: A Description of One Deaf Person's Experiences with Literacy*, Robert Perry (1995) told the story of his wife's virtual isolation from the spoken language around her since she was 6 months of age. Suffering from a severe skin ailment, Jane had been administered three shots of streptomycin within a week's time in the early 1950s. (Streptomycin was one of several antibiotics later shown to damage the neural structure of infants' ears.) Relying primarily on lipreading until she became an adult and learned American Sign Language, Jane and her mother collaborated with Perry to tell a story that spans two continents, two spoken languages, and a lifetime of experiences related to learning to read. Included are a number of comprehension and vocabulary strategies that Jane developed without formal instruction, a history of her development as a concert pianist, an original poem by Jane titled "The Artist's Life," and a thoughtful discussion of how her deafness has limited the knowledge she needs to make inferences while reading. Much of what Jane has shared in her role as coresearcher on this biography project is interpreted within a theoretical framework that honors the social nature of language and literacy.

Two other approaches to narrative inquiry can be found in Lorri Neilsen's writings on literacy and educational change. The first is a book of narrative essays by Neilsen (1994) titled *A Stone in My Shoe: Teaching Literacy in Times of Change*. In one of the essays, "Bring on the Children," Neilsen began her story this way:

> I had a sassy red planbook, a teaching certificate, and a nameplate on my door. I had a storehouse of language arts guides, a fat file of mimeographed story starters, boxes of paint and clay, and a black light poster of the Beatles. At twenty-one, I was prepared to transform children's minds through language and art. Bring on the children. (p. 1)

After tracing several changes in her thinking about what makes a good literacy teacher, Neilsen concluded by saying:

> But what I now know about teaching reading and writing, I know not only in my mind, but in my bones. This knowing transcends words on the page and goes deep into that twilight zone that makes all researchers wary: personal knowledge. Because this wisdom of practice is difficult to see, label, measure, count, or stamp, we call it intuition, sixth sense, or—strangely, considering its status—common sense. It is the essence of good teaching, the root source of improvisation, and traditionally the most undervalued knowledge in the educational enterprise. (p. 5)

Elsewhere, Neilsen (1998) experimented with performative texts as a narrative approach to understanding how two adolescents (one of them her 15-year-old son) experience literacy in and out of school. As Neilsen described this approach, performance and role playing were central to what she hoped the reader would take from her study:

Some of this study is reported as stage setting, some as conventional discursive analysis, and some as dialogue and monologue. The play, as it were, is in the reading of the juxtaposed texts. Readers become both participants and audience as these texts weave through one another. As narrator and participant, I become, as does the reader, part of the intertextual dynamics. The players, the texts, the readings, and the contexts are presented in an attempt to create an interplay that is not linear—a text about text that does not adhere to Western rhetorical and narrative conventions. (p. 5)

The use of narrative inquiry to understand one's own life and the lives of others is but part of the story. Literacy researchers are also exploring a variety of narrative devices that have potential for opening up new ways of making visible to their reading audiences how the choices they make in collecting, analyzing, and representing their data reflect the theoretical frameworks within which they work. Three examples of such devices are presented next, the first of which is an *aside*.

According to *The American Heritage Dictionary*, an *aside* is a theatrical term used to denote "a piece of dialogue intended for the audience and supposedly not heard by the other actors on stage" or "a parenthetical departure; a digression" (Soukhanov, 1996, p. 108). A few researchers in literacy related areas have begun to use the aside as a narrative device—as a textual method of discovery. For instance, St. Pierre (1997), working from Deleuze and Guattari's (1980/1987) theoretical image of the nomad deterritorializing space, used the aside in search of her warrant for credibility in studying how older, white Southern women care for their intellectual and literary selves. Upon returning to the site where she originally had collected her data, St. Pierre wrote:

Aside: I have been to Milton since I last wrote. I returned to collect more data, to get a "feel" for the place, so that I could refresh and deploy my ethnographic authority in this aside, my warrant for credibility that Clifford (1988) describes as an "accumulated savvy and a sense of the style of a people or a place" (p. 35). I wanted to look around again and listen to the women talk so that I could write with what Geertz (cited in Olson, 1991) describes as that "sense of circumstantiality and of power in reserve ... [so that] an anecdote or an example doesn't sound strained but sounds like you've got fifty others and this is the best one you chose" (p. 191). I know, however, that I am always an "unreliable narrator" (Visweswaran, 1994, p. 62) and can never produce a traditional authoritative account. Nevertheless, I might manage to construct some semblance of Essex County women for you in this space.

During my days there, I was much concerned about this telling and rehearsed first one story and then another and composed bits of text in my head as I tried once again to put myself in the dubious scientific position of participant-observer. I am just about ready to give up on that signifier, since I am always sucked right into the middle of things, barely able to maintain the status of fieldworker, once more just Bettie Adams, come home to celebrate her mother's birthday. (p. 372)

In this aside, which continues for several more paragraphs, St. Pierre laid out in narrative form why she is suspicious of ethnographic methods and how they intrude on her interactions with the women of Essex County. Offered in a narrative aside, her critique of ethnography as a viable methodology for her own work is meant to speak to her audience of readers only if they wish to attend to it. Those not wishing to attend need only skip over the aside to get to the rest of her article.

The aside has also been used to provide a temporary release from the constraints of academic writing. For example, Young (1998) used asides at the beginning of each of her chapters in her dissertation on the critical literacies of young adolescent boys who were part of a home schooling project that she initiated. In introducing the aside in Chapter 1 of her dissertation, Young advised her readers that what she wrote would add context to her study—in fact, would tell another story—but only if they chose to read it. The asides were used to share her personal thoughts as a writer, a researcher, and the mother of two of the boys in the project.

A second narrative device that has been used by literacy researchers involves what Fitzgerald and Noblit (1999) described as a "think scene"—that is, "think how I [the researcher] can *show* this, not tell it" (p. 60). Showing (rather than merely talking about) their data was Fitzgerald and Noblit's way of conveying to their reading audience what their field notes and videotapes revealed about the two English-language learners, Roberto and Carlos, who were at the center of their study on emergent reading. As Fitzgerald and Noblit worked to analyze their data within what is referred to as the "I-witnessing" or "confessional" narrative genre (Geertz, 1988; Van Maanen, 1988), they orally constructed stories about the "think scenes" that they had identified as being representative of their year-long study.

In similar fashion, Schaafsma (1993) shared stories orally with members of his research team—stories that he had originally jotted in his journal while teaching in an inner-city Detroit summer writing program. Later, in writing about this kind of oral-sharing activity, which he "re-presented" narratively in his book, *Eating on the Street: Teaching Literacy in a Multicultural Society*, Schaafsma made visible to his readers how his perspective on literacy as social action influenced the way he collected and analyzed the data.

A third narrative device, a layered participant profile for representing the multiple views of a multiple author team, was developed by my colleagues and me (Alvermann, Commeyras, Young, Randall, & Hinson, 1997) in our study of gendered discursive practices in text-oriented classroom discussions. Although I wrote the first layer of each of five profiles, the other four members of the research team wove their own views into that initial layer. Profiling the participants' personal histories in this way was a conscious effort to interrupt the modernist emphasis on individualism, wherein *I* is separable and identifiable from *we* (Harre & Gillet, 1994). Identities were blurred as we wrote about ourselves, one over the other, until we had confounded our individual voices—a practice in keeping with the two theoretical constructs that framed our study: Messer-Davidow's (1985) perspectivity and Alcoff's (1988) positionality. In the following truncated version of one of the five participants' profiles (that of David Hinson), David's contributions are italicized to distinguish his views from those of the other four authors.

> He [David] told us there are two kinds of teachers. One is the "guide on the side," whereas the other is the "sage on the stage." He sees himself as the latter.... David's vision of himself as a sage on the stage seems ... [congruent with] his life as a disc jockey. For 9 years, he was accustomed to playing the winners and shelving the losers. He wouldn't have kept his job any other way. Is it David the disc jockey or David the teacher we are observing? Both descriptions ... imply that David is an actor and performs daily for his students. *How unusual is this? I like the give-and-take with an audience. For me, it's more enjoyable to view teaching as "show business."* And he's good! I think that is one reason why I never voiced any of my criticism about his tendency to control students' discussions. Why should I criticize something that was working for David and his class? *What exactly was there to criticize?* I feel I have not been honest with David. I remember being shocked when I heard David say he finds himself having to fight the tendency to call on the attractive, verbose students over the unattractive, passive students during class discussions. Later, I thought it was good David was aware of his biases and wanted to alter them. (pp. 81–82)

In sum, as this brief overview suggests, literacy researchers are engaged in a variety of narrative approaches. Although grounding their studies in a narrative framework necessarily put these researchers in touch with issues related to subjectivity, truth claims, and representation, by and large the published reports of their work (mostly chapters or journal length articles) did not permit an extended discussion of how they dealt with these issues. The dual purpose, therefore, of the remaining two sections of this chapter is to provide a detailed look at the three issues in terms of how they may influence a study's findings, and the implications they hold for future research and practice.

A DETAILED LOOK AT THREE CURRENT ISSUES

Knowledge grounded in stories is suspect in some people's minds. As one critic (Cizek, 1995) observed, "if all knowledge is a personalized construction ... then can any interpretivist claims be rejected?" (p. 27). This question of whether or not narrative research is falsifiable is also reflected in Fenstermacher's (1994) question, "How, in the use of stories and narratives, are such problems as self-deception, false claims, and distorted perceptions confronted and resolved?" (p. 218). In an attempt to address some of the concerns raised by Cizek and Fenstermacher, I turn to a body of literature that deals with subjectivity and the twin problems of legitimation and representation.

Subjectivity and the Reflexive Self

The concern that a distinction be made between what seems apparent to us and what is in fact "reality" has been part of humankind's search for truth and certainty since ancient times. In forging notions of the need to maintain a distance between the knower and what can be known or between one's personal orientations and the scientific project, scholars writing from the empiricist tradition have demonstrated little patience with narrative approaches. Generally, they have tended to regard interactions between researchers and their research participants (or between researchers and narrators in the case of storytelling approaches) as potential sources of distortion and bias (Jansen & Peshkin, 1992). For instance, literary critic Linda Kauffman (1993) warned that because in autobiographical work "there is something fatally alluring about personal testimony" (p. 132), it behooves us to be wary of a rear-view mirror enchantment with ourselves. This allusion to autobiographers' purportedly narcissistic tendencies has been challenged by scholars sympathetic to the idea that "autobiographical reflection is not a symptom of but a solution to contemporary psychosocial problems" (Casey, 1995, p. 217). Sympathetic to this view, Pinar (1988) argued, "Understanding of self is not narcissism; it is a precondition and concomitant condition to the understanding of others" (p. 150).

Other criticisms involving charges of solipsism and risk of alienation have also been leveled against narrative inquiry. To counter the charge that such inquiry assumes the self is the only thing that can be known and verified, researchers have relied upon a technique they call *methodological reflexivity*. Perhaps one of the better known illustrations of this technique is Wolf's (1992) *A Thrice Told Tale* in which the author records the same set of events using three different forms of writing: a narrative (short story), a social science article, and her anthropological field notes. The assumption is that this type of reflexive writing forces one to turn a critical eye to one's own prejudices and distortions (or at least as the self perceives them). In Wolf's case, "The Hot Spell" was written as a piece of fiction in which the narrator revealed her biases and her state of mind (boredom, discomfort, insecurity) during a dramatic unfolding of events that took place while she was doing fieldwork in Taiwan in 1960. Wolf's field notes, which cover the events written about in the short story, and the article she published some 30 years later in *American Ethnologist* (Wolf, 1990) can be read against and within the short story as a way of locating the author's subjective involvement and the attention she paid it.

A second criticism—the potential for self-revelations to invite alienation—stems from the fact that narrative tellings often diminish the teller, or, equally damaging, they turn the teller into a crafty narrator. In Grumet's (1987) words, "Our stories are the masks through which we can be seen, and with every telling we stop the flood and swirl of thought so someone can get a glimpse of us, and maybe catch us if they can" (p. 322). Acknowledging the politics of personal knowledge and the potentially alienating aspects of the self-story, Grumet made it a practice to use Pinar's (1976b) method of *currere* in her work with teachers who examine their own practices through autobiographical writing. This method requires that, instead of a single text, the teachers write three separate accounts of their lives—a triple retelling organized into past experience, present situation, and future images. Grumet used this approach to autobiographical writing as a way of partially addressing the dangers involved in asking others to reveal themselves in a single telling, for as she pointed out, if multiple accounts undermine the authority of the teller, they at least protect him or her "from being captured by the reflection provided in a single narrative" (p. 324).

Finally, an ethical concern posed by those who work within narrative as a form of inquiry is the degree to which we should expect our work to enable those who tell us their stories to take actions that will change their own conditions or the conditions of others living in similar circumstances. In *Troubling the Angels: Women Living with HIV/AIDS* (Lather & Smithies, 1997), the researchers held themselves accountable as the authors of the text for getting the women's stories out to the general public in what was called the "K-Mart" version of the later published work. The women, whose stories Lather and Smithies told, served as the authors' editorial board. In this capacity, the women had final say as to how they would be portrayed and to whom they would speak (e.g., their choice of the general public, not the academic world, as their initial audience). In making the personal lives of these women who were living with HIV/AIDS part of their scholarship, Lather and Smithies found ways of textually representing the relationship between themselves and the women's selves. For example, they used split pages on which the women's voices were positioned above their own, and they boxed in the women's poems as a way of setting them apart, out of reach of their own authorial control.

In summary, the relationship between the knower and the known is made less obscure and perhaps "safer" when researchers practice reflexivity and take steps to ensure that ethical consideration is given to their participants' needs. However, in the long run, as Haraway (1991) cogently pointed out, our subjectivities are "always constructed and stitched together imperfectly" (p. 193)—a point that one might argue also suggests that narrative approaches are no more susceptible to problems of self-deception than are other forms of research. Or, as Nespor and Barber (1995) succinctly put it, "No one is detached or 'neutral'" (p. 53).

Crisis of Legitimation (Truth Claims)

The belief that "truth and validity claims reflect historically determined values and interests of different groups ... [and that] reality is mediated by conceptual schemes (Kant), ideologies (Marx), language games (Wittgenstein), and paradigms (Kuhn)" (Jansen & Peshkin, 1992, p. 688) is part of a tradition that views knowledge as being at least partially dependent on the knower. It is a tradition influenced in post-World War II Europe by existentialist thinking according to Casey (1995), who, in her analysis of the education field's current enthusiasm for narrative research, finds a connection between certain narrative approaches and existentialism's emphasis on the need for individuals to make sense of a senseless world.

But how is one to address the issues surrounding validity in current-day discussions of the so-called legitimation crisis? I suggest that French literary theorist Helene

Cixous's (Cixous & Calle-Gruber, 1997) interpretation of Archimedes' thoughts on Truth is a good starting place:

> Archimedes is someone who never believed in the truth of something;
> that something was the truth, no.
> To believe in the Truth as tension, as movement, yes.
>   — Helene Cixous (Cixous & Calle-Gruber, 1997, p. 5)

Viewing the Truth as tension, as movement, seems a good way to characterize contemporary writers' handling of narrative inquiry and truth claims. Although some narrative analysts (see Cortazzi, 1993) assume that the language used by their participants captures the reality of lived experiences, others view language as actually constituting that reality (Denzin, 1997; Gilbert, 1993). Still others (The Personal Narratives Group, cited in Riessman, 1993) believe that people fabricate their stories, not so much with an intent to deceive as with a desire to make their fictions become realities. In describing this phenomenon, Riessman (1993) noted that interpretive narratives require interpretation:

> When talking about their lives, people lie sometimes, forget a lot, exaggerate, become confused, and get things wrong. Yet they *are* revealing truths. These truths don't reveal the past "as it actually was," aspiring to a standard of objectivity. They give us instead the truths of our experiences.... Unlike the Truth of the scientific ideal, the truths of personal narratives are neither open to proof nor self-evident. We come to understand them only through interpretation, paying careful attention to the contexts that shape their creation and to the world views that inform them. Sometimes the truths we see in personal narratives jar us from our complacent security as interpreters "outside" the story and make us aware that our own place in the world plays a part in our interpretation and shapes the meanings we derive from them. (The Personal Narratives Group, cited in Riessman, 1993, p. 22)

The criteria that might be applied in determining a narrative's authority, legitimacy, or trustworthiness (Denzin, 1997; Riessman, 1993) vary with the type of narrative under consideration (e.g., oral, first-person, written, biographical, and so on). Generally, those who work with narrative forms of inquiry agree that valid[3] research is well grounded and supportable—it has what Polkinghorne (1988) referred to as *verisimilitude*, or the appearance of truth.

Transgressive validity (Richardson, 1997), as its name implies, violates what many working within the narrative paradigm would consider "acceptable" social science. In transforming her notes of an oral history of an unwed mother into the poem "Louisa May," Richardson (1997), in her words, transgressed "the normative constraints for social science writing" (p. 167). She crossed the invisible line separating social science from literary craft (Manning, 1987). Although she initially found her work trivialized and vulnerable to dismissal among colleagues in her field (sociology), today Richardson's scholarship is considered an important move in engaging narrative researchers in serious discussions of authorship, authority, validity, and aesthetics (Lenzo, 1995).

One such discussion focuses on Lawrence-Lightfoot's (1997) recounting of a paradox that argues for a very different way of thinking about validity and generalization. She contextualized this paradox within her own method of inquiry, portraiture, which

---

[3]Here, Polkinghorne (1988) used the ordinary, or nontechnical, meaning of *valid*, as in well-grounded and supportable. He distinguished its ordinary meaning from two of its more technical ones—the first being a valid conclusion drawn in the context of formal logic, and the second being a valid relationship between an instrument and the concept it purports to measure.

blends aesthetics and empiricism while drawing on features of the narrative, case study, and ethnography. In her words:

> Not only is the portraitist interested in developing a narrative that is both convincing and authentic, she is also interested in recording the subtle details of human experience. She wants to capture the specifics, the nuance, the detailed description of a thing, a gesture, a voice, an attitude as a way of illustrating more universal patterns. A persistent irony—recognized and celebrated by novelists, poets, playwrights—is that as one moves closer to the unique characteristics of a person or a place, one discovers the universal.... Eudora Welty (1983) offers a wonderful insight gained from her experience as a storyteller. She says forcefully: "What discoveries I have made in the process of writing stories, all begin with the particular, never the general." Clifford Geertz (1973) puts it another way when he refers to the paradoxical experience of theory development, the emergence of concepts from the gathering of specific detail. Geertz (1973) says, "Small facts are the grist for the social theory mill" (p. 23). The scientist and the artist are both claiming that *in the particular resides the general*. (Lawrence-Lightfoot, 1997, p. 14)

In summary, in the same way that traditional concerns for validity and generalizability can get in the way of how narrative researchers like to tell their stories, so also can the evolving notions of what ought to constitute truth claims beget angst among the traditionalists (Smith, 1997). In the end, however, it may be the work of individuals such as those whose research has just been described that will prevent the balkanization of education research. For if agreement can be reached on how to accept and work from one another's stories, it will be due in no small measure to their ability, and ours, to see Truth as tension, and as movement.

Crisis of Representation

Making problematic the assumed link between experience and text has created what is known in anthropology circles as the crisis of representation (Clifford & Marcus, 1986; Denzin, 1994). An argument that supports the existence of such a crisis is this: Because we can never suppress ourselves in the texts we write (or read), we in fact create the persons we write about. An example of the dilemma that the crisis of representation poses for researchers can be found in Denzin's (1989) work on the crisis of representation in biographical studies:

> When a writer writes a biography, he or she writes him[self] or herself into the life of the subject written about. When the reader reads a biographical text, that text is read through the life of the reader. Hence, writers and readers conspire to create the lives they write and read about. Along the way, the produced text is cluttered by the traces of the life of the "real" person being written about. (p. 26)

Questioning the assumed link between a narrative that tells about a real person's life and the text which represents that life (or, as Denzin noted, "traces of [that] life") opens the door to exploring two related phenomena. The first has to do with performance and the inadequacy of written texts for depicting lived experience (Denzin, 1997; Eisner, 1997) and the second with the blurring of genres (Geertz, 1980, 1983).

The inadequacy of written texts for depicting lived experience has led some researchers to explore ways of presenting their data through various performance modes. For example, Neilsen (1998) represented a series of in-depth interviews on teenagers' literate experiences as a play; Paget (1995) offered a dramatic reading of her research on conversations between a doctor and a patient; and Richardson (1993) performed an oral rendition of her data poem, "Louisa May," before a group of her peers at a national meeting of sociologists. By performing their texts, Neilsen, Paget, and Richardson established a different kind of communicative relation with their audiences.

Even so, by its very nature, performance relies on language to mediate experience—a point Denzin (1997) makes in drawing from Derrida (1976) to explain why neither the written word nor the performance (that is, no text) is ever final or complete:

> There is no clear window into the inner life of a person, for any window is always filtered through the glaze of language, signs, and the process of signification. And language, in both its written and spoken forms, is always inherently unstable, in flux, and made up of the traces of other signs and symbolic statements. Hence, there can never be a clear, unambiguous statement of anything, including an intention or a meaning. (Denzin, 1997, p. 14)

The publication of Geertz's two books, *The Interpretation of Cultures* (1973) and *Local Knowledge* (1983), helped to usher in the crisis of representation by introducing the notion of blurred genres. Although the first of these two volumes set the stage for reconceptualizing interpretive research generally, it is the latter, with its chapter on blurred genres, and Pratt's (1986) work on the relation of narrative to ethnographic writing that are at the heart of the representational crisis in narrative inquiry. This crisis, which dismisses the assumption that narrative approaches directly capture lived experience, argues instead that the texts written by researchers using these approaches create such experience (Denzin, 1997). Just as importantly, the work of Geertz (1983) and Pratt (1986) is recognized for having elevated storytelling from mere anecdotal writing to its current status as a vehicle in which empirical and aesthetic descriptions of the human condition find articulation. For example, Pratt (1986) has advocated blurring the genre boundaries between the personal narrative and ethnographic writing:

> I think it is fairly clear that personal narrative persists alongside objectifying description in ethnographic writing because it mediates a contradiction within the discipline between personal and scientific authority, a contradiction that has become especially acute since the advent of fieldwork as a methodological norm.... Fieldwork produces a kind of authority that is anchored to a large extent in subjective, sensuous experience. One experiences the indigenous environment and lifeways for oneself, sees with one's own eyes, even plays some roles, albeit contrived ones, in the daily life of the community. (p. 32)

In a move to extend Pratt's (1986) endorsement of blurring narrative and ethnographic boundaries as a means of circumventing problems associated with texts that separate the researcher from the researched and the literary from the scientific,[4] Richardson (1997) and Eisner (1997) argued for a style of academic writing that blurs narrative knowing, sociological telling, poetry, and film making. Although both Richardson and Eisner personally research and write in ways that displace (and, at times, erase) boundaries between art and science, both are also fully cognizant of the need to avoid turning this new approach to narrative inquiry into a petrified discourse—one that is no longer open to resistance and rewriting.

In sum, exploring alternative ways of representing ourselves and the people we write about in our research comes at a defining moment in the history of narrative inquiry—when the question of what counts (or should count) as legitimate research has been settled to some degree by what Eisner (1997) described as the long-overdue insight that "research [does] not belong to science alone" (p. 5). Although this insight is not recognized as such in all corners of the research world, Eisner's thinking, which is grounded in Geertz's (1983) work on blurred genres, lends credence to the continuing

---

[4]In 16th-century European travel accounts, first-person narrations of the traveler's journey predominated over the empirical descriptions of the flora and fauna of the regions he or she described. Ironically, "the descriptive portions were sometimes seen as dumping grounds for the 'surplus data' that could not be fitted into the narrative" (Pratt, 1986, p. 33).

search for better ways of representing lived experience, given the inadequacy of all texts, written and performed, for depicting such experience presently.

IMPLICATIONS

Of interest here are the implications of the issues raised by the postmodern or poststructural turn in narrative inquiry. Specifically, how has this turn affected the way researchers and practitioners think about subjectivity, truth claims, and representation? For instance, what methodological considerations do researchers need to take into account when using narrative approaches? Who might be an audience for academic writing that purposefully blurs borders separating the scholarly from the everyday world of practice, and why might this audience be a valuable one to seek?

Research

Regardless of the type of narrative inquiry undertaken, the postmodern critique calls attention to the researcher's presence and why it must be taken into account from the start (Brodkey, 1987). Such an accounting involves making decisions about whose stories to tell, which parts of a story to omit when it comes time to publish the research, how much of the narrator's voice to include, when to interrupt that voice with the researcher's commentary, and so on. The implications such reflexive practices hold for literacy researchers are numerous. Perhaps understanding the complex system of power relations embedded in the narrative interview is as good a starting point as any. As Emihovich (1995) noted, the interview process is complicated by the privileged position of the researcher in relation to the researched (e.g., the researcher can leave the scene after recording the narrator's story, whereas the narrator often does not have this choice). A more subtle form of privilege is to be found in the decisions that lead to the researcher taking on the voice of the narrator/storyteller. Such decisions often alter the way in which the voice of the storied participant can be heard (Polkinghorne, 1997).

Another aspect of the power relationship present in the narrative interview that has implications for literacy researchers is documented by Scheurich (1995) in his postmodernist critique of the traditional interview process. Arguing from the perspective that "the researcher has multiple intentions and desires, some of which are consciously known and some of which are not" (p. 240), as does the person being interviewed, Scheurich believed we should highlight, not hide, the so-called baggage that is brought to the interview process. Admitting that it is simply impossible to name all that baggage, Scheurich opted for what he termed "a reasonably comprehensive statement of disciplinary training, epistemological orientation, social positionality, institutional imperatives, and funding sources and requirement" (pp. 249–250). Providing readers with such a statement is, to Scheurich's way of thinking, a way of enabling them to make their own evaluations of the research enterprise.

Experimenting with alternative ways of writing, such as those encountered in the newer forms of narrative research in education (see Casey, 1995, for a comprehensive listing of these forms and examples of each), is never without controversy. But it is especially the case when such experimentation crosses boundaries traditionally thought to separate academic scholarship from the more mundane world in which we all live. This kind of boundary crossing has appeal for literacy researchers working in areas where representing in writing what their participants tell them is not viewed as simply a matter of mirroring lived experience, as if that were possible in the first place. As Denzin (1997), following Derrida (1976), pointed out, "Language and speech do not mirror experience; they create experience and in the process of creation constantly transform and defer that which is being described" (p. 5).

For theorists writing about narrative inquiry, however, the issue lies not so much with representation per se as with the truth claims that can be made about one's story (Bruner, 1987; Gilmore, 1994; Tonkin, 1992; Trinh, 1991). Rejecting the notion that narrative texts need only "move us" to establish their truth claims, Riessman (1993, p. 64) and Polkinghorne (1995) argued for judging a text's authority in terms of its coherence (explanatory power), correspondence (achieved through member checks), persuasiveness, and pragmatic use (the insights and understandings it provides the field). That there is no agreement on what constitutes the legitimacy of narrative texts is part of the larger debate surrounding the notion of truth as both tension and movement. Nowhere is this debate more evident than in our own field. In literacy research, the criteria used in establishing truth claims for narratives are numerous, ranging from those that refuse to endorse any single interpretation of the data to those that seek convergence, if not consensus (Alvermann & Hruby, 2000).

Opening up our research agendas in literacy education to include alternative forms of data representation typically associated with narrative inquiry can increase the variety of questions we ask about reading and writing as processes and about literacy instruction in general. As Eisner (1997) pointed out, agendas open to alternative forms of data representation hold promise for developing a field's awareness in ways that may lead to new ways of thinking:

> Put another way, our capacity to wonder is stimulated by the possibilities that new forms of representation suggest. As we learn to think within the medium we choose to use, we also become more able to raise questions that the media themselves suggest; tools, among other things, are also heuristics. (p. 8)

But with this opening up of agendas to include new forms of data representation comes a need to avoid substituting creativity and cleverness for substance. In Eisner's (1997) words, "We need to be our own toughest critics" (p. 9). This advice seems sound if the goal is to experiment with less technical forms of scientific writing but not at the expense of methodological rigor.

Practice

To whom do we tell our stories as literacy researchers engaged in narrative inquiry? More often than not, these stories are shared professionally with a relatively small group of like-minded peers. As Lawrence-Lightfoot (1997) reminded us in her introduction to *The Art and Science of Portraiture*, rarely does the work produced in the academy reach beyond its walls:

> Academicians tend to speak to one another in a language that is often opaque and esoteric. Rarely do the analyses and texts we produce invite dialogue with people in the "real world." Instead, academic documents—even those that focus on issues of broad public concern—are read by a small audience of people in the same disciplinary field, who often share similar conceptual frameworks and rhetoric. (pp. 9–10)

However, this situation appears to be changing. A growing number of scholars working within the realm of narrative inquiry are beginning to argue forcefully for reaching out to audiences other than one's academic peer group. For example, Tierney (1997) pressed for an openness in narrative writing, one that enables others to exercise greater awareness of the debates that rage in the academic community. He also pushed for dissertation committees to consider experimental fiction as a viable form of doctoral research. Although less radical in his approach to reaching out to audiences beyond the academic community, Polkinghorne (1997) posited that "by changing their voice to storyteller, researchers will also change the way in which the voices of their 'subjects' or participants can be heard" (p. 3). This change has implications, in turn, for what those outside the academic community "hear" and value or reject in our research. Polkinghorne also advocated writing separate reports for different audiences, thus improving the chances that one's story is read beyond the academic community.

Implications of the socially constructed nature of narrative inquiry for literacy teaching and learning are also numerous. For example, the potential for storytelling to renew and regulate our ways of ordering and naming literacy practices at all levels of instruction is profound, as Gilbert (1989, 1993) repeatedly showed. This renewal process continually provides the framework through which we act as we go about our work in search of different story lines for language research. In Gilbert's (1993) words:

> In our personal lives, we tell stories as a way of structuring and giving significance to lived experience, and as a way of positioning ourselves in particular ways with our friends, our colleagues, our families. And this is not only so for our personal lives. It applies equally to our professional lives and to the stories that sustain us there. We tell stories of our research experiences, stories of the texts we read, stories of our classrooms, and stories of the children we teach. And our stories keep changing as our ways of reading stories (and therefore of making new stories) change. (p. 211)

Narrative research that is grounded in the everyday world of literacy and teaching provides entry into that world. Stories of how local knowledge of literacy conditions can help shape policy decisions are few and far between; however, where they do exist (e.g., Quint, 1996; Rist, 1994), they signal still further the collapsing of boundaries once thought to separate the research community from the world of practice—the knower from the known. In the wake of this collapse, at least two key questions have surfaced that have implications for the field of practice. First is the question of whether or not a level of discourse can be found that encourages communication between researchers and practitioners in literacy education. A second question asks what impact narrative research is having on classroom literacy practices. To some degree, the difficulty in answering these questions lies with literacy researchers' partial, as opposed to full, specification of the educational phenomena that they observe. More generally, however, the difficulty seems to stem from the literacy community's disinclination (or inability) to set a collective research agenda (Mosenthal, 1985, 1993). For whatever reason, the situation is made even more complex by postmodernist critiques that challenge the authority of the author–storyteller–researcher.

Writing in a different context, but on a theme related to decentering the author–storyteller–researcher's authority, Grumet (1987) made the following observation about truth claims in relation to first-person narratives:

> Viewed against the background of bureaucratic, depersonalized institutions, storytelling seems pretty authentic, or at least expressive. It seems natural to assume that the first person is closer to us than the third, an intimacy that Sartre [1972] repudiates emphatically in *The Transcendence of the Ego*, arguing that we do not know ourselves any better than we know others, and reminding us not to confuse familiarity with knowledge. (p. 321)

This observation calls to mind one of Eisner's (1997) several cautions concerning the use of alternative forms of data representation. In essence, Eisner is concerned that narrative researchers—in their effort to paint classroom life and all its complexities in a way that is understandable to the general public—all too often settle for a kind of ambiguity in their reporting that is reminiscent of the Rorschach syndrome. That is, "Everyone confers his or her own idiosyncratic meaning on the data. No consensus is possible. The data mean whatever anyone wants them to mean; or worse, no [one] knows what they mean" (Eisner, 1997, p. 9).

On a more positive ending note, it is important to bear in mind educational philosopher Maxine Greene's (1994) thinking on the postmodernist critique of narrative inquiry and how we might choose to respond to the problem that Eisner (1997) has identified. Writing from the perspective of someone who has observed many changes come and go in the name of educational research, Greene quoted Kathy Carter (1993) on the place of story in teaching and teacher education to make the point that what matters is not the label of one's truth claims but rather the problems such claims pose for representing one's data:

> We may need, [Carter wrote], to continue to challenge the tradition of truth claims that largely ignored context, character, contradiction, and complexity. We may have to run against the winds of the sometimes warped ways of gaining acceptance by the scientific community, a community that has systematically excluded particular problematics, voices, values, and experiences from its intellectual pursuits. (Carter, cited in Greene, 1994, p. 455)

The appealing nature of Carter's argument notwithstanding, to Greene's way of thinking (and, I might add, my own), the "problems of relativism and representation will have to be confronted" (Greene, 1994, p. 455) if the metanarratives of yesteryear are not to replace the stories of today. This chapter is offered as an invitation to the conversation surrounding these problems, or at least as I have interpreted them.

REFERENCES

Alcoff, L. (1988). Cultural feminism versus post-structuralism: The identity crisis in feminist theory. *Signs*, *13*, 405–436.

Allen, J., Michalove, B., & Shockley, B. (1993). *Engaging children*. Portsmouth, NH: Heinemann.

Alvermann, D. E., & Hruby, G. G. (2000). Mentoring and reporting research: A concern for aesthetics. *Reading Research Quarterly*, *35*(1), 46–63.

Alvermann, D. E., Commeyras, M., Young, J. P., Randall, S., & Hinson, D. (1997). Interrupting gendered discursive practices in classroom talk about texts: Easy to think about, difficult to do. *Journal of Literacy Research*, *29*, 73–104.

Au, K. H. (1997). Schooling, literacy, and cultural diversity in research and personal experience. In A. Neumann & P. L. Peterson (Eds.), *Women, research, and autobiography in education* (pp. 71–90). New York: Teachers College Press.

Britzman, D. (1995). "The question of belief": Writing poststructural ethnography. *Qualitative Studies in Education*, *8*, 233–242.

Brodkey, L. (1987). Writing ethnographic narratives. *Written Communication*, *4*, 25–50.

Bruner, J. (1986). *Actual minds, possible worlds*. Cambridge, MA: Harvard University Press.

Bruner, J. (1987). Life as narrative. *Social Research*, *54*(1), 11–32.

Carter, K. (1993). The place of story in the study of teaching and teacher education. *Educational Researcher*, *22*(1), 5–18.

Casey, K. (1995). The new narrative research in education. In L. Darling-Hammond (Ed.), *Review of research in education* (Vol. 21, pp. 211–253). Washington, DC: American Educational Research Association.

Cixous, H., & Calle-Gruber, M. (1997). *Helene Cixous rootprints: Memory and life writing*. London: Routledge.

Cizek, G. J. (1995). Crunchy granola and the hegemony of the narrative. *Educational Researcher*, *24*(2), 26–28.

Clifford, J. (1988). *The predicament of culture: Twentieth-century ethnography, literature, and art*. Cambridge, MA: Harvard University Press.

Clifford, J., & Marcus, G. E. (Eds.). (1986). *Writing culture*. Berkeley: University of California Press.

Cochran-Smith, M., & Lytle, S. L. (Eds.). (1993). *Inside/outside: Teacher research and knowledge*. New York: Teachers College Press.

Constas, M. A. (1998). The changing nature of educational research and a critique of postmodernism. *Educational Researcher*, *27*(2), 26–33.

Cortazzi, M. (1993). *Narrative analysis*. London: Falmer.

de la Luna, L., & Kamberelis, G. (1997). Refracted discourses/disrupted practices: Possibilities and challenges of collaborative action research in classrooms. In C. K. Kinzer, K. A. Hinchman, & D. J. Leu (Eds.), *Inquiries in literacy theory and practice: 46th Yearbook of the National Reading Conference* (pp. 213–228). Chicago: National Reading Conference.

Deleuze, G., & Guattari, F. (1987). *A thousand plateaus: Capitalism and schizophrenia* (B. Massumi, Trans.). Minneapolis, MN: University of Minnesota Press. (Original work published 1980)

Denzin, N. (1989). *Interpretive biography*. Newbury Park, CA: Sage.

Denzin, N. (1994). Evaluating qualitative research in the poststructural moment: The lessons James Joyce teaches us. *International Journal of Qualitative Studies in Education, 7*, 295–308.

Denzin, N. (1997). *Interpretive ethnography*. Thousand Oaks, CA: Sage.

Derrida, J. (1976). *Of grammatology*. (G. C. Spivak, Trans.). Baltimore, MD: Johns Hopkins University Press.

Dyson, A. H. (1997). *Writing superheroes: Contemporary childhood, popular culture, and classroom literacy*. New York: Teachers College Press.

Eisner, E. W. (1997). The promise and perils of alternative forms of data representation. *Educational Researcher, 26*(6), 4–10.

Emihovich, C. (1995). Distancing passion: Narratives in social science. *International Journal of Qualitative Studies in Education, 8*, 37–48.

Featherstone, J. (1989). To make the wounded whole. *Harvard Educational Review, 59*, 367–378.

Fenstermacher, G. D. (1994). Argument: A response to "Pedagogy, virtue, and narrative identity in teaching." *Curriculum Inquiry, 24*, 215–220.

Fishman, A. (1988). *Amish literacy: What and how it means*. Portsmouth, NH: Heinemann.

Fitzgerald, J., & Noblit, G. (1999). About hopes, aspirations, and uncertainty: First-grade English-language learners' emergent reading. *Journal of Literacy Research, 31*(2), 133–182.

Geertz, C. (1973). *The interpretation of cultures*. New York: Basic Books.

Geertz, C. (1980). Blurred genres. *American Scholar, 49*, 165–179.

Geertz, C. (1983). *Local knowledge: Further essays in interpretive anthropology*. New York: Basic Books.

Geertz, C. (1988). *Works and lives*. Stanford, CA: Stanford University Press.

Gilbert, P. (1989). *Writing, schooling and deconstruction: From voice to text in the classroom*. London: Routledge.

Gilbert, P. (1993). Narrative as gendered social practice: In search of different story lines for language research. *Linguistics and Education, 5*, 211–218.

Gilmore, L. (1994). *Autobiographics*. Ithaca, NY: Cornell University Press.

Greene, M. (1994). Epistemology and educational research: The influence of recent approaches to knowledge. In L. Darling-Hammond (Ed.), *Review of research in education* (Vol. 20, pp. 423–464). Washington, DC: American Educational Research Association.

Grumet, M. (1987). The politics of personal knowledge. *Curriculum Inquiry, 17*, 319–329.

Hankins, K. H. (1998). Cacophony to symphony: Memoirs in teacher research. *Harvard Educational Review, 68*, 80–95.

Haraway, D. J. (1991). *Simians, cyborgs, and women*. New York: Routledge.

Harre, R., & Gillet, G. (1994). *The discursive mind*. Thousand Oaks, CA: Sage.

Heath, S. B. (1983). *Ways with words: Language, life, and work in communities and classrooms*. New York: Cambridge University Press.

hooks, b. (1991). Narratives of struggle. In P. Mariani (Ed.), *Critical fictions: The politics of imaginative writing* (pp. 53–61). Seattle, WA: Bay.

Jansen, G., & Peshkin, A. (1992). Subjectivity in qualitative research. In M. D. LeCompte, W. L. Millroy, & J. Preissle (Eds.), *The handbook of qualitative research in education* (pp. 681–725). New York: Academic Press.

Kauffman, L. S. (1993). The long goodbye: Against personal testimony, or an infant grifter grows up. In G. Greene & C. Kahn (Eds.), *Changing subjects: The making of feminist literary criticism* (pp. 129–146). London: Routledge.

Lalik, R., Dellinger, L., & Druggish, R. (1996). Appalachian literacies at school. In D. J. Leu, C. K. Kinzer, & K. A. Hinchman (Eds.), *Literacies for the 21st century: Research and practice: 45th Yearbook of the National Reading Conference* (pp. 345–358). Chicago: National Reading Conference.

Lather, P., & Smithies, C. (1997). *Troubling the angels: Women living with HIV/AIDS*. Boulder, CO: Westview Press.

Lawrence-Lightfoot, S. (1997). A view of the whole: Origins and purposes. In S. Lawrence-Lightfoot & J. H. Davis (Eds.), *The art and science of portraiture* (pp. 1–16). San Francisco, CA: Jossey-Bass.

Lawrence-Lightfoot, S., & Davis, J. H. (1997). *The art and science of portraiture*. San Francisco: Jossey-Bass.

Lenzo, K. (1995). Validity and self-reflexivity meet poststructuralism: Scientific ethos and the transgressive self. *Educational Researcher, 24*(4), 17–23, 45.

Manning, P. K. (1987). *Semiotics and fieldwork*. Newbury Park, CA: Sage.

Manning, P. K., & Cullum-Swan, B. (1994). Narrative, content, and semiotic analysis. In N. K. Denzin & Y. S. Lincoln (Eds.), *Handbook of qualitative research* (pp. 463–477). Thousand Oaks, CA: Sage.

Marcus, G. E. (1994). What comes (just) after "post"? In N. K. Denzin & Y. S. Lincoln (Eds.), *Handbook of qualitative research* (pp. 563–574). Thousand Oaks, CA: Sage.

Messer-Davidow, E. (1985). Knowers, knowing, knowledge: Feminist theory and education. *Journal of Thought, 20*, 8–24.

Mosenthal, P. B. (1985). Defining progress in educational research. *Educational Researcher, 14*(9), 3–9.

Mosenthal, P. B. (1993). Understanding agenda setting in reading research. In A. P. Sweet & J. I. Anderson (Eds.), *Reading research into the year 2000* (pp. 115–128). Hillsdale, NJ: Lawrence Erlbaum Associates.

Neilsen, L. (1994). *A stone in my shoe: Teaching literacy in times of change*. Winnipeg, Canada: Peguis.

Neilsen, L. (1998). Playing for real: Performative texts and adolescent identities. In D. E. Alvermann, K. A. Hinchman, D. W. Moore, S. F. Phelps, & D. R. Waff (Eds.), *Reconceptualizing the literacies in adolescents' lives* (pp. 3–26). Mahwah, NJ: Lawrence Erlbaum Associates.

Nespor, J., & Barber, L. (1995). Audience and the politics of narrative. *International Journal of Qualitative Studies in Education, 8*, 49–62.

Neumann, A., & Peterson, P. L. (1997). *Learning from our lives: Women, research, and autobiography in education.* New York: Teachers College Press.

Olson, G. A. (1991). The social scientist as author: Clifford Geertz on ethnography and social construction [Interview with Clifford Geertz]. In G. A. Olson & I. Gale (Eds.), *(Inter)views: Cross-disciplinary perspectives on rhetoric and literacy* (pp. 187–210). Carbondale, IL: Southern Illinois University Press.

Paget, M. A. (1995). Performing the text. In J. Van Maanen (Ed.), *Representation in ethnography* (pp. 222–244). Thousand Oaks, CA: Sage.

Perry, R. C. (1995). *Jane's story: A description of one deaf person's experiences with literacy.* Unpublished dissertation, University of Georgia, Athens.

Pinar, W. F. (1976a). Introduction. In W. F. Pinar & M. R. Grumet, *Toward a poor curriculum* (pp. iii–viii). Dubuque, IA: Kendall/Hunt.

Pinar, W. F. (1976b). The method. In W. F. Pinar & M. R. Grumet, *Toward a poor curriculum* (pp. 51–65). Dubuque, IA: Kendall/Hunt.

Pinar, W. F. (1988). "Whole, bright, deep with understanding": Issues in qualitative research and autobiographical method. In W. Pinar (Ed.), *Contemporary curriculum discourses* (pp. 134–153). Scottsdale, AZ: Gorsuch Scarisbrick.

Pinar, W. F., & Grumet, M. R. (1976). *Toward a poor curriculum.* Dubuque, IA: Kendall/Hunt.

Polkinghorne, D. E. (1988). *Narrative knowing and the human sciences.* Albany: State University of New York Press.

Polkinghorne, D. E. (1995). Narrative configuration in qualitative analysis. *International Journal of Qualitative Studies in Education, 8*, 5–23.

Polkinghorne, D. E. (1997). Reporting qualitative research as practice. In W. G. Tierney & Y. S. Lincoln (Eds.), *Representation and the text: Re-framing the narrative voice* (pp. 3–21). Albany: State University of New York Press.

Pratt, M. L. (1986). Fieldwork in common places. In J. Clifford & G. E. Marcus (Eds.), *Writing culture: The poetics and politics of ethnography* (pp. 27–50). Berkeley: University of California Press.

Quint, S. (1996). "Cause you talkin' about a whole person": A new path for schooling and literacy in troubled times and spaces. *Journal of Literacy Research, 28*, 310–319.

Richardson, L. (1993). Poetics, dramatics, and transgressive validity: The case of the skipped line. *Sociological Quarterly, 35*, 695–710.

Richardson, L. (1997). *Fields of play: Constructing an academic life.* New Brunswick, NJ: Rutgers University Press.

Riessman, C. K. (1993). *Narrative analysis.* Newbury Park, CA: Sage.

Rist, R. (1994). Influencing the policy process with qualitative research. In N. K. Denzin & Y. S. Lincoln (Eds.), *Handbook of qualitative research* (pp. 545–557). Thousand Oaks, CA: Sage.

Sartre, J. P. (1972). *The transcendence of the ego* (F. Williams & R. Kirkpatrick, Trans.). New York: Octagon Books.

Schaafsma, D. (1993). *Eating on the street: Teaching literacy in a multicultural society.* Pittsburgh, PA: University of Pittsburgh Press.

Scheurich, J. J. (1995). A postmodernist critique of research interviewing. *International Journal of Qualitative Studies in Education, 8*, 239–252.

Smith, J. K. (1997). The stories educational researchers tell about themselves. *Educational Researcher, 26*(5), 4–11.

Soukhanov, A. H. (1996). *The American heritage dictionary of the English language* (3rd ed.) Boston: Houghton Mifflin.

St. Pierre, E. A. (1997). Nomadic inquiry in the smooth spaces of the field: A preface. *International Journal of Qualitative Studies in Education, 10*, 365–383.

Tierney, W. G. (1997). Lost in translation: Time and voice in qualitative research. In W. G. Tierney & Y. S. Lincoln (Eds.), *Representation and the text: Re-framing the narrative voice* (pp. 23–36). Albany: State University of New York Press.

Tierney, W. G., & Lincoln, Y. S. (Eds.). (1997). *Representation and the text: Re-framing the narrative voice.* Albany: State University of New York Press.

Tonkin, E. (1992). *Narrating our pasts: The social construction of oral history.* Cambridge, UK: Cambridge University Press.

Trinh, T. M-ha. (1991). *When the moon waxes red: Representation, gender and cultural politics.* New York: Routledge.

Van Maanen, J. (Ed.). (1988). *Tales of the field.* Chicago: University of Chicago Press.

Visweswaran, K. (1994). *Fictions of feminist ethnography.* Minneapolis: University of Minnesota Press.

Welty, E. (1983). *One writer's beginnings.* Cambridge, MA: Harvard University Press.

Wolf, M. (1990). The woman who didn't become a shaman. *American Ethnologist, 17*, 419–430.

Wolf, M. (1992). *A thrice-told tale.* Stanford, CA: Stanford University Press.

Young, J. P. (1998). *Critical literacy, homeschooling, and masculinities: Young adolescent boys talk about gender.* Unpublished doctoral dissertation, University of Georgia, Athens.

CHAPTER 5

Critical Approaches

Marjorie Siegel
Teachers College, Columbia University

Susana Laura Fernandez
University of Buenos Aires

Why is it that there is so much intellectual activity around issues of power and politics in the social sciences and the humanities, yet so little of it has influenced theory, research, and practice in the field of literacy education? This is indeed a curious situation, especially when we consider that by 1984—the publication year of the first *Handbook of Reading Research* (Pearson, Barr, Kamil, & Mosenthal, 1984)—critical perspectives on teaching, curriculum, and schooling had begun to take hold in schools of education. The publication of books like *Knowledge and Control* (Young, 1971) and *Schooling in Capitalist Society* (Bowles & Gintis, 1976) challenged the long-standing fiction that schooling is a neutral activity, and proposed, instead, that teaching and curriculum are political practices inasmuch as they produce knowledge for purposes of social regulation. As such, critical approaches represent a critique of widely held functionalist views about the role of schooling in society, which suggest that schooling is "an efficient and rational way of sorting and selecting talented people so that the most able and motivated attain the highest status positions" (Hurn, 1993, p. 45). For example, the image of schooling as an opportunity for social mobility based on merit is replaced, in critical thought, by one that shows how schools reproduce the unequal distribution of wealth and power that is the hallmark of capitalist societies, and in so doing contribute to the maintenance of the status quo (Shannon, 1996).

Even a brief consideration of why "critical approaches" are just beginning to find a place in the discourse on literacy will allow us to highlight some of the themes that distinguish critical approaches from those theories and methods that have dominated reading research thus far. We begin, therefore, with a brief look at what was included and excluded from the first two volumes of the *Handbook of Reading Research* (hereafter *HRR1* and *HRR2*), and then turn to the problem of defining critical approaches, working historically from the critical theory of the Frankfurt School, to Paulo Freire's work on literacy as the development of critical consciousness, to contemporary critical scholarship, especially the ideas of Michel Foucault. We conclude with some observations on current trends in critical studies of literacy education. In taking on the challenge of mapping the discourse on critical approaches to reading and literacy education, we are mindful of the fact that chapters such as these are "acts of cultural production" (Noblit & Pink, 1995, cited in Apple, 1997, p. xi) that construct the field they purport to "describe." Hence, our reading of this rapidly expanding field of studies is by no means definitive but, rather, suggestive of the multiple meanings critical approaches have today.

CRITICAL APPROACHES AND THE DISCOURSE ON READING

However problematic the exclusion of critical approaches from the discourse on reading and literacy may seem to us now, the reasons for this exclusion become clear when we consider the history of reading research. From its earliest beginnings as a field of study, reading research has followed the currents of academic psychology (cf. Luke & Freebody, 1997a; Venezky, 1984), resulting in a particular view of both the object of study and the method for studying it. This dominance is evident in *HRR1* (Pearson et al., 1984), which can be read as a tribute to psychological theories and methods and a celebration of the knowledge about reading they produced. With few exceptions, the chapters constructed reading as an autonomous (Street, 1984), psychological process unrelated to any of the social, political, cultural, and economic patterns that shape schooling, and thus treated science, schooling, and language unproblematically as neutral, rational activities unaffected by power and ideology. The few chapters that interrupted this narrative (e.g., ethnographic approaches [Guthrie & Hall, 1984], sociolinguistic directions [Bloome & Green, 1984], and social and motivational influences [Wigfield & Asher, 1984]) were quite important, as they introduced ways of conceptualizing reading and reading research drawn from anthropology and sociology. In these chapters, reading was characterized as a social and cultural activity, research methods emphasized meanings and contexts, and schools were found to play a role in producing the low levels of reading achievement among African-American and Hispanic students, although explanations for this finding tended toward theories of cultural discontinuity rather than structural inequalities (Au, 1993).

The interpretative turn that refigured the social sciences in the 1970s was fully evident when *HRR2* (Barr, Kamil, Mosenthal, & Pearson) appeared in 1991, and this shift was marked by an expanded vocabulary: *literacy*, not just *reading*, had become an object of study. For some, this meant that in addition to a psychological dimension, "literacy has acquired … a sociopolitical dimension, associated with its role within society and the ways in which it is deployed for political, cultural, and economic ends" (Venezky, 1991, p. 46). Yet, the meaning of *sociopolitical* remained largely unexamined, as evidenced by the field's uncritical acceptance of the "literacy myth," that is, the belief that literacy leads to economic and political progress (Graff, 1987). Absent from the historical treatment of literacy in *HRR2* was research that showed how literacy was used to "solidify the social hierarchy, empower elites and ensure that people lower on the hierarchy accept the values, norms, and beliefs of the elites, even when it is not in their interest to do so" (Gee, 1990, p. 40). Even when an overtly economic topic was examined, as in the chapter on the production of commercial materials (Chall & Squire, 1991), the ideological process whereby cultural material is selected and shaped for consumption in schools was taken for granted. From this brief discussion, it seems clear that although the study of reading was no longer decontextualized, the meaning of context had not yet been expanded to include the political and economic contexts. In light of this, it should probably not be surprising to find that Paulo Freire's work on critical literacy received only one mention in *HRR2*, despite the worldwide acclaim that *Pedagogy of the Oppressed* had received since its publication in 1970.

Patrick Shannon's chapter, "Politics, Policy, and Reading Research" (1991), was the one exception to this, and his opening comments on educational policy analysis can provide an introduction to the meaning of *critical* in critical approaches. He argued that educational policy analysis:

> can no longer be discussed as the natural evolution of scientific progress, neutral or benign. Rather, with political discussions included, specific policies can be identified as particular historical constructions negotiated among people with unequal power and authority to make decisions, often pursuing differing visions of how we should live together in and out of schools. (p. 47)

What makes this characterization of policy analysis "critical" is its rejection of naturalism (the assumption that policies represent unmediated reality), rationality (the assumption that policies are the result of science and logic), neutrality (the assumption that policies are not reflective of any particular interests), and individualism (the assumption that policies affect individuals without regard for their membership in particular social groups) (Popkewitz, 1990). Critical policy research, instead, assumes that educational problems must be conceptualized as part of the social, political, cultural, and economic patterns by which schooling is formed, patterns that reflect the unequal power and access of some groups in society. As Shannon noted, "critical" policy research employs a range of methods, but what sets this work apart from that of liberal and conservative policy research are the assumptions researchers make, the questions they pursue, and the value commitments they bring to their work. He wrote:

> In their attempts to identify how this imbalance of power exerts itself in specific situations, critical policy researchers use history to access the past policy negotiations and social relations that set the parameters for the current negotiations; they employ survey and statistical analyses to gather information about how the larger social structure affects all reading policies; and they utilize naturalistic methods to understand how both the powerful and the powerless cope with policy negotiations and the consequent situations.… This sense of injustice and the advocacy position in favor of teachers and students leads critical policy researchers to select questions that illuminate the power relations of reading policy and programs … and that can expose the contradictions in reading education policy as opportunities for change. (p. 164)

Embedded in this description of critical policy research are themes that are characteristic of critical approaches to the study of literacy education: the emphasis on historical analyses of the social construction of educational problems, policies, and practices; the awareness of schooling as a site for the production and reproduction of social, economic, and political inequities; and the desire to use research to achieve social change. With these themes in mind, we turn now to the problem of understanding critical approaches.

UNDERSTANDING CRITICAL APPROACHES

There are a number of difficulties in attempting to understand "critical approaches." First, there is no single "critical approach." The word *critical* has begun to appear as a descriptor for approaches to research that are already common in education, as in "critical" ethnography (Anderson, 1989; Carspecken, 1996; Quantz, 1992; Simon & Dippo, 1986), "critical" discourse analysis (Bloome & Talwalkar, 1997; Fairclough, 1989, 1992; Gee, 1990; Luke, 1995), and "critical" action research (Carr & Kemmis, 1986; Noffke, 1997). Is there something that these approaches could be said to share? Would that shared element be "critical theory," "critical literacy," or "critical pedagogy," or perhaps a commitment to aligning purpose and method (Gitlin, Siegel, & Boru, 1989)?

These questions point to a second difficulty in understanding critical approaches, and that is that the word *critical* has no single meaning. Although it is tempting to seek a single meaning, doing so may result in forcing a uniformity of meaning where none exits or smoothing over what is in fact contested (Kincheloe & McLaren, 1994; Lankshear & McLaren, 1993). In light of these difficulties, we have chosen to present a brief overview of the historical formation of the meaning of the word *critical* because we believe understanding "critical approaches" depends on understanding the multiple meanings this word has in educational discourse. In this regard, we think it important to keep in mind Martin Jay's (1973) observation on the work of the Frankfurt School: "At the very heart of Critical Theory was an aversion to closed philosophical systems. To present it as such would therefore distort its essentially open-ended, probing, and unfinished quality" (p. 41).

The Critical Theory of the Frankfurt School

Any discussion of the meaning of *critical* must begin with a reference to the critical theory of the Frankfurt School, a group of scholars—including Max Horkheimer, Theodor Adorno, and Herbert Marcuse, among others—who formed the Institute of Social Research at the University of Frankfurt in 1923. Although the rise of Nazism forced the Institute into exile in 1935, first at Columbia University and later in California, their writings were not translated into English until the 1960s. Hence, the impact of their ideas only began to be felt when they captured the attention of students and intellectuals in the 1960s and 1970s, and later through the writings of Jurgen Habermas (Held, 1980).

Critical theory had two major thrusts: (a) a critique of positivism, which, by reducing reasoning to instrumental rationality and separating fact from values, had not only linked science to new forms of domination, but had privileged forms of reasoning that gave little emphasis to human consciousness and action; and (b) a concern for the relationship of theory and society, seeking a theory that would connect institutions, the activities of daily life, and the forces that shape the larger society—that is, connections among the economy, the culture industry, and the psychology of individuals.

Horkheimer set the stage for the idea of critical theory in his 1932 essay "Notes on Science and the Crisis" (1972), and introduced the term itself in 1937 in "Traditional and Critical Theory" (1972). The crisis that concerned Horkheimer was the failure of science to contribute to the betterment of society as a whole, and the source of this crisis was positivism (i.e., the description, classification, and generalization of facts). Horkheimer criticized positivists for reducing reasoning to formal logic, for making a fetish of facts, and for pretending to have "disentangled facts from values" (Jay, 1973, p. 62). The result, he argued, was "the abdication of reflection ... and the reification of the existing order" (Jay, 1973, p. 62). In short, science had become scientistic, something set apart from the workings of society; questions about value (i.e., deciding which problems should be addressed, deciding which course of action to take) were set aside in favor of questions about technique. Horkheimer argued that human reasoning could not simply involve passive sense-perception of reality because the world is "a product of the activity of society as a whole" (p. 200)—something made rather than given. In the following passage, Horkheimer rejected the idea of naturalism and highlighted the historical formation of both the objects perceived and the individual:

> The facts which our senses present to us are socially performed in two ways: through the historical character of the object perceived and through the historical character of the perceiving organ. Both are not simply natural; they are shaped by human activity, and yet the individual perceives himself [sic] as receptive and passive in the act of perception. (p. 200)

A central criticism of positivism, therefore, was that treating things as natural placed "questions about the genesis, development, and normative nature of the conceptual systems that select, organize, and define the facts" (Giroux, 1981, p. 14) outside the purview of science. Because the facts could not be questioned, the evaluative dimension of theory was eliminated and science became a tool of prevailing interests.

What was needed, instead, was a theory that served an unmasking function and could be used to "penetrate the world of things to show the underlying relations between persons … and demystify the surface forms of equality" (Aronowitz, 1972, p. xiii). This involved both immanent critique and dialectical thought (Giroux, 1981). Immanent critique is the analysis of "reality" by comparing "the pretensions of bourgeois ideology with the reality of its social conditions" (Jay, 1973, p. 63) or the appearance of a social fact (e.g., money, consumption, production) and what lay behind it. Dialectical thought was a style of analysis that attempted to trace out the historical formation of facts and their mediation by social forces. The goal of this analysis was not only to unmask the connections between knowledge, power, and domination, but to construct a more just society through praxis, defined as a kind of "self-creating action" (Jay, 1973, p. 4) that was both informed by theory and controlled by people. To summarize, reason and praxis were the two poles of critical theory (Jay, 1973). One could not separate knowledge from either values or action; moreover, the researcher was never a disinterested investigator inasmuch as the investigator's reasoning was mediated by the very social categories that were the focus of study. It was this striving for critical awareness of the historical formation of human thinking and social relations that would serve as the starting point for emancipation from exploitative and oppressive social conditions.

The influence of critical theory was not felt in American intellectual circles until the 1960s, when sociologists of education (among others) grew disenchanted with the optimism of the functionalist view of schooling, and skeptical of the benefits of science and technology. Arguing that "we live in a divided and conflict-ridded society [and] groups who compete for control of schooling use the rhetoric of societal needs to conceal the fact that it is their interests and their demands they are trying to advance" (Hurn, 1993, p. 57–58), scholars began to enunciate a conflict view of schooling that questioned the rhetoric of equal opportunity and pointed out the role schools played in reproducing inequalities. Correspondence (Bowles & Gintis, 1976) and reproduction (Bourdieu & Passeron, 1977) theories offered Marxist analyses of schooling that purported to show that schools met "the needs of capital by mirroring the class-differentiated, alienated social relations of the workplace" (Wexler, 1987, p. 40). Members of the Frankfurt School rejected orthodox Marxism as overly deterministic and lacking a consideration of human consciousness, and their empirical work focused on the psychology of domination and the creation of mass deception by the emerging culture industry. Sociologists of education drew on this work to criticize the economic reductionism of correspondence and reproduction theories (e.g., Bowles & Gintis, 1976); culture, not just the economy, thus became a focal point in the cultural reproduction theory neo-Marxist scholars developed. These theories suggested that schools reproduced class relations by selecting and transmitting the culture of dominant groups as if it were universal and legitimate knowledge. Willis (1977) later argued that cultural reproduction theory ignored human agency and the internal contradictions and forms of resistance that served as sources for social change, and schools eventually came to be seen as sites for production as well as reproduction, a perspective that allowed for struggle and possibility (Wexler, 1987).

Paulo Freire and the Idea of Critical Literacy

Among literacy educators, the person most associated with critical approaches is Paulo Freire, the Brazilian philosopher and teacher whose death in 1997 was mourned by radical educators around the world. Freire's work emerged from social and political conditions that existed in Brazil in the 1960s, which he described as stratified by race and class, with a very large and very poor working class population with little or no education. He argued, further, that Brazil's history of colonialism "bred the habits of domination and dependence which still prevail among us in the form of paternalistic approaches to problems" (1973, p. 22) and "did not constitute the cultural climate necessary for the rise of democratic regimes" (1973, p. 29). In this context, Freire began to develop a pedagogy of liberation, working with adults to break what he called "the culture of silence" (1973, p. 24) and enable them to overcome the oppression they experienced. Working from Marxist theory, he rejected the idea that the "oppressed" are "marginals" living "outside" of society, and argued, instead, that "they have always been 'inside'—inside the structure which made them 'beings for others'" (Freire, 1970, p. 55). "Illiteracy" is thus regarded not as an individual failing but as a historically constructed product of a society structured to produce inequality. Freire's first literacy campaign, carried out in northeast Brazil where 15 of the 25 million people in the region were illiterate, was so successful (300 workers became literate in 45 days) that the government decided to apply his method throughout Brazil. From these experiences, Freire developed a theory of education that was radical both in its politics and its methods, and successful enough as to become a threat to those in power. When a right-wing government came to power in 1964, Freire was jailed and then exiled.

The starting point of his theory was the observation that humans, unlike animals, are culture makers who use language to mediate their world. Freire argued that the human capacity to name the world enables humans to reflect on their worlds and become aware of their social and political location in those worlds, and this awareness, in turn, creates the urge to act on the world and remake culture. This kind of awareness, which he called *conscientizacao* or critical consciousness, cannot be developed through education practiced as banking because such practices regard knowledge as "a gift bestowed" (Freire, 1970, p. 53) and students as objects into which knowledge is deposited. In contrast, problem-posing education starts with people's knowledge and, through a dialogue among equals, attempts to expose—"demythologize"—the historical conditions that create their reality so that they may act to transform those conditions. It is in this way that education becomes the practice of freedom.

The method Freire developed to engage people in dialogues that would lead to critical consciousness was grounded in language. He wrote:

> Consistent with the liberating purpose of dialogical education, the object of investigation is not persons … but rather the thought-language with which men and women refer to reality, the levels at which they perceive that reality, and their view of the world, in which their generative themes are found. (1970, p. 78)

By examining a series of generative themes represented pictorially (what Freire called codifications of the participants' world), participants in the culture circles can begin to name their world and by decoding it begin to transform that reality. This is followed by work with syllables carefully selected for their ability to generate a range of words that can be used to examine the codifications. As even this brief description indicates, this approach to teaching literacy does not treat reading as a technical matter of reading words, but a political matter of reading the world and rewriting that world (Freire, 1987). Critical literacy can thus be defined as the practice of demystifying the conditions that oppress and working toward the transformation of those conditions. From this has come the idea of critical pedagogy as "classroom practice consistent with liberatory politics" (Gore, 1993, p. 42), a definition that attends "both to social vision and to instruction" (p. 42).

Contemporary Perspectives on the Meaning of "Critical"[1]

In recent years, these interpretations of *critical* have themselves been criticized, due in part to what these perspectives have ignored as well as to new social theories that have been taken up in the academy. Feminists, for example, have argued that Freire's theory emphasizes forms of oppression that result from an inequitable class structure over those that result from gender and racial inequalities. By speaking about oppression in abstract and universal terms, Freire ignores the ways in which gender and race, as well as class, serve as oppressive forces (Weiler, 1991). Feminists, among others, have also argued that critical pedagogy, which was meant to serve as a "pedagogy of hope" against the despair of reproduction theories of education, became as dominating and limiting as more traditional educational practices (e.g., Ellsworth, 1989; Gore, 1993; Knoblach & Brannon, 1993; Luke & Gore, 1992). Critical scholars have also argued that critical theory needs to be rethought or modified, given the shift from industrialism to postindustrialism, and the limitations of structuralism and modernism (Gee, 1990; Lankshear & McLaren, 1993; Wexler, 1987). Indeed, critical approaches have been profoundly reshaped by postmodernism, which critiques grand narratives about the direction of history (e.g., the Marxist narrative of class conflict and revolution), poststructuralism, which critiques the Enlightenment idea of progress, reason, and power (Popkewitz & Brennan, 1998), and postcolonialism, which rereads western knowledge as forged in the context of relationships between the west and the non-west. Because Michel Foucault's work has been so influential in reformulating critical scholarship, we comment briefly on his contributions to contemporary critical approaches.

Although Foucault knew the work of the Frankfurt School, and regarded its examination of rationality important, he did not accept its belief that enlightenment—the development of consciousness—would free people. As Popkewitz and Brennan (1998) explained, the philosophy of consciousness, the cornerstone of critical theory and critical literacy as well as of functionalist views of schooling, was rooted in two ideas from 19th-century thought: (a) the idea that rational knowledge was the engine of progress, and (b) the idea that the avenue of social progress was through individual human consciousness and action. Foucault upset these foundations of knowing and rationality when he suggested that our very concepts (such as individual agency, reason, abnormality, the child, etc.) were already *effects* of power; thus he questioned whether critical theory hid more than it revealed. As a result of this inquiry, he shifted his emphasis from human consciousness and agency to the changing ways in which knowledge and humanness were historically constituted. This approach to studying knowledge as a social practice is called *decentering the subject* and provides a way to understand how the subject is produced by systems of ideas that relate power and knowledge. Foucault called these systems of ideas *discourses* and turned his attention from the study of "autonomous" subjects to the study of how discourses, as historical practices, construct objects. Discourses operate both across disciplinary boundaries (e.g., across medicine, law, education, and social work) and within material practices across social locations (e.g., juvenile courts, hospitals, schools, and social service agencies).

Another aspect of critical theory and critical literacy that Foucault reconceptualized was power. In these theories, power is regarded as something people do or do not have, but Foucault (1977) argued that power is diffused through all social relationships in concrete and detailed specificity (pp. 115–116). Thus, he rejected the notion that power is primarily repressive and juridical, and proposed, instead, that power "tra-

---

[1]The contemporary landscape of critical work is more complex than what we can present here; our hope is that this brief overview can give a sense of the issues being developed in the discourse.

verses and produces things, it induces pleasure, forms knowledge, produces discourse. It needs to be considered as a productive network which runs through the whole social body" (p. 119). Knowledge or truth, on the other hand,

> isn't outside power or lacking in power.... Truth is a thing of this world: it is produced only by virtue of multiple forms of constraint. And it induces regular effects of power. Each society has its regime of truth, its "general politics" of truth: that is, the types of discourse which it accepts and makes function as true; the mechanisms and instances which enable one to distinguish true and false statements, the means by which each is sanctioned; the techniques and procedures accorded value in the acquisition of truth; the status of those who are charged with saying what counts as true. (p. 131)

Knowledge and power are thus inextricably intertwined in that what counts as knowledge is related to and may indeed arise from the ways in which power is diffused throughout society and within social relationships. From a Foucauldian perspective, then, *"critical* refers to a broad band of disciplined questioning of the ways in which power works through the discursive practices and performances of schooling" (emphasis in the original, Popkewitz & Brennan, 1998, p. 4).

CRITICAL APPROACHES TO STUDYING LITERACY EDUCATION

Locating the literature that could be characterized as *critical* within the field of literacy education is not as straightforward as it may seem, largely because, until quite recently, there were few such studies, and those that were published tended to appear as books, book chapters, and articles in general educational journals (e.g., *Harvard Educational Review*) and practitioner-oriented journals (e.g., *Rethinking Schools*) rather than in the mainstream research journals in the field (e.g., *Reading Research Quarterly, Journal of Literacy Research*). Despite these problems, several lines of work can be identified. One line of work, inspired by neo-Marxist critical theory, examines the political economy of reading instruction (a study of the historical relations between means of production and state structures) in order to show the ideological dimensions of what are thought to be neutral technologies (i.e., commercially published materials and instructional practices) of reading instruction (Luke, 1989, 1991; Shannon, 1989). Shannon (1989) extended his work on basal reading materials by examining the ways these materials serve to deskill teachers, whereas Luke (1988, 1989), showed how particular literacy practices come to be selected and authorized in the official discourse on literacy education.

A second line of work attempts to move beyond cultural discontinuity explanations for the low levels of reading achievement among African-American and Hispanic students by considering issues of power and politics as well as cultural differences. Drawing on Freire's theory, this work explores the ways that students' positioning in the larger society intersects with school literacy practices to silence them and construct them as school failures rather than literate persons, or, in other cases, to enable them to give voice to their knowledge and begin to read their world and rewrite it (e.g., Mitchell & Weiler, 1991; Walsh, 1991a). Other literacy scholars have woven together Freirean ideas with those of Russian language and social philosopher Mikhail Bakhtin to show how power works through language and how acknowledging students' voices can inform pedagogy and expand students' possibilities (e.g., Gutierrez, Rymes, & Larson, 1995; Walsh, 1991b). A few progressive literacy educators (e.g., Edelsky, 1991) have used critical theory and Freirean theory to articulate their underlying political commitment to challenging social and economic inequalities, something others are less sanguine about because they believe whole language and process writing instruction have taken hold, in part, because they serve corporate interests in an information society (Willinsky, 1990).[2]

One of the most fertile strands of critical work on literacy education is inspired by poststructuralist theories, as indicated by the interest in critical discourse analysis (e.g., Bloome & Talwalkar, 1997; Fairclough, 1989, 1992; Gee, 1990; Luke, 1995) and in feminist poststructuralist studies of literacy education (e.g., Davies, 1989, 1993; Gilbert, 1991, 1993, 1997). In some cases, this work combines critical theory, sociocultural theories of literacy (e.g., Street, 1984), and poststructuralist theory to critique progressive literacy pedagogies such as process writing and whole language (Luke & Freebody, 1997a, 1997b). This line of scholarship points up the contradictions in these practices and shows that what are thought to be "natural," "authentic," and "empowering" pedagogies may unintentionally reinforce the status quo by valorizing particular kinds of literacy practices or allowing oppressive practices to enter the classroom in an attempt to value students' "voices" or encourage teachers to serve as "facilitators" (e.g., Gilbert, 1991, 1997).

Despite the differences in the meaning of *critical* within critical scholarship on literacy education, we can (tentatively) note some themes that this work seems to share. One is that literacy is conceptualized as a social and political practice rather than a set of neutral, psychological skills. Another is that critical approaches look beyond the taken-for-granted explanations of practices and policies to understand their historical formation, especially the ways in which discourses—systems of ideas traditionally thought to be "outside" of schooling—work to construct the instructional practices and social relations that constitute literacy education in schools. And, finally, critical approaches seek to challenge and transform the status quo by engaging people in a "collective process of re-naming, re-writing, re-positioning oneself in relation to coercive structures" (Davies, 1993, p. 199).

CONCLUDING THOUGHTS

We began this chapter by asking why critical approaches had been excluded from the discourse on literacy education, and this question continues to trouble us, especially at a time when bilingual education and affirmative action are under attack. Why have we agreed not to frame literacy education as political? One explanation is that we, as a field, have made a fetish of the search for the "correct" methods of teaching reading. Yet, as Bartolome (1994) noted, this "methods fetish" only serves to deflect our attention from questions about the inequalities and injustices that persist in schools and society. Critical approaches to the study of literacy education examine the ways in which literacy instruction participates in the production of these persistent inequalities but also how literacy instruction may become a site for contesting the status quo. Although this line of scholarship is just beginning to receive attention within the field of literacy education, the need for work that addresses these issues is more urgent than ever as new literacies, along with new modes of exploitation, multiply in our increasingly globalized and digitalized world.

---

[2]This debate reflects the ambiguous legacy of the Progressivism (the social movement critical of the urban, capitalist, industrial society that was emerging at the turn of the 20th century); although progressives were committed to social progress and believed in equality, efficiency, and science, there is disagreement as to whether this movement was liberal or conservative because, it is argued, it helped consolidate the emerging corporate capitalism (Wexler, 1976).

ACKNOWLEDGMENTS

We acknowledge the contributions of Desiree Baird, Nadine Bryce, Peggy McNamara, Anastasia Maroulis, Hannah Schneewind, and Susan Stires—whose efforts to locate the literature on critical approaches to literacy research did much to shape this chapter. Special thanks go to Nancy Lesko and Michelle Knight for their careful readings and constructive comments on an earlier draft of this chapter, and to David Pearson for his support and patience.

REFERENCES

Anderson, G. (1989). Critical ethnography in education: Origins, current status, and new directions. *Review of Educational Research, 59*, 249–270.

Apple, M. (1997). Introduction. In M. Apple (Ed.), *Review of research in education* (Vol. 22, pp. xi–xxi). Washington, DC: American Educational Research Association.

Aronowitz, S. (1972). Introduction. In M. Horkheimer, *Critical theory: Selected essays* (pp. xi–xxi). New York: Herder & Herder.

Au, K. (1993). *Literacy instruction in multicultural settings.* Fort Worth, TX: Harcourt Brace.

Barr, R., Kamil, M., Mosenthal, P., & Pearson, P. D. (Eds.). (1991). *Handbook of reading research* (Vol. 2). New York: Longman.

Bartolome, L. (1994). Beyond the methods fetish: Toward a humanizing pedagogy. *Harvard Educational Review, 64*(2), 173–194.

Bloome, D., & Green, J. (1984). Directions in the sociolinguistic study of reading. In P. D. Pearson (Ed.), *Handbook of reading research* (Vol. 1, pp. 395–422). New York: Longman.

Bloome, D., & Talwalkar, S. (1997). Critical discourse analysis and the study of reading and writing. *Reading Research Quarterly, 32*(1), 104–112.

Bourdieu, P., & Passeron, J. (1977). *Reproduction in education, society, and culture.* London: Sage.

Bowles, S., & Gintis, H. (1976). *Schooling in capitalist America.* New York: Basic Books.

Carr, S., & Kemmis, W. (1986). *Becoming critical: Education, knowledge, and action research.* London: Falmer Press.

Carspecken, P. (1996). *Critical ethnography in educational research.* New York: Routledge.

Chall, J., & Squire, J. (1991). The publishing industry and textbooks. In R. Barr, M. Kamil, P. Mosenthal, & P. D. Pearson (Eds.), *Handbook of reading research* (Vol. 2, pp. 120–146). New York: Longman.

Davies, B. (1989). *Frogs and snails and feminist tales: Preschool children and gender.* Sydney: Allen & Unwin.

Davies, B. (1993). *Shards of glass: Children reading and writing beyond gendered identities.* Cresskill, NJ: Hampton Press.

Edelsky, C. (1991). *With literacy and justice for all.* London: Falmer Press.

Ellsworth, E. (1989). Why doesn't this feel empowering?: Working through the repressive myths of critical pedagogy. *Harvard Educational Review, 59*(3), 297–324.

Fairclough, N. (1989). *Language and power.* London: Longman.

Fairclough, N. (1992). *Discourse and social change.* Cambridge: Polity Press.

Foucault, M. (1977). *Power/knowledge: Selected interviews and other writings (1972–1977)* (C. Gordon, L. Marshall, J. Mepham, & K. Soper, Trans.). New York: Pantheon Books.

Freire, P. (1970). *Pedagogy of the oppressed.* New York: Continuum.

Freire, P. (1973). *Education for critical consciousness.* New York: Continuum.

Freire, P. (1987). *Literacy: Reading the word and the world.* South Hadley, MA: Bergin & Garvey.

Gee, J. P. (1990). *Social linguistics and literacies: Ideologies in discourses.* London: Falmer Press.

Gilbert, P. (1991, June). *The story so far: Gender, literacy and social regulation.* Paper presented at the Rejuvenation Conference of the Center for the Expansion of Language and Thinking, Amherst, MA.

Gilbert, P. (1993). Dolly fictions: Teen romance down under. In L. Christian-Smith (Ed.), *Texts of desire: Essays on fiction, femininity and schooling* (pp. 69–86). London: Falmer Press.

Gilbert, P. (1997). Discourses on gender and literacy: Changing the stories. In S. Muspratt, A. Luke, & P. Freebody (Eds.), *Constructing critical literacies: Teaching and learning textual practice* (pp. 59–75). Cresskill, NJ: Hampton Press.

Giroux, H. (1981). *Critical theory and educational practice.* Victoria, Australia: Deakin University Press.

Gitlin, A., Siegel, M., & Boru, K. (1989). The politics of method: From leftist ethnography to educative research. *International Journal of Qualitative Studies in Education, 2*(3), 237–253.

Gore, J. (1993). *The struggle for pedagogies: Critical and feminist pedagogies as regimes of truth.* New York: Routledge.

Graff, H. (1987). *The legacies of literacy: Continuities and contradictions in western culture and society.* Bloomington, IN: Indiana University Press.

Guthrie, L., & W. Hall. (1984). Ethnographic approaches to reading research. In P. D. Pearson (Ed.), *Handbook of reading research* (Vol. 1, pp. 91–110). New York: Longman.

Gutierrez, K., Rymes, B., & Larson, J. (1995). Script, counterscript, and underlife in the classroom: James Brown *versus* Brown v. Board of Education. *Harvard Educational Review, 65*(3), 445–471.

Held, D. (1980). *Introduction to critical theory: Horkheimer to Habermas.* Berkeley: University of California Press.

Horkheimer, M. (1972). *Critical theory: Selected essays.* New York: Herder & Herder.

Hurn, C. (1993). *The limits and possibilities of schooling* (3rd ed.). Boston: Allyn & Bacon.

Jay, M. (1973). *The dialectical imagination: A history of the Frankfurt School and the Institute of Social Research 1923–1950.* Boston: Little, Brown.

Kincheloe, J., & McLaren, P. (1994). Rethinking critical theory and qualitative research. In N. Denzin & Y. Lincoln (Eds.), *Handbook of qualitative research* (pp. 138–157). Thousand Oaks, CA: Sage.

Knoblach, C., & Brannon, L. (1993). *Critical teaching and the idea of literacy.* Portsmouth, NH: Boyton/Cook.

Lankshear, C., & McLaren, P. (Eds.). (1993). *Critical literacy: Politics, praxis, and the postmodern.* Albany: State University of New York Press.

Luke, A. (1989). *Literacy, textbooks, and ideology: Postwar literacy instruction and the mythology of Dick and Jane.* London: Falmer.

Luke, A. (1991). The political economy of reading instruction. In C. Baker & A. Luke (Eds.), *Towards a critical sociology of reading pedagogy* (pp. 3–25). Amsterdam: John Benjamins.

Luke, A. (1995). Text and discourse in education: An introduction to critical discourse analysis. In M. Apple (Ed.), *Review of research in education* (Vol. 21, pp. 3–48). Washington, DC: American Educational Research Association.

Luke, A., & Freebody, P. (1997a). Critical literacy and the question of normativity: An introduction. In S. Muspratt, A. Luke, & P. Freebody (Eds.), *Constructing critical literacies: Teaching and learning textual practice* (pp. 1–18). Cresskill, NJ: Hampton Press.

Luke, A., & Freebody, P. (1997b). The social practices of reading. In S. Muspratt, A. Luke, & P. Freebody (Eds.), *Constructing critical literacies: Teaching and learning textual practice* (pp. 185–225). Cresskill, NJ: Hampton Press.

Luke, C., & Gore, J. (Eds.). (1992). *Feminisms and critical pedagogy.* New York: Routledge.

Mitchell, C., & Weiler, K. (Eds.). (1991). *Rewriting literacy: Culture and the discourse of the other.* New York: Bergin & Garvey.

Noffke, S. (1997). Professional, personal, and political dimensions of action research. In M. Apple (Ed.), *Review of research in education* (Vol. 22, pp. 305–343). Washington, DC: American Educational Research Association.

Pearson, P. D., Barr, R., Kamil, M., & Mosenthal, P. (Eds.). (1984). *Handbook of reading research* (Vol. 1). New York: Longman.

Popkewitz, T. (1990). Whose future? Whose past? Notes on critical theory and methodology. In E. Guba (Ed.), *The paradigm dialog* (pp. 46–66). Newbury Park, CA: Sage.

Popkewitz, T., & Brennan, M. (1998). Introduction. In T. Popkewitz & M. Brennan (Eds.), *Foucault's challenge: Discourse, knowledge, and power in education* (pp. 3–35). New York: Teachers College Press.

Quantz, R. (1992). On critical ethnography (with some postmodern considerations). In M. LeCompte, W. Millroy, & J. Preissle (Eds.), *The handbook of qualitative research in education* (pp. 447–505). San Diego: Academic Press.

Shannon, P. (1989). *Broken promises: Reading instruction in twentieth-century America.* Granby, MA: Bergin & Garvey.

Shannon, P. (1991). Politics, policy, and reading research. In R. Barr, M. Kamil, P. Mosenthal, & P. D. Pearson (Eds.), *Handbook of reading research* (Vol. 2, pp. 147–168). New York: Longman.

Shannon, P. (1996). Critical issues: Literacy and educational policy. Part two (Poverty, literacy, and politics: Living in the USA). *Journal of Literacy Research, 28*(3), 429–449.

Simon, R., & Dippo, D. (1986). On critical ethnographic work. *Anthropology and Education Quarterly, 17,* 195–202.

Street, B. (1984). *Literacy in theory and practice.* Cambridge: Cambridge University Press.

Venezky, R. (1984). The history of reading research. In P. D. Pearson (Ed.), *Handbook of reading research* (Vol. 1, pp. 3–38). New York: Longman.

Venezky, R. (1991). The development of literacy in the industrialized nations of the west. In R. Barr, M. Kamil, P. Mosenthal, & P. D. Pearson (Eds.), *Handbook of reading research* (Vol. 2, pp. 46–67). New York: Longman.

Walsh, C. (Ed.). (1991a). *Literacy as praxis: Culture, language, and pedagogy.* Norwood, NJ: Ablex.

Walsh, C. (1991b). *Pedagogy and the struggle for voice.* New York: Bergin & Garvey.

Weiler, K. (1991). Freire and a feminist pedagogy of difference. *Harvard Educational Review, 61*(4), 449–474.

Wexler, P. (1976). *The sociology of education: Beyond equality.* Indianapolis, IN: Bobbs-Merrill.

Wexler, P. (1987). *Social analysis of education: After the new sociology.* London: Routledge & Kegan Paul.

Wigfield, A., & Asher, S. (1984). Social and motivational influences on reading. In P. D. Pearson (Ed.), *Handbook of reading research* (Vol. 1, pp. 423–452). New York: Longman.

Willinsky, J. (1990). *The new literacy.* New York: Routledge.

Willis, P. (1977). *Learning to labor.* Westmead, England: Saxon House.

Young, M. F. D. (Ed.). (1971). *Knowledge and control.* London: Collier-Macmillan.

CHAPTER 6

Ethnographic Approaches to Literacy Research

Susan Florio-Ruane
Michigan State University
Mary McVee
University of Nevada, Reno

ETHNOGRAPHY OLD AND NEW: UNDERSTANDING LANGUAGE, CULTURE, AND EDUCATION

When the first *Handbook of Reading Research* was published in 1984, it included a chapter on ethnography by Larry F. Guthrie and William S. Hall. Joining a related chapter on sociolinguistics (by David Bloome and Judith Green), the chapter reviewed the interpretive study of literacy education in U.S. schools. Shortly thereafter, related reviews were published in the third edition of the *Handbook of Research on Teaching* (1986), including a chapter on qualitative research (by Frederick Erickson) and one on classroom discourse (by Courtney Cazden). Ethnography dominated educators' interest in interpretive research. Noting that by 1984 ethnography was fast "approaching the status of a catchword" (p. 91), Guthrie and Hall reviewed its contributions to literacy research. In this, the second chapter on ethnography, we examine some of the ways in which the approach continues to inform research on language, culture, and education.

Although ethnography was new to many educational researchers in the early 1980s, it has a long history. Literally "a picture of the people," ethnography is the study of culture. It offers a holistic theoretical perspective from which to view education, an array of accessible research tools, and a narrative genre for research reporting. Shirley Brice Heath instructed educational researchers that an understanding of ethnography "depends on linking it to its traditional disciplinary base in anthropology and its role in the anthropologist's study of human behavior in cross-cultural perspective" (1982, p. 33). Heath's comment underscores the disciplinary roots of ethnography in *studies of culture* and the importance of *comparison and contrast across cultures* as a part of such study.

Human beings have been studying culture more or less systematically as long as they have been traveling. Using observation, participation, comparison, and contrast, people have exploited their visits to unfamiliar places to learn about others' ways of life and to reflect on their own. Ethnography was born out of our curiosity about different ways of behaving and making sense. Hymes noted in this regard that:

If one traces the history of ethnography where it leads, one goes back centuries, indeed, to the ancient Mediterranean world, … Herodotus being its most famous, but not only exemplar. With regard to just the Americas, one can trace a fairly continuous history of the ethnographic reports, interacting with the posing of ethnological questions, from the first discovery of the New World.… If ethnography is new to some in education, certainly it is not new to the world. (1982, p. 21)

Yet, despite its long history and disciplinary pedigree, two related problems have complicated the application of ethnography to contemporary research on literacy education in the United States:

1. The definition of culture, and hence the clarification of ethnography's purposes, method, and texts, is under transformation within anthropology (Behar & Gordon, 1995; Clifford & Marcus, 1986; Rosaldo, 1989).
2. The field of anthropology lacks, in Hymes's words, "a unified conception of ethnography in relation to the study of institutions in our own society, such as education" (1982, p. 21).

Anthropologists were grappling with these issues as their ways of working came to the attention of the educational research community in the mid 20th century. The cross-fertilization of ethnography with questions of educational policy and practice has advanced work in both domains.

In colonial times, ethnographers considered culture to be a static state, isomorphic with bounded ethnic or language groups. In the postcolonial world, however, culture has taken on kaleidoscopic complexity. Certainly cultural contact and transformation have always been present in human society, but their dynamics are more starkly visible in the 20th century's global, economic interdependence and technologies for rapid travel and communication. "Triangulating" cultural identity, people cross borders of all kinds as a part of their daily life (Florio-Ruane, 1997; Hoffman, 1989). The following vignette illustrates this.

In the early 1980s, one of the authors of this chapter (Florio-Ruane) traveled to rural Alaska shortly after the completion of the Alaska pipeline. She arrived on a frigid November evening, invited by the Teacher Corps at the University of Alaska in Fairbanks to offer a workshop on writing instruction for teacher educators. Working in a pilot field-based program, these young men and women crisscrossed Alaska to instruct and supervise native Alaskans learning to teach in their home villages. For the Athabaskans who lived in the interior, this would be the first generation of native school teachers, yet another aspect of the 20th-century cultural transformation they experienced as they abandoned nomadic life and became literate in English.

Stepping off the small plane in Fort Yukon, a village north of the Arctic Circle, Florio-Ruane was whisked into the frigid night on a dogsled. Although dogsleds were rapidly being replaced by snow mobiles, they were still in use, especially for treating visitors to an authentic Alaskan experience. (The next day, however, she would mount a Ski-doo when invited to check hand-made rabbit traps on the arctic tundra.) Florio-Ruane was delivered to a rustic cabin on the outskirts of town and greeted warmly by its owners. Their children barely looked away from the television set to acknowledge their guest's arrival. They were engrossed in watching a tight-trousered John Travolta strut down a New York street to the disco rhythms of the Bee Gees, a popular Australian band.

Contemporary anthropologists can no longer afford to engage exclusively in the description and comparison of "cultures" as static systems. In James Clifford's words, "people and things are increasingly out of place" (1988, p. 6). This forces a shift in the focus of cultural inquiry to what Bhabha calls those "in between spaces" where the self is elaborated as people engage with one another (1994, pp. 1–2). Just at the point when U.S. educational researchers were beginning to employ the cultural lens, the very idea of "culture" was under transformation. Eisenhart commented that in our time, "older views of culture as a group's distinct pattern of behaviors, or coherent 'way-of-life,' lost ground to an interpretive view of culture as 'webs of significance,' or meanings partially shared and manipulated by those who knew them" (Eisenhart, in press, p. 2).

Thus anthropologists found themselves addressing education as a process that not only transmits culture but also transforms it as diverse people come together within the institutions of complex society (Eisenhart, 1995). Yet, coming newly to ethnography, educational researchers did not immediately to grasp this shift in thinking about culture or its significance for research on teaching and learning. Some early ethnographic studies of education presumed a relatively static model of culture (Eisenhart, in press). Others, perhaps uninspired by the flatness of such a model, disregarded culture altogether and drew from ethnography only its narrative-style data collection and reporting techniques. But, as educational researchers first encountered it, ethnography was old—and it was new. Ethnography was emerging as a way of seeing that might be usefully applied to studying education in the complex institutions of our own society and in others worldwide. Concomitantly, this application would contribute to the ferment within anthropology around the concept of culture or the function of education as cultural praxis.

THE ETHNOGRAPHIC STUDY OF EDUCATION AS CULTURAL PRAXIS

Educational anthropology gathered itself into a field of study in the United States in the 1960s. It formalized that process with the establishment of the Council on Anthropology and Education (CAE) in 1970. From the outset, the blending of anthropology and education pushed the limits of theory and method in both fields. This was especially the case in ethnographic research on the teaching and learning of literacy. Reading, writing, and oral language were viewed by cultural anthropologists as a constellation of communicative tools and practices essential to the reflexive process of constructing culture by participating in it. To study literacy education as cultural praxis required interpretive, field-based methods of data collection, analysis, and reporting.

This shift in research question and method captured the attention of literacy researchers in the 1960s and 1970s but was anticipated as early as 1936. In that year, Bradislaw Malinowski, a pioneer of modern ethnography, urged anthropologists who wanted to study language and its acquisition to go to the people. He reasoned that if we want to understand how language is learned and used, we should, as participant observers, study and describe "living speech in its actual context of situation" (Malinowski, 1936, cited in Hymes, 1964, p. 63, and Florio-Ruane, 1987, p. 187). Malinowski's dictum was striking in its advancement of three key ideas:

1. Language, although rule governed, is living and, as such, is subject to improvisation, negotiation, and change—it has a history, a present, and a future.
2. People use language (both oral and written) to communicate within activities, settings, and relationships.
3. Meaning resides in the relationship of language forms to the functions they serve in those activities, settings, and relationships.

More than a half century later, these features of language and culture continue to inform research on literacy education.

By the 1970s, educational researchers had devised a robust method for studying the effects of teaching on the learning of students. According to Koehler (1978), this method, known as "process-product," described "which teaching processes are effective in relation to desired outcomes such as student achievement" (cited in Cazden, 1986, p. 432). Yet powerful as this method is for testing the outcomes of instructional interventions, it is limited in its ability "to define or describe the process" by which the outcomes are achieved (Koehler, 1978, cited in Cazden, 1986, p. 432). To theorize about the dynamic processes of teaching and learning, researchers needed to know more about the "hidden dimensions" of what Erickson called, "taught cognitive learning" in both its immediate and wider sociocultural contexts (Erickson, 1982).

For contemporary literacy researchers, the ethnographic turn brought new ways to think about their work. Literacy could be thought of not only as a constellation of school subjects (reading, writing, speaking, and listening) or a private intellectual achievement, but as observable practices, learned and used within communities and constituent of social and cultural identity (Bauman & Sherzer, 1974; Gee, 1989). In this spirit, literacy is studied within an "ecology" that is cultural, social, historical, and psychological (Barton, 1994). Researchers look at the role of written language in the "total communicative economy" of a society (Basso, 1974). They analyze the multiple and situated "literacies" individuals learn and practice (e.g., Scribner, 1984; Scribner & Cole, 1981), and describe the forms and functions of those literate practices as well as their distribution across status, role, activity, situation, and community (e.g., Heath, 1983).

Since the late 1970s, we have seen ethnographic studies of school structuring and classroom social organization as these shape literacy teaching and learning; case studies and cross-case comparisons of literate practices taught and learned within schools, families, and communities; studies of differential treatment and access to knowledge among literacy learners from diverse social and linguistic backgrounds; and studies of text-related discourse, both oral and written, as the social construction of knowledge among members of a community (see reviews by Bloome, 1991; Cazden, 1987; Erickson, 1986; Florio-Ruane, 1994; Jacob & Jordan, 1987; and Raphael & Brock, 1997). Throughout, ethnographic research on education has retained an interest in cross-cultural comparison, focusing primarily on differential treatment and access to knowledge within the schools of a society characterized by diversity in race, language, ethnicity, and social class (Hess, 1998). These have been important issues for applied research because, as Scribner (1984) noted, how we think about literacy profoundly informs the policies (both explicit and implicit) that guide formal education. In her words:

> The definitional controversy has more than academic significance. Each formulation of an answer to the question, 'What is literacy?' leads to a different evaluation of the scope of the problem (i.e., the extent of *il* literacy) and to different objectives for programs aimed at the formation of a literate citizenry. Definitions of literacy shape our perceptions of individuals who fall on either side of the standard (what a 'literate' or 'nonliterate' is like) and thus in a deep way affect both the substance and style of educational programs. (p. 6, parentheses and emphasis in original)

DEVELOPMENTS IN ETHNOGRAPHIC RESEARCH ON LITERACY EDUCATION

In 1982, Dell Hymes challenged anthropologists and educational researchers to work together not simply to apply or import research techniques from anthropology to education, but to create a field, an *educational* anthropology. As we prepared this chapter, we considered various ways to illustrate developments in educational anthropology. We noted that, in 1984, one literacy researcher, Kathryn Au, was noted by Guthrie and

Hall for her "studies of reading as a social activity" (p. 102). As such, Au's work had three important characteristics: It applied ethnography to investigating educational practice; it undertook comparative analysis by considering the mismatch of norms for literate practices across pupils' home and school experiences; and it applied insights about language use in diverse cultural contexts to the improvement of teaching and learning within classrooms.

We returned to Au's work as we drafted this chapter in 1998. In addition to reading or rereading many of her writings, we asked her to reflect on her work and the field in terms of the following important developments in educational ethnography since the last *Handbook* chapter was published:

1. Research in the context of reform, especially instructional research grounded in thoughtful ethnography.
2. Ethnographic studies of literacy in relation to social historical theory.
3. The influence of postmodern thought in educational ethnography, especially feminism, which emphasizes the transactional nature of research and teaching. We close our chapter by looking at these three issues with particular reference to Au's research and commentary.

ETHNOGRAPHICALLY GROUNDED INSTRUCTIONAL RESEARCH IN THE CONTEXT OF REFORM

Like her contemporaries (several of whom were cited in 1984 by Guthrie and Hall), Au's early research focused on comparisons of literacy and learning at home and at school. Well-known ethnographic research among Hawaiian youngsters (e.g., Boggs, 1972; Watson-Gegeo & Boggs, 1977) had documented differences in narrative practices across these settings. Informed by this body of research, Au worked with teachers and children in the Kamehameha Early Education Program (KEEP) to study approaches to literacy instruction that might more effectively support the school literacy learning of Hawaiian youngsters (e.g., Au, 1980).

From the outset, however, Au was less than sanguine about the contributions to education of a theoretical frame that presumed a static conception of culture. An experienced teacher and teacher educator, she found no easy instructional "matches" for what had allegedly been "mismatched" as children made the transition into school and its literate practices. Recognizing that neither children's cultural experiences nor the practice of teaching were that discretely simple, Au and Mason wrote that while the idea that

> culturally congruent elements in lessons given to minority children may help to prevent damaging conflicts between teacher and students ... has much intuitive appeal, ... we have very little evidence to support the notion that the presence of school situations resembling those in the home leads to improved academic achievement by minority children (1981, p. 150)

In the ensuing years, Au and her colleagues sought to move beyond descriptions of home and school as isolated places whose borders diverse children crossed at their peril. Instead, focusing on culturally responsive educational practice, Au engaged in a program of research to create, document and evaluated transactional ways of teaching that might enhance the learning of low-achieving young readers (e.g., Au & Carroll, 1997). For Au, the most important test of a method is the consequences of what can be learned by using it for the benefit of those studied. Thus, although descriptive studies are interesting, Au told us recently that educational ethnographers need to continue to ask of their work: *What is educational about educational anthropology?*

Trying to take from ethnography useful constructs for education, Au trained her gaze on the points of contact between teachers and young readers and writers. These encounters are viewed as not only points of contact among people whose prior cultural experiences may differ, but as occasions that are cultural in their own right—places of learning and transformation. Au has said in this regard that as we consider contexts (e.g., language use, cultural practices) for learning, we must examine instruction. Her ethnographically informed instructional research has been directly applied to the improvement of teaching and teacher education, both preservice education within the university and in-service education in the profession at large (Au, 1995).

In 1981, Au lamented (with Cathie Jordan) that research on cultural differences had not "substantially changed the situation for minority culture children" (p. 139). Au told us that in the 1980s she found it "very discouraging how little impact research has had on policy and teacher education." She noted that by using ethnography we "can further refine our understandings and descriptions" of the processes by which literacy is learned. But there is a danger that our descriptions will not inform subsequent practice. In her words, "it is more critical at this juncture for us to be reform minded" (interview, February, 1998).

Au is one of a number of educational ethnographers whose descriptive studies of the discontinuity between learning at home and at school, especially for economically disadvantaged and/or ethnic minority children, have given way to research in sites of their own and others' reform-oriented practice (Hess, 1998). Ray McDermott, whose research was also described in Guthrie and Hall's chapter, recently wrote (with Shelley Goldman) of the proliferation of applied studies by educational ethnographers, that "good theory and successfully changing the world do not have to be completely overlapping, but we cannot afford to let them be antithetical" (McDermott & Goldman, 1998, p. 126).

Ethnographic Research on Literacy, Culture, and Thought

Au's work exemplifies another development of ethnography since the mid 1980s, that of the integration of social historical theory (Vygotsky, 1978) with educational anthropology. Researchers from a hybrid of traditions including anthropology and psychology have probed how literacy as both cultural tool and cultural practice is influenced by social and historical factors as well as the micro-politics of face to face interaction (e.g., Scribner & Cole, 1981; Moll, 1992). Au's work has been influenced by this exploration. Yet as we merge the study of culture with the study of individuals' learning in dialogue with one another, Au believed there remains a need to "take adequate account of differences in ethnicity, primary language, and social class that may affect students' school literacy learning" (1998, p. 306). This statement echoes the commitment that Au and her colleagues held when they conducted their work at KEEP in the 1980s. However, Au's reading of social historical theory led her to a more complex understanding of culture as a process of identification of self in and by means of contact with others.

Au fears that when educators hear the phrase "literacy as a cultural tool," they may tend to think of "culture" and "tools" as static. Given the history of research in the field, it is easy to make this assumption and to disregard the possibility that new forms of literacy can and do happen as a part of teaching and learning (see, e.g., New London Group, 1996). During an interview with Au preparatory to the writing of this chapter, she stressed the idea that tools for communication are human creations that arise out of the "hybrid culture" of interactions among people. This is true in both within and outside the classroom. In this sense, a classroom can become a cultural setting in which participants develop common expressive ground as they undertake meaningful activities in support of learning.

Looking back on Au's earlier research, it is notable that teachers adopted and adapted not perfect "matches" of ways of talking about text at home to ways of talking about text at school, but hybrid forms of text-based talk that drew on the meanings, intentions, and prior knowledge of both teachers and pupils. Learning about Hawaiian children's entering knowledge of "talk-story" gave teachers insight into the meaning that youngsters were making of oral response to narrative selections read in school. This insight can be thought of as transforming the relationship between teacher and learner (and among learners) as teachers found ways of conversationally calling up appropriate and familiar ways of speaking to support the further development of school-based cognitive skills. To this end, teachers were initially learners not unlike ethnographic field workers. It was their responsibility to understand youngsters' understandings, especially their prior knowledge and experience with text-based talk. Their pedagogical task was to engage in relationships with youngsters and around stories by "mutual participation" (Au & Jordan, 1981, p. 146). Ultimately, the teachers made these transactions educational as they interwove the threads of school literacy into the fabric of youngsters' prior, informal learning.

Viewed this way, culturally responsive instruction involves identifying features of both teachers' and students' experiences that can be drawn on and transformed to create educationally productive dialogue. Its purpose is not to give teachers a recipe or set of rules that might further separate them from meaningful encounters with youngsters and text, but to help them think from observant participation toward more educational ways to engage with youngsters around text. To respond to another is not simply to match one person's behavior to another's, but to construct ways of behaving and making sense together. This insight parallels changes in anthropology moving toward the webs of meaning that people weave, rather than the cultural boxes they inhabit. In that spirit, Au currently works with teachers to transform instruction by exploring their own cultural identities and those of their students, in particular, around issues of "ethnicity and primary language" (Au, 1996).

Other Voices: Cultural Study and Literacy Education in a New Key

A third issue related to the fusion of theoretical and practical work described earlier is the movement to address the transactional aspects of ethnographic research—what Erickson (1996) referred to as "Eve's task." Citing the influence of feminism on ethnography, Erickson pointed out that 25 years earlier the anthropologist's professed aim was to describe others and their points of view. In Erickson's view, this naming function is akin to the Biblical imperative Adam was given by God to name and thus to claim dominion over the "others" in the Garden. A form of "Adam's task" was undertaken by ethnographers who sought to describe others and thereby gain some control over them—both literally, as ethnography served colonialism, and perhaps more insidiously today as descriptions of others can tend to freeze or stereotype their realities, rendering them voiceless in the creation of those descriptions.

Cultural description was considered novel, even controversial, as social research in the first part of this century. It has since become a valued and familiar part of the educational research landscape. As such, its biases and limitations are exposed along with its contributions to knowledge. Ethnography is vulnerable to critique. New controversies have arisen about the very presumption that ethnographer can or should speak for and about others. Of this Erickson said,

> ethnographic realism is no longer credible to many of us within ethnography itself. We have come to realize that the so-called "participant observer" is only minimally participating, and is mostly outside the social gravity within which the "observed" live. (1996, p. 7)

To redress this problem, educational ethnographers have begun trying to add "Eve's task" to their work. Moving from participant observer to "observant participant," ethnographers are beginning to acknowledge that the work of understanding and describing others' lives is inevitably mediated by our own autobiographies. Ruth Behar makes this point in her ethnographic study, *Translated Woman* (1993), where the "story" of her key informant, a Mexican woman named Esperanza, is jointly constructed by and serves the authorial purposes of both Esperanza and Ruth. Behar further notes that although this idea may be a new one to contemporary ethnographers, it is not new to feminists, for whom Eve's task has been a long-standing, if undervalued, one in their scholarship (Behar & Gordon, 1995).

In exploring how researchers and informants construct meaning in relationship with one another, Au and other ethnographic researchers working in literacy education (e.g., Florio-Ruane, Raphael, Glazier, McVee, & Wallace, 1997; Brock, 1997) are examining the "self–other dialogue" (Tedlock, 1991) foundational to both research and teaching. About this effort, Au recently wrote that "educators' recognition of the inequities possible in a given educational situation depends on an understanding of their own cultural identities as well as the cultural identities of their students" (1998, p. 308).

Using literacy activities such as writing workshop, mini-lessons, individual conferences, author's chair, personal literacy portfolios, and publication, Au encourages her own students' exploration of the cultural foundations of their literate practices. As her students write and rework narratives relating to their past, Au does the same. Thus Au's pedagogy and research exemplify the weaving of "Adam's task" of description with "Eve's task" of revealing the ways self and other are entwined in education and research. Especially in literacy education, the idea that teachers as well as students bring to communication knowledge, beliefs and values that are culturally acquired is fundamental. This idea underscores language use and language learning as living processes with a past, present, and certainly a future. As such, they are appropriately studied ethnographically.

REFERENCES

Au, K. H. (1980). Participation structures in a reading lesson with Hawaiian children: Analysis of a culturally appropriate instructional event. *Anthropology and Education Quarterly, 11*(2), 91–115.
Au, K. H. (1995). Multicultural perspectives on literacy research. *Journal of Reading Behavior, 27*(1), 85–100.
Au, K. H. (1996, November). *Personal narratives, literacy portfolios, and cultural identity.* Paper presented at the meetings of the American Anthropological Association, Washington, DC.
Au, K. H. (1998). Social constructivism and the school literacy learning of students of diverse cultural backgrounds. *Journal of Literacy Research, 30*(2), 297–319.
Au, K. H., & Carroll, J. H. (1997). Improving literacy achievement through a constructivist approach: The KEEP demonstration classroom project. *Elementary School Journal, 97*(3), 203–221.
Au, K. H., & Jordan, C. (1981). Teaching reading to Hawaiian children: Finding a culturally appropriate solution. In H. T. Trueba, G. P. Guthrie, & K. H. Au (Eds.), *Culture and the bilingual classroom: Studies in classroom ethnography* (pp. 139–152). Rowley, MA: Newbury House.
Au, K. H., & Mason, J. M. (1981). Social organizational factors in learning to read: The balance of rights hypothesis. *Reading Research Quarterly, 17*(1), 115–152.
Barton, D. (1994). *Literacy: An introduction to the ecology of written language.* Oxford: Blackwell.
Basso, K. (1974). The ethnography of writing. In R. Bauman & J. Sherzer (Eds.), *Explorations in the ethnography of speaking* (pp. 425–432). Cambridge: Cambridge University Press.
Bauman, R., & Sherzer, J. (Eds.). (1974). *Explorations in the ethnography of speaking.* Cambridge: Cambridge University Press.
Behar, R. (1993). *Translated woman: Crossing the border with Esperanza's story.* Boston: Beacon Press.
Behar, R., & Gordon, D. A. (Eds.). (1995). *Women writing culture.* Berkeley: University of California Press.
Bhabha, H. K. (1994). *The location of culture.* London: Routledge.
Bloome, D. (1991). Anthropology and research on teaching the English language arts. In J. Flood, J. M. Jensen, D. Lapp, & J. Squire (Eds.), *Handbook of research on teaching the English language arts* (pp. 46–56). New York: Macmillan.

Bloome, D., & Green, J. (1984). Directions in the sociolinguistic study of reading. In P. D. Pearson, R. Barr, M. L. Kamil, & P. Mosenthal (Eds.), *Handbook of reading research* (1st ed. pp. 395–421). New York: Longman.

Boggs, S. T. (1972). The meaning of questions and narratives to Hawaiian children. In C. B. Cazden, V. P. John, & D. Hymes (Eds.), *Functions of language in the classroom* (pp. 299–327). New York: Teachers College Press.

Brock, C. (1997). *Exploring a second language student's literacy learning opportunities: A collaborative case study analysis.* Unpublished doctoral dissertation, Michigan State University, East Lansing.

Cazden, C. B. (1986). Classroom discourse. In M. C. Wittrock (Ed.), *Handbook of research on teaching* (3rd ed., pp. 432–463). New York: Macmillan.

Cazden, C. B. (1987). *Classroom discourse: The language of teaching and learning.* Portsmouth, NH: Heinemann.

Clifford, J. (1988). *The predicament of culture: Twentieth-Century Ethnography, Literature, and Art.* Cambridge: Harvard University Press.

Clifford, J., & Marcus, G. E. (1986). *Writing culture: The poetics and politics of ethnography.* Berkeley: University of California Press.

Eisenhart, M. (1995). The fax, the jazz player, and the self-story teller: How do people organize culture? *Anthropology and Education Quarterly, 26*(1), 3–26.

Eisenhart, M. (in press). Changing conceptions of culture and ethnographic methodology: Recent thematic shifts and their implications of research on teaching. In V. Richardson (Ed.), *Handbook of research on teaching* (4th ed.). New York: Macmillan.

Erickson, F. (1982). Taught cognitive learning in its immediate environments: A neglected topic in the anthropology of educators. *Anthropology and Education Quarterly, 13*(2), 149–180.

Erickson, F. (1986). Qualitative methods in research on teaching. In M. C. Wittrock (Ed.), *Handbook of research on teaching* (3rd ed., pp. 119–161). New York: Macmillan.

Erickson, F. (1996). On the evolution of qualitative approaches in educational research: From Adam's task to Eve's. *Australian Educational Researcher, 23*(2), 1–15.

Florio-Ruane, S. (1987). Sociolinguistics for educational researchers. *American Educational Research Journal, 24*(2), 185–197.

Florio-Ruane, S. (1994). Anthropological study of classroom culture and social organization. In T. Hussein & T. N. Postlethwaite (Eds.), *The international encyclopedia of education* (2nd ed., pp. 796–803). Oxford: Pergamon.

Florio-Ruane, S. (1997). To tell a new story: Reinventing narratives of culture, identity and education. *Anthropology and Education Quarterly, 28*(2), 152–162.

Florio-Ruane, S., Raphael, T. E., Glazier, J., McVee, M., & Wallace, S. (1997). Discovering culture in discussion of autobiographical literature: Transforming the education of literacy teachers. In C. K. Kinzer, K. A. Hinchman, & D. J. Leu (Eds.), *Inquiries in literacy theory and practice: Forty-sixth Yearbook of the National Reading Conference* (pp. 452–464). Chicago: National Reading Conference.

Gee, J. P. (1989). *What is literacy?* Brookline, MA: The Literacies Institute, Educational Development Corporation.

Guthrie, L. F. & Hall, W. S. (1984). Ethnographic approaches to reading research. In P. D. Pearson, R. Barr, M. L. Kamil, & P. Mosenthal (Eds.), *Handbook of reading research* (1st ed., pp. 91–109). New York: Longman. 91–109.

Heath, S. B. (1983). *Ways with words: Language, life and work in communities and classrooms.* New York: Cambridge University Press.

Heath, S. B. (1982). Ethnography in education: Defining the essentials. In P. Gilmore & A. A. Glatthorn (Eds.), *Children in and out of school: Ethnography and education* (pp. 33–55). Washington, DC: Center for Applied Linguistics.

Hess, G. A. (1998, December). *Keeping educational anthropology relevant: Asking good questions rather than trivial ones.* Presidential address to the Council on Anthropology and Education, Meetings of the American Anthropological Association, Philadelphia.

Hoffman, E. (1989). *Lost in translation: A new life in a new language.* New York: Penguin.

Hymes, D. (1964). *Language in culture and society.* New York: Harper and Row.

Hymes, D. (1982). What is ethnography? In P. Gilmore & A. A. Glatthorn (Eds.), *Children in and out of school: Ethnography and education* (pp. 21–32). Washington, DC: Center for Applied Linguistics.

Jacob, E., & Jordan, C. (Eds.). (1987). Explaining the school performance of minority students. *Anthropology and Education Quarterly, 18*(4).

Koehler, V. (1978). Classroom process research: Present and future. *Journal of Classroom Interaction, 13*(2), 3–11.

McDermott, R., & Goldman, S. (1998). Review of *Constructing School Success*: The consequences of untracking low-achieving students. *Anthropology and Education Quarterly, 29*(1) , 125–127.

Moll, L. (1992). Bilingual classroom studies and community analysis. *Educational Researcher, 21*(2), 20–24.

New London Group. (1996). A pedagogy of multiple literacies: Designing social futures. *Harvard Educational Review, 66*(1), 60–92.

Raphael, T. E., & Brock, C. H. (1997). Instructional research in literacy: Changing paradigms. In C. K. Kinzer, K. A. Hinchman, & D. J. Leu (Eds.), *Inquiries in literacy theory and practice: Forty-sixth Yearbook of the National Reading Conference* (pp. 13–36). Chicago: National Reading Conferences.

Rosaldo, R. (1989). *Culture and truth: The remaking of social analysis.* Boston: Beacon Press.

Scribner, S. (1984, November). Literacy in three metaphors. *American Journal of Education,* (pp. 6–21).

Scribner, S., & Cole, M. (1981). *The psychology of literacy.* Cambridge, MA: Harvard University Press.

Tedlock, B. (1991). From participant observation to the observation of participation: The emergence of narrative ethnography. *Journal of Anthropological Research, 47*, 69–94.

Vygotsky, L. (1978). *Mind in society: The development of higher psychological processes.* Cambridge, MA: Harvard University Press.

Watson-Gegeo, K. A., & Boggs, S. T. (1977). From verbal play to talk story: The role of routine in speech events among Hawaiian children. In S. Ervin-Tripp & C. Mitchell-Kernan (Eds.), *Child discourse* (pp. 67–90). New York: Academic Press.

CHAPTER 7

Verbal Reports and Protocol Analysis

Peter Afflerbach
University of Maryland at College Park

Protocol analysis offers the opportunity to gather detailed understandings of reading and reading-related phenomena. The ongoing evolution of theories of mind and reading combined with the suitability of the verbal report methodology contribute to the considerable popularity of protocol analysis (Ericsson & Simon, 1984/1993; Kucan & Beck, 1997; Pressley & Afflerbach, 1995). The convergence of theory and method offers rich opportunities for reading researchers. This chapter provides an overview of the history of use of verbal reports and protocol analysis in reading research, a discussion of current understandings and uses of verbal reports and protocol analysis, and an examination of ongoing challenges and future directions for protocol research.

A BRIEF HISTORY OF VERBAL REPORTS AND PROTOCOL ANALYSIS

Verbal reports and subsequent protocols have been elicited and analyzed for centuries. The question "What's on your mind?" and the offer "A penny for your thoughts" both reflect an abiding interest in understanding how and what people think. In this sense, verbal reports and protocol analysis represent one evolution of the human habit of asking people to share their thoughts into a useful form of scientific inquiry. Evidence of interest in people's thinking exists in the works of Aristotle and Plato, both of whom encouraged colleagues to discuss the things they thought about. Thousands of years later, James (1890) used subjects' reports of their thinking to inform his theories of psychology. Reviews of introspection (Boring, 1953; Pritchard, 1990a) demonstrate that asking people to discuss and describe their thoughts has been a continuous, if sporadic, general methodology in psychology. The increasing permanence of records of scientific inquiry and the emergence of the expectation that the methods of this inquiry be described in detail contribute to our understanding of the legacy and promise of protocol analysis. It is probable that verbal report and protocol analysis will continue as a popular methodology to describe cognitive, affective, and social aspects of reading.

The use of protocol analysis is marked by a fair amount of controversy. The first half of the 20th century is notable for the tension between behaviorists and those interested in describing processes of reading. Researchers examining the workings of the mind needed methodologies that could describe mental processes. One result was the use of introspection at the turn of the century (Marbe, 1901/1964; Titchener, 1912a, 1912b) and its application in reading inquiry (Huey, 1908). However, the early and mid 20th century saw protocol analysis relegated to occasional use, as introspection was challenged by behaviorists. Behaviorism dictated that peoples' verbalizations were not theoretically important (Watson, 1913, 1920). Verbal reports and protocol analysis were suspect as behaviorists doubted the veridicality of introspective reports and challenged the notion that individuals mediate their mental processes. Methodology that sought subjects' reports of thinking was consigned to relatively dusty shelves, and protocol analysis saw only limited use. Yet inquiry using verbal reports did continue. For example, McAllister (1930) described the difficulties in identifying readers' processes through inferences based on products, such as reading test scores, readers' retellings of text, or their answers to comprehension questions. Protocol analysis provided a new class of data that changed the inferential path, and allowed for hypothesizing about reading processes from more process-oriented data. Detailed accounts of reading processes, specifically cognition and response, have become one grail of users of protocol analysis (Afflerbach & Johnston, 1984).

A sample of research published during (and in spite of) the reign of behaviorism emphasized the dynamic nature of reading. This work focused on readers' difficulty with content-area learning and responses to questions (McAllister, 1930); readers' use of context to develop word meanings and vocabulary understanding (Werner & Kaplan, 1950); and readers' responses to texts (Piekarz, 1954). Concurrent with the relatively spare use of protocol analysis in reading was protocol-based research investigating a range of thinking tasks and situations, including medical problem solving (Duncker, 1945), mathematical problem solving (Polya, 1954a, 1954b), and chess (de Groot, 1965). These inquiries served as both demonstration and reminder for once and future reading researchers. They demonstrated the suitability of the methodology for revealing thinking and problem solving, mental processes that figure largely in reading. They reminded that under appropriate conditions, verbal reports yield rich and compelling protocol data. Kucan and Beck (1997) noted that the occasional use of protocol analysis during the reign of behaviorism was crucial not only for keeping verbal reports on the radar screen, but for shaping their use. That is, findings from verbal report studies helped demonstrate that foundational work was needed in theory building to accommodate and logically organize the processes and responses revealed by protocol analysis. Subjects' utterances could not be interpreted as reports of cognitive processes or responses until theories of cognition and response were more fully developed. Accompanying the nascent cognitive revolution was the increasing realization that understanding reading required the detailed descriptions of reading processes that protocol analysis could provide.

Increasing interest in the use of protocol analysis was supported by detailed characterizations of human problem solving (Newell & Simon, 1972), which in turn supported research that conceptualized reading as strategic problem solving. An example is the work of Olshavsky (1976–1977), conducted on the cusp of the cognitive revolution as it applied to reading. Olshavsky's findings demonstrated that reading is clearly strategic, as well as the need for detailed accounts of the nature of reading strategies. Her work demonstrated that the complexity of reading demanded research designs that accommodate both a breadth and depth of examination. It also hinted that the cognitive strategy use of accomplished readers was accompanied by response and engagement. The strong conceptualization of reading as cognition and the strong defense of protocol analysis as a means to investigate reading contributed to initial investigations of readers' strategies including inferences (Collins, Brown, & Larkin, 1980), summarization (Brown & Day, 1983), and general cognitive strategy use while reading (Garner, 1982; Hare, 1981). Critical analysis of the methodology of verbal reports and protocol analysis was provided by Ericsson and Simon (1980, 1984/1993). Their work continues to influence the conceptualization and use of protocol analysis related to information processing and cognition, and the authors present a compelling case for protocol analysis as a methodology with flexibility of application that can help describe the breadth of cognition. Ericsson and Simon provided strong evidence of the prospective validity of protocol analysis, and they proffered specific methodological recommendations for using protocol analysis.

The increasing use of verbal reports and protocol analysis in reading research led to a state of the methodological art summary (Afflerbach & Johnston, 1984) that described their potential advantages. First, they provide access to the constructive and responsive processes that comprise reading. This information is accretive to our understanding of the complex constructs of cognition and response that might otherwise be investigated in an indirect manner. Second, protocol analysis allows for the examination of important but often neglected reader characteristics, including motivation and affect. Moreover, protocol analysis may explain the relationships and interactions of motivation and affect with cognitive processes and responses. Third, protocol analysis allows for the examination of the influence of contextual variables (e.g., text, task, setting, reader ability) on the act of reading. Finally, protocol analysis provides valuable information on a range of processes related to reading, such as instruction, assessment, discussion, and teacher decisionmaking. Fairly regular reviews of the intersection of reading research and protocol analysis critically examine the accomplishments and challenges related to the methodology and reading research (Deffner, 1988; Ericsson, 1988; Kucan & Beck, 1997; Pressley & Afflerbach, 1995; Pritchard, 1990a; Waern, 1988).

The historical path to contemporary applications of protocol analysis and current conceptualizations of readers' thoughts and actions is continually marked by symbiosis. Protocol analysis continues to influence the very constructs it is used to investigate, in the "bootstrap operation" first alluded to by Ericsson and Simon (1980). That is, protocol analysis may first contribute to the initial building of theories that represent progress in the understanding of reading. These theories help us chart a course of the work that remains to fill the gaps in this understanding, and protocol analysis serves ably in the second role of focused research tool. The last two decades have witnessed burgeoning use of protocol analysis to investigate acts of cognition, response, and reading related phenomena. In turn, the refinement of cognitive theory (Anderson & Pearson, 1984; van Dijk & Kintsch, 1983) and literary theory (Beach & Hynds, 1991; Eco, 1990) have helped steer protocol analyses to positions in which it can both refine existing theory and break ground for new theory. Although protocol analysis provides compelling evidence that constructive cognition is central to reading, it also proves that reading is more than cognition. The symbiotic relationship of the methodology and the aspects of reading it investigates should continue.

The history of verbal reports and protocol analysis is marked by controversy over the veridicality of the data provided. There are numerous challenges to the validity and use of verbal reports and protocol analysis. These challenges are ably addressed in theory, whereas in practice they receive intermittent attention. Less attention is paid to the caveats that are provided by both users and skeptics of the methodology (cf. Afflerbach & Johnston, 1984; Nisbett & Wilson, 1977; Pressley & Afflerbach, 1995), all of whom insist that integrity of method influences quality of data. Although behaviorism posed a major obstacle to the acceptance and use of protocol analysis, there are more recent claims against the validity of verbal reports and protocol analysis (Nisbett & Wilson, 1977). The increasing use of protocol analysis within reading research indicates a general acceptance of the methodology, but inappropriate use of verbal reports and protocol analysis can quickly revive claims against validity. The diminution of claims for protocol analysis will not stem from the lack of a theory of how verbal reports and protocol analysis provide legitimate data. Rather, it may result from a lack of attention to the details of appropriate use of the methodology.

WHAT VERBAL REPORTS AND PROTOCOL ANALYSIS TELL US ABOUT READING

The close relationship between protocol analysis and the investigation of readers' cognition and response leads to both predictable and novel applications of the methodology in reading research. The suitability of the method to different areas of inquiry within the broad discipline of reading has provided rich accounts of reading (Pressley & Afflerbach, 1995). At the same time, the broad range of reading research that uses protocol analysis defies easy categorization. There are several prominent themes that emerge from this research, including the investigation and description of a predetermined and relatively finite aspect of reading (e.g., a cognitive strategy), and the exploration of the complexity of cognition, social meaning construction, and response within situated acts of reading (e.g., reading a newspaper article on a controversial topic). The use of protocol analysis to investigate single phenomena, be it process or strategy, reflects the close relationship of protocol analysis with cognitive psychology. Protocol research within cognitive psychology often focused on relatively simple problems. This served to constrain subjects' thoughts and verbalizations and allowed researchers to focus on the cognitive aspects of human-task interactions within small and well-defined problem spaces (Newell & Simon, 1972). Because the nature of readers' thoughts and actions is often complex, a focus on single aspects of reading may contribute detailed accounts of aspects of reading. Examples of studies with a single focus within reading research (a focus that is often expanded, based on the consideration of the richness of a set of protocol data) include determining main ideas (Afflerbach, 1990a; Johnston & Afflerbach, 1985), generating inferences (Collins et al., 1980; Magliano & Graesser, 1993; Phillips, 1988), hypothesizing and predicting the contents of texts (Afflerbach, 1990b; Bruce & Rubin, 1984), summarizing texts (Brown & Day, 1983), searching for information (Guthrie, Britten, & Barker, 1991), demonstrating awareness of text cohesion (Bridge & Winograd, 1982), and the monitoring of cognition (Garner & Reis, 1981; Lundeberg, 1987; Lytle, 1982). These studies demonstrate that protocol analysis can focus on particular reader process and strategy, and they often include research designs that provide the means to quantify reader strategy use. Often, the research involves manipulations of independent variables such as readers' prior knowledge (Afflerbach, 1990a) or text genre (Olson, Mack, & Duffy, 1981). I note that many of these studies evolve to adopt a dual focus, as it is determined that the original focus strategy (e.g., summarization) is situated in the rich context that is described by serendipitous verbal reports of what else is going on in the reader's head. It is often the case that reports of these studies combine both quantitative and qualitative (descriptive) data. Many single-focus reading studies supplement and complement researchers' initial hypothesis testing with protocol data that serve exploratory, discovery, and descriptive purposes that help situate a reading strategy or reading stance, continuing the bootstrap operation (Ericsson & Simon, 1980).

The majority of research that is conceptualized with a single focus demonstrates that protocol analysis was suitable for describing the reading strategies that are selected a priori by researchers and that are encouraged through manipulation of text, reader, context, and instructions. These studies also demonstrate that the target reading processes and strategies occur as situated in complex problem spaces. Increasingly, the interrelationships and interdependencies of strategy, skill, response, motivation, and affect must be more fully understood. Although we possess a fairly comprehensive catalog of the strategies that good readers use, by no means do we have complete understanding of the strategic, responsive, and social reader.

A second body of work focuses on reading writ more broad, related to what Earthman (1992) calls the "concert" of readers orchestrating complex strategies of cognition, knowledge construction, and response within acts of reading. This work is anticipated by cognitive psychology (Schoenfeld, 1983) and literary criticism (Rosenblatt, 1978). Protocol analysis tells more than the story of cognitive strategies. Changing the investigative lens, it can describe the influence of contextual variables on strategy and process use. The study of interrelationships and interdependencies of strategies, skills, stances, goals, and reader affect and motivation proves challenging for practitioners of protocol analysis: The problem spaces within which readers work are broad and ill-defined. Numerous inquiries focus on acts of reading (as opposed to isolate factors within an act of reading). These inquiries attempt to describe the totality of the reading task and seek protocols from which case accounts of reading can be constructed (Schmalhofer & Boschert, 1988; Schwegler & Shamoon, 1991). Studies focus on acts of reading such as reading to evaluate legal texts (Neutelings & Maat, 1997), physicists reading professional journal articles (Bazerman, 1985), biologists reading a divisive article of evolutionary biology (Charney, 1993), professors and students reading primary source texts in history (Leinhardt & Young, 1996; Wineburg, 1991, 1998; Young & Leinhardt, 1998), and social science professors reading professional articles in their fields of specialization (Wyatt et al., 1993). The results of such studies help describe the complex thought and action that characterize accomplished reading. In general, these studies honor a cognitive heritage but increasingly describe critical noncognitive aspects of acts of reading (Smagorinsky, 1998).

The cognitive focus in research using protocol analysis is complemented by work from the literary tradition. Literary theory has a long history of describing the possible relationships between the text and the reader. For example, new criticism (Ransom, 1979, pp. 12–33; Wimsatt & Beardsley, 1954) and reader response (Fish, 1980; Rosenblatt, 1978) propose significantly different stances between the reader and the text. Protocol analysis provides data that help describe and gauge the legitimacy of these proposed stances. In a manner similar to Olshavsky's (1976–1977) pursuit of the strategic reader, Squire (1964) conducted research that helped set the stage for future investigations of the responsive reader. His investigation of short-story reading demonstrated both the richness of readers' literary responses and the need for conceptualizations of reading that might describe and accommodate these responses. Subsequent protocol analysis studies described readers' interactions and transactions with literary texts, including reading and discussing poems (Beach, 1972; Kintgen, 1983; Peskin, 1998), the construction of meaning within the genre of short story (Earthman, 1992; Rogers, 1991), and describing narratives in relation to excerpts from novels (Graves & Frederiksen, 1991). There are several important outcomes from these studies. First, the response and transactions that readers have with literature are varied and often intensely individualistic. As important is the demonstration that there is no response to literature without cognition (Langer, 1990), just as research focused on expository and informational text demonstrates that there is no cognition without response.

Pressley and Afflerbach (1995) synthesized the results of reading research that utilized think-aloud protocols to describe constructively responsive reading. Their work emanates from the realization that within and across research paradigms and traditions of cognition and response there is a corpus of work that shares both the verbal reporting methodology and a focus on readers' thoughts and actions. These investigations involve complex variables and their interactions, including text types, reader characteristics, and reading situations and tasks. The corpus of work demonstrates that competent readers report similar strategies and responses, regardless of the paradigms undergirding a particular research study, the focus of research, the reading text or task, or the particular directions given to subjects. Thus, protocol analysis studies from both the cognitive and literary response traditions, and studies with both broad and narrow foci yield verbal reports with often strikingly similar contents. Lacking, however, is a "common language" (Rich, 1974) to describe core aspects of competent reading that are based on data from protocol analysis. Pressley and Afflerbach believed that readers' verbal reports can be central to the development of both a common language and reading theory. Their meta-analysis of extant protocol studies involved the categorization and sorting of readers' verbalizations across studies and paradigms, and allowed for the concatenation of strategies and responses as reported in studies with foundations in cognitive psychology and literary response. From this synthesis of readers' verbal reports came the model of constructively responsive reading: constructive as knowledge is constructive, and responsive as readers respond to the texts that they read in relation to the contexts in which reading occurs. Pressley and Afflerbach's portrait of the constructively responsive reader offered a comprehensive list of what readers do, grouped under three general categories of strategy and response. Accomplished readers identify and remember important information, they monitor their reading, and they evaluate their reading. Further, Pressley and Afflerbach determined that constructively responsive reading is marked by four characteristics. Readers seek to identify the overall meaning of the text by actively searching, reflecting on, and responding to text in pursuit of main ideas. Readers respond to text with predictions and hypotheses that reflect their prior knowledge. Readers are passionate in their responses to text. Readers' prior knowledge predicts their comprehension and responses to texts.

Pressley and Afflerbach's (1995) synthesis was informed both by the results of individual studies that used verbal reports and by existing models of reading. Thus, the theory of constructively responsive reading incorporates critical aspects of previous text processing theories. For example, readers' verbalizations describe the processing of text information that helps readers construct micro and macro text structures through the use of corresponding text-processing strategies (van Dijk & Kintsch, 1983). The top-down aspects of text processing and the importance of prior knowledge as described in schema theory (Anderson & Pearson, 1984) are present in many verbal reports and are both accommodated in constructively responsive reading. The transaction between reader and text and the stance that a reader takes toward a text, both conceptualizations of literary theorists (Beach & Hynds, 1991; Rosenblatt, 1978), are part of constructively responsive reading. So is readers' comprehension monitoring and metacognition (Baker & Brown, 1984), constructs most often associated with cognitive theorists. The massive amounts of inferencing that occur in reading (Graesser & Bower, 1990) are a hallmark of constructively responsive reading, as is reader awareness of the social space in which reading and meaning-making are situated (Geisler, 1991; Smagorinsky, 1998). Constructively responsive reading is based on the detailed descriptions of the things that talented readers do when reading different texts for different purposes. In addition to providing the initial attempt to describe competent reading as revealed by aggregate think-aloud protocol data, Pressley and Afflerbach demonstrated the suitability of verbal reports for describing complex acts of reading, the relationship of the research traditions of cognitive psychology and literary response, and the usefulness of verbal reports for theory building.

The majority of protocol analysis research focuses on talented readers. This is of practical and theoretical importance. Practically, better readers are often more verbal, make better use of their limited working memory, and may better verbalize the things they do in a think-aloud. These readers may be more sophisticated, diverse, and successful in the application of reading strategies and in responding to what they read.

Implicit in much of the protocol-based research is the notion that the detailed description of talented readers can inform our efforts to teach less expert readers. The detailed descriptions of talented reading can provide the detailed information that can be incorporated into instruction in the strategies, skills, and other knowledge that developing readers need to become expert. Bruner (1985) noted that there is not a well-defined path from novice to expert, because we lack a theory of what each one is, and how one progresses from novice to expert. It may be that our understanding of the nature of reading and reading instruction, critically informed by protocol analysis, can help describe that path. That is, verbal reports may serve as a means of helping teach the very strategies they have helped describe. This idea is addressed in a recent review of think-aloud protocols by Kucan and Beck (1997), which describes the relationship of verbal reports and protocol analysis to reading comprehension instruction. Their review serves as an indicator of progress from the prolegomenon for identifying, specifying, and teaching reading strategies provided by Collins and Smith (1982). One result of research using protocol analysis is the provision of detailed and explicit accounts of reading processes and strategies. This fine-grained detail can inform instruction and external modeling of competent strategy use, which eventually becomes internalized as a student's reading routine. This use of verbal report data with scaffolded instruction and work across zones of proximal development derives from the work of Vygotsky (1978), and it fits well with the notion of the development of cognitive strategy use and the incremental differences between novice and expert performance (Palincsar & Brown, 1984; Paris, Lipson, & Wixson, 1983).

The detailed accounting of readers' strategies, motivations, and mindsets that is provided by protocol analysis may prove as valuable for determining the detail and focus of reading instruction as it is for building models of reading (Pearson & Fielding, 1991). These instructional efforts follow from earlier work that sought to describe and teach reading strategies using explicit instruction (e.g., Bereiter and Bird, 1985; Palincsar & Brown, 1984; Pressley, Harris, & Marks, 1992). For example, verbal reports are used in efforts to help students better comprehend text (Loxterman, Beck, & McKeown, 1994) and participate in discussions of authors and texts (Trabasso & Magliano, 1996). A result is that verbal reports and protocol analysis have influenced thinking about what to teach (the strategies and responses revealed in expert readers' protocols) and how to teach (the verbal description and explicit modeling of strategy instruction derived, in part, from think-aloud protocols). An additional value of thinking aloud is that it encourages children to spend time with their thinking. The promise of this aspect of verbal reports and protocol analysis is that they may provide the opportunity for readers to better mediate their learning by becoming better acquainted with it. An intriguing possibility is that classroom discussions can provide models of thinking and social interaction (Kucan & Beck, 1997). This suggestion adds to the conceptualization of verbal reports as aides for learning, and returns to the notion that verbal reports are closely related to inner speech (Vygotsky, 1978). As such, verbal reporting may serve an important regulatory function in learning (Feuerstein, 1980) as learners situate themselves in relation to a particular reading and learning task (Wertsch, 1991). The classroom discussions and social interactions can be considered verbal reports that provide models for students who are keyed into the critical features of such phenomena (Gambrell & Almasi, 1996).

Protocol analysis can also help us better understand the diverse strategies and processes which may ultimately impact students' reading achievement. Understanding the detail and focus of student thought during instruction (Peterson, Swing, Braverman, & Buss, 1982), the differences in how teachers and students determine main ideas (Schellings & Van Hout Walters, 1995), teachers' evolving understanding of writing processes (Afflerbach et al., 1988), the procedural and declarative knowledge that teachers use to evaluate and grade students' literacy achievement (Afflerbach &

Johnston, 1993), and the manner in which students reason their way through test items (DuBois, 1998; Norris, 1990, 1992; Nuthall & Alton-Lee, 1995) have all been investigated using think-aloud protocols. Results from these studies may contribute to optimizing the processes and strategies that support successful reading instruction. In addition, these studies demonstrate the flexibility and suitability of the verbal report methodology for investigating reading related phenomena. Future investigations may use protocol analysis to examine the social contexts of reading and the situated nature of reading and tasks related to reading (Greeno, Pearson, & Schoenfeld, 1996). Such inquiry should contribute to a more complete understanding of acts, strategies, and responses within the culture of reading (Bruner, 1996). The research findings yielded through the use of protocol analysis continue to demonstrate the accuracy of Huey's (1908) claim that reading well is one of the most compelling human accomplishments.

ONGOING CHALLENGES TO THE USE OF PROTOCOL ANALYSIS TO STUDY AND DESCRIBE READING AND READING-RELATED PHENOMENA

Protocol analysis helps describe strategies for understanding words (Werner & Kaplan, 1950), paragraphs (Afflerbach, 1990a; Collins et al., 1980), textbook excerpts (Haas & Flower, 1988), legal documents (Deegan, 1995; Lundeberg, 1987), historical documents (Wineburg, 1991), the subtexts of teachers' and children's history texts (Afflerbach & VanSledright, 1999), professional articles (Wyatt et al., 1993), and the intertextuality between texts (Hartmann, 1995). Protocol analysis also has informed our understanding of reading poems (Beach, 1972; Kintgen, 1983), short stories (Rogers, 1991; Squire, 1964), and excerpts from novels (Graves & Frederiksen, 1991). The past and present use of protocol analysis helps describe the promise and challenge of their future use. The worth of verbal reports and protocol analysis for investigating reading and reading-related phenomena will be demonstrated through both methodological rigor and flexible use. The movement from a developing to a mature protocol analysis methodology is fueled, in part, by the ability to identify and anticipate strengths and weaknesses of the methodology and to design research that reflects this knowledge.

As verbal reports and protocol analysis are utilized, several methodological concerns demand close attention. These include full disclosure of the nature of the use of the verbal reporting methodology, the triangulation of verbal protocol data, the distinction between concurrent and retrospective reports, and the intimate nature of think-aloud protocols. The lack of complete reporting of the details of the verbal report and protocol analysis methodology represents a lost opportunity to build knowledge of the method—especially as it is increasingly applied to the complex problem spaces that are replete with the interactions of readers, tasks, texts, and intervening variables. The distinct lack of convention and comprehensiveness in many research accounts of the methodology is not surprising, as published accounts of research reflect different traditions of inquiry and the norms of different research communities. Protocol analysis is often treated as a mature methodology, as if everything about eliciting, collecting, and interpreting verbal reports has been learned. There is often a startling lack of detail provided in published research reports. The result is lack of further understanding of the intricacies of the method. Less than full disclosure of method thwarts critical evaluation of the reading research process and product. Scant accounting of the details of design, instructions to subjects, prompting, selection of tasks, coding of transcripts, and classification of phenomena influences the research consumer's ability to understand and accept or reject a researcher's claims. Concise descriptions provide a gloss for better understanding of researcher intent and method and of research results. A lack of detail of how the protocol analysis method is used creates questions that the accompanying research text cannot answer.

Consistent and detailed description of the methodology facilitates the examination of commonalties across investigations and across paradigms in reading research that uses protocol analysis (Pressley & Afflerbach, 1995). Researchers investigating readers' use of cognitive strategies as situated in reading a scientific text should be able to divine commonalities and differences in research on readers' literary responses. This should contribute to better understanding of the aggregate findings of reading research using the verbal reporting methodology. Attention also must be given to characteristics of every aspect of reader–text interaction to better understand what is revealed in verbal reports. A key tenet of Ericsson and Simon's (1980, 1984/1993) work is that people can self-report the contents of their working memory. This provides the "stuff" of think-aloud protocols, and it is critical to understand how contextual variables influence the availability of information to report and the process of reporting. Table 12.1 contains representative aspects of the verbal report methodology that demand comprehensive description, including the characteristics of subjects, texts, tasks, directions to subjects, the transcription of the verbal protocols, the selection of protocol excerpts and their representativeness, the categories used to score think-alouds, and the reliability of coding of protocol contents. Each is worthy of careful attention in the design and execution of research using protocol analysis.

The results of protocol analysis should be triangulated with information from complementary methodologies. Data from process measures, product measures, and comparisons of online performance can strengthen the claims made with verbal report data. Magliano and Graesser (1993) suggested a three-pronged approach to drawing

TABLE 7.1

Aspects of the Verbal Reporting and Protocol Analysis Methodology
That Require Detailed Descriptions

Aspect of Methodology	Representative Concerns
Subjects	Verbal ability
	Familiarity with the methodology
	Knowledge of text content and structure
	Relationship with researcher
Texts	Degree of intactness
	Difficulty or familiarity
	Mode of text presentation
Tasks	Influence of verbal reporting task on designated reading task
	Automatic or nonautomatic processing
	Novelty of task
	Amount of text available for previewing or rereading
Directions to subjects	Focus on specific or general reading strategies
	To read as one "normally would"
Transcription process	Faithfulness of print to tape
	Status of nonverbal utterances
	Treatment of pause time
Selection of protocol excerpts	Representativeness and typicality
Categories used to score think-alouds	Relationship to previous research and theory
Coding of protocol excerpts	Reliability

conclusions about cognitive aspects of text processing. The first involves theoretical analysis of the processing that might be expected of a particular reader of a particular text, as determined by expert consensus (e.g., van den Broek, Fletcher, & Risden, 1993). For example, accomplished readers identify portions of a poem that are expected to elicit a strong emotional response. The second prong is verbal reports and protocol analysis, with protocol data analyzed in relation to the triangulation measures. The third prong involves the collection of behavioral measures, such as reading time, objective memory of text, and readers' eye movements (e.g., Just & Carpenter, 1980). The greater the degree of alignment of all three measures, the greater confidence research producers and consumers may place in verbal report data. Pressley and Afflerbach (1995) noted that the weakest link in the aggregate of verbal report data and triangulation measures is the demonstrated correlations between objective measures of text processing and subjects' verbal reports (e.g., Wade, Trathen, & Schraw, 1990). Efforts to seek such a three-pronged alignment will do much to move protocol analysis to the status of mature methodology. Ericsson and Simon's (1984/1993) observations and recommendations are related to verbal reports of cognition: the processes and strategies readers use to comprehend text. The majority of reading research that uses protocol analysis has a cognitive focus. As reading research evolves and investigates acts of reading in which cognition is packaged with affect and motivation, and situated in diverse social contexts, participants may be viewed as readers, negotiators, and collaborators. It is necessary to examine these aspects of reading and their relationship to the verbal reporting methodology. As protocol analysis evolves to examine situated acts of reading (and their attendant social, affective, and motivational aspects), the type of data that can provide triangulation will change. For example, motivation that is present in a protocol might receive support from the triangulation provided by a motivation observation checklist, or readers' retrospective self-reports of motivation.

Future inquiry should carefully consider the delineation between concurrent verbal reports and other verbal reports within a protocol. A central argument of Ericsson and Simon (1980, 1984/1993) is that the contents of working memory are available for verbal report. Given the process and storage constraints that working memory places on reading (Britton, Glynn, & Smith, 1985), there is clear need to determine at what point a reader is accessing and reporting working memory contents and when the same reader is leaving working memory to access recent long-term memory. What is concurrent and what is retrospective? Theoretical descriptions clearly delineate between the two, and they revolve around the notion of the reportability of the contents of working (or short-term) memory. Concurrent reports are online accounts of the contents of working memory. Retrospective reports rely, in part, on subjects' long-term memory. However, in real time the differences blur. An online and concurrent verbal report can dodge in and out of retrospection based on the length of the verbalization, the instructions to subjects, and the nature of the task. If concurrent and retrospective reports are purported to be qualitatively different in theory, we need to better know their characteristics, interactions, and relationship as they may be embedded within a single verbal report transcript. This is especially critical in light of our increasing awareness of the cognitive, affective, and social aspects of reading, all of which can muddle the fine line between concurrent and other verbalizations. Promising work demonstrates that concurrent verbal reports and retrospective debriefing from subjects can enrich our understanding of complex phenomena. Thus, the two distinct types of verbal report may be mutually supportive (Haastrup, 1987; Lundeberg, 1987).

There is no more intimate reading research methodology than protocol analysis. It is typical for the array of verbal protocols collected from different readers in the same study to exhibit variance in terms of reader focus, strategies used, responses elicited, feelings emoted, and how the act of reading is situated in a social context. Verbal reports and protocol analysis reveal considerable individual differences in how people read. These differences may be masked or ignored if the purpose of the research is to quantify the use of a particular cognitive strategy or literary response. Although research has paid attention to the individual differences in reading that are revealed by protocol analysis, it has not adequately considered how the intimate nature of the method may influence the data gathered. Verbal reports depend on subjects' ability to verbalize what they are thinking. The verbalization may be influenced by the relationship between the participant and the researcher, gender differences between subject and researcher, cultural differences in reporting and using language, or differences in how the subject conceptualizes her or his role as a reporter of reading phenomena (Belenky, Clinchy, Goldberger, & Tarule, 1986; Smagorinsky, 1998). Individuals use language differently, and any comprehensive theory of the methodology of verbal reports must account for how individual language differences may influence the eliciting, giving, and subsequent analysis of verbal reports.

THE FUTURE FOCI OF PROTOCOL ANALYSIS AND READING

Verbal reports and protocol analysis enrich our understanding of reading. They played a central role in developing detailed descriptions of cognition and response in reading. Future applications of protocol analysis will continue to provide information about reading as our understanding of reading and how to profitably apply protocol analysis evolve. An immediate application of protocol analysis will be to help describe reading at the intersection of cognition, response, and the social world of the reader. Situated cognition and situated response provide compelling protocol data. Protocol analysis should also help describe developing readers, and provide a contrast to the expert reader descriptions of reading that dominate.

Protocol analysis provides much information about how expert readers read. In fact, it is not a stretch to say that protocol analysis has contributed greatly to our understanding of how academics read texts within their areas of expertise. The focus on expert performance contributes to our understanding of talented reading. However, the resource of protocol analysis has not been fully realized in the investigation of the developmental nature of reading, the growth of ability to read, and the growth of ability to provide verbal reports. Reading inquiry using protocol analysis has generally been guided by the notion that less able readers will not provide useful verbal reports. This assumption needs careful examination. Less able readers are often less verbal, and their reports might be more unduly influenced by the burden of the task of reading and reporting. This could contribute to both qualitative and quantitative differences in the uses of strategies and responses. However, lacking protocol studies of how developing readers read, we forego the development of a potentially rich database that could inform our understanding of how children read, their nascent theories of reading, their lack of convention, and their creativity in approaching and overcoming reading challenges. The verbal reports of such readers may provide diagnostic information that describes the processing, comprehension, interpretation, and motivation challenges less able readers face.

The preeminent focus of verbal reports and protocol analysis remains cognition. Our understanding of readers' cognitive strategy use is rich but incomplete. Cognition has received the majority of attention from reading researchers using protocol analysis. An initial model of cognition, knowledge construction, and response (Pressley & Afflerbach, 1995) invites challenge and revision. Researchers should continue the rich cognitive tradition, and future research should more clearly delineate between the shared and unique aspects of cognition and response, and how each figures in particular reading situations.

Each investigation of reading strategies is socially situated. Thus, it is not surprising that subjects' verbal reports, which are most often directed to cognitive events, spill over into the realm of the context. In fact, readers' verbal reports related to the contextual factors of a reading act (even when they are not requested) serve as support for the veridicality or authenticity of the report, and the social nature of reading. The noncognitive aspects of reading are rarely the focus of think-aloud protocol directives. Yet, it is difficult to transcribe verbal protocols of reading without encountering affect and motivation, which are evinced by readers' exclamations, expletives, grunts, groans, and affirmations. In addition to proving difficult to transcribe to English, these interjections demonstrate above all that readers are more than cognitive in their reading. That considerable affect and motivation are revealed in verbal reports suggests that a systematic approach to their investigation and the systematic variation of instructions to subjects and requests for the focus of their reporting might contribute to new insights about reading.

As our understandings of curriculum, instruction, and learning evolve, so too should our research foci. There are rich opportunities for examining the interface of reading with traditional content learning areas. It will be beneficial to examine protocol studies in other domains: investigations of writing (Flower & Hayes, 1977), physics problem solving (Simon & Simon, 1978) and students' cognitions during instruction (Peterson et al., 1982) contributed to our understanding of theories of problem solving and cognition that may help frame inquiry in reading. As cognitive psychology maintains a strong paradigmatical position, we see the continued use of protocol analysis for inquiry of writing (Breetveldt, van den Bergh, & Rijlaarsdam, 1994), problem solving in physics (Slotta, Chi, & Joram, 1995), genetics (Smith, 1990), mathematics (Hall, Kibler, Wenger, & Truxaw, 1989; Miller & Stigler, 1991), and the programming of intelligent tutoring systems (Pirolli & Recker, 1994). These studies offer the opportunity to examine the relationship of reading to other cognitive, responsive, and constructive acts of mind. They may help inform the design and focus of future protocol studies of reading.

Future use of protocol analysis should also focus on the teaching and learning of reading. Verbal protocols have "the potential to reveal" (Kucan & Beck, 1997, p. 292) aspects of thinking and reading, including the development of self-awareness and metacognition. To the extent that verbal reports help developing readers better understand themselves, this form of encouraged inner speech should prove valuable. In addition to further specification of current models of reading, protocol analysis should help describe emerging realities of reading and literacy. Searching for information (Guthrie, Britten, & Barker, 1991) and interacting with hypertext (Reinking, 1992) are two examples of phenomena that are increasingly important to the literate individual, as are comprehending and responding to combinations of print and graphics. As curricular materials change, protocol analysis may help describe the benefits and challenges of this change for teachers and students. For example, Afflerbach and VanSledright (2000) investigated fifth graders reading of American history texts related to the Jamestown colony. They found that although nontraditional, primary source texts (e.g., excerpts from colonists' diaries, poems) proved captivating and motivating for some students, other students were significantly challenged by the unfamiliar syntax and archaic vocabulary found in the texts. VanSledright and Afflerbach (1999) also investigated the manner in which preservice teachers navigate revisionist history texts, with a focus on how future teachers reconcile existing historical knowledge with contradictory accounts, and how they approach teaching contentious historical topics to students.

Additional uses of verbal reports and protocol analysis may be found in the areas of teacher decision making, teachers' professional development, and reading assessment. Teacher decision making is a complex and rapid phenomenon, and verbal protocols may help us better understand how reading teachers make critical decisions. Teachers' professional development is critical to successful reading programs, and verbal protocols may also help describe the experiences, processes, and materials that contribute to this professional development. For example, knowing how teachers select, read, and use professional journals (Shearer, Coballes-Vega, & Lundeberg, 1993) may positively influence teachers' professional development, and ultimately student achievement. Reading assessment continues to evolve. A frequent criticism of many reading assessments is that they provide information about products, and not reading processes. Think-aloud protocols have been used to investigate the processes used by reading test-takers (Kavale & Schreiner, 1979; Norris, 1990, 1992; Pritchard, 1990b). New forms of reading assessment may help describe the reading and test-taking processes of students, but also the relationship of reading to performance in an assessment situation (DuBois, 1998).

Verbal reports and protocol analysis should continue to play a central role in defining the problem spaces within which it is used. The traditions of use of the methodology for inquiry in cognition (Pressley & Afflerbach, 1995) and literary response (Beach & Hynds, 1991) have been joined with inquiry that seeks to describe the teaching and learning of cognitive strategy and literary response (Kucan & Beck, 1997). The conceptualization of the nature of verbal reports and protocol analysis is continually debated (Ericsson & Simon, 1998; Smagorinsky, 1998) and from this ongoing debate should evolve new areas of inquiry. In summary, verbal reports and protocol analysis prove valuable in describing reading and charting one course of reading research. The flexibility and suitability of the methodology are demonstrated by increasingly diverse applications in the study of reading. The appeal of verbal reports and protocol analysis must be complemented by careful attention to aspects of the methodology that either undergird or undermine the validity of verbal report data. Be it cognition and response, reading instruction and learning, or the socially situated nature of each, verbal reports and protocol analysis may serve the reading research enterprise well.

REFERENCES

Afflerbach, P. (1990a). The influence of prior knowledge on expert readers' main idea construction strategies. *Reading Research Quarterly, 25,* 31–46.

Afflerbach, P. (1990b). The influence of prior knowledge and text genre on readers' prediction strategies. *Journal of Reading Behavior, 22,* 131–148.

Afflerbach, P., Bass, L., Hoo, D., Smith, S., Weiss, L., & Williams, L. (1988). Pre-service teachers use think-aloud protocols to study writing. *Language Arts, 65,* 693–701.

Afflerbach, P., & Johnston, P. (1984). Research methodology: On the use of verbal reports in reading research. *Journal of Reading Behavior, 16,* 307–322.

Afflerbach, P., & Johnston, P. (1993). Eleven teachers composing language arts report cards: Conflicts in knowing and communicating. *Elementary School Journal, 94,* 73–86.

Afflerbach, P., & VanSledright, B. (1999). *The challenge of understanding the past. How do fifth graders construct meaning from diverse history texts?* Elva Knight Research Presentation, International Reading Association, San Diego, CA.

Anderson, R., & Pearson, P. (1984). A schema-theoretic view of basic processes in reading. In P. D. Pearson (Ed.), *Handbook of reading research* (pp. 225–291). New York: Longman.

Baker, L., & Brown, A. (1984). Metacognitive skills and reading. In P. D. Pearson, R. Barr, M. Kamil, & P. Mosenthal (Eds.), *Handbook of reading research* (pp. 353–394). New York: Longman.

Bazerman, C. (1985). Physicists reading physics: Schema-laden purposes and purpose-laden schema. *Written Communication, 2,* 3–24.

Beach, R. (1972). *The literary response process of college students while reading and discussing three poems.* Doctoral dissertation, University of Illinois. (Dissertation Abstracts International Order No. 73–17112)

Beach, R., & Hynds, S. (1991). Research on response to literature. In R. Barr, M. L. Kamil, P. B. Mosenthal, & P. D. Pearson (Eds.), *Handbook of reading research* (Vol. 2, pp. 453–489). New York: Longman.

Belenky, M., Clinchy, B., Goldberger, N., & Tarule, J. (1986). *Woman's ways of knowing: The development of self, voice, and mind.* New York: Basic Books.

Bereiter, C., & Bird, M. (1985). Use of thinking aloud in identification and teaching of reading comprehension strategies. *Cognition and Instruction, 2,* 131–156.

Boring, E. (1953). A history of introspection. *Psychological Bulletin, 50*, 169–189.

Breetveldt, I., van den Bergh, H., & Rijlaarsdam, G. (1994). Relations between writing processes and text quality: When and how? *Cognition and Instruction, 12*, 103–123.

Bridge, C., & Winograd, P. (1982). Readers' awareness of cohesive relationships during cloze comprehension. *Journal of Reading Behavior, 14*, 299–312.

Britton, B., Glynn, S., & Smith, E. (1985). Cognitive demands of processing expository text. In B. Britton & J. Black (Eds.) *Understanding expository text* (pp. 227–248). Hillsdale, NJ: Lawrence Erlbaum Associates.

Brown, A., & Day, J. (1983). Macrorules for summarizing strategies: The development of expertise. *Journal of Verbal Learning and Verbal Behavior, 22*, 1–14.

Bruce, B., & Rubin, A. (1984). Strategies for controlling hypothesis formation in reading. In J. Flood (Ed.), *Promoting reading comprehension* (pp. 97–112). Newark, DE: International Reading Association.

Bruner, J. (1985). Models of the learner. *Educational Researcher, 14*, 5–8.

Bruner, J. (1996). *The culture of education.* Cambridge, MA: Harvard University Press.

Charney, D. (1993). A study in rhetorical reading: How evolutionists read "The spandrels of San Marco." In J. Selzer (Eds.), *Understanding scientific prose* (pp. 203–231). Madison: University of Wisconsin Press.

Collins, A., Brown, J., & Larkin, K. (1980). Inferences in text understanding. In R J. Spiro, B. C. Bruce, & W. F. Brewer (Eds.), *Theoretical issues in reading comprehension* (pp. 385–407). Hillsdale, NJ: Lawrence Erlbaum Associates.

Collins, A., & Smith, E. (1982). Teaching the process of reading comprehension. In D. Detterman & R. Sternberg (Eds.), *How and how much can intelligence be increased?* (pp. 173–185). Norwood, NJ: Ablex.

Deegan, D. (1995). Exploring individual differences among novices reading in a specific domain: The case of law. *Reading Research Quarterly, 30*, 154–170.

Deffner, G. (1988). Concurrent thinking aloud: An on-line tool for studying representations used in text understanding. *Text, 8*, 351–367.

de Groot, A. (1965). *Thought and choice in chess.* The Hague, Netherlands: Mouton.

DuBois, P. (1998). Evaluating test items in AIR's cognitive survey lab. *Internet report: What's new.* Washington, DC: American Institutes for Research.

Duncker, K. (1945). On problem solving. *Psychological Monographs, 58*, 1–113 (whole no. 270).

Earthman, E. (1992). Creating the virtual work: Readers' processes in understanding literary texts. *Research in the Teaching of English, 26*, 351–384.

Eco, U. (1990). *The limits of interpretation.* Bloomington: Indiana University Press.

Ericsson, K. (1988). Concurrent verbal reports on text comprehension: A review. *Text, 8*, 295–325.

Ericsson, K., & Simon, H. (1980). Verbal reports as data. *Psychological Review, 87*, 215–253.

Ericsson, K., & Simon, H. (1993). *Protocol analysis: Verbal reports as data.* Cambridge, MA: MIT Press. (Original work published 1984)

Ericsson, K. & Simon, H. (1998). How to study thinking in everyday life: Contrasting think-aloud protocols with descriptions and explanations of thinking. *Mind, Culture, and Activity, 5*, 178–186

Feuerstein, R. (1980). *The dynamic assessment of retarded performers: The learning potential assessment, device, theory, instrument, and techniques.* Baltimore, MD: University Park Press.

Fish, S. (1980). *Is there a text in this class? The authority of interpretive communities.* Cambridge, MA: Harvard University Press.

Flower, L., & Hayes, J. (1977). Problem-solving strategies and the writing process. *College English, 39*, 449–461.

Gambrell, L., & Almasi, J. (1996). *Lively discussions! Fostering engaged reading.* Newark, DE: International Reading Association.

Garner, R. (1982). Verbal report data on reading strategies. *Journal of Reading Behavior, 14*, 159–167.

Garner, R., & Reis, R. (1981). Monitoring and resolving comprehension obstacles: An investigation of spontaneous lookbacks among upper-grade good and poor comprehenders. *Reading Research Quarterly, 16*, 569–582.

Geisler, C. (1991). Toward a sociocognitive model of literacy: Constructing mental models in philosophical conversation. In C. Bazerman & J. Paradis (Eds.). *Textual dynamics of the professions* (pp. 171–190). Madison: University of Wisconsin Press.

Graesser, A., & Bower, G. (1990). *Inferences and text comprehension.* San Diego, CA: Academic Press.

Graves, B., & Frederiksen, C. (1991). Literary expertise in the description of fictional narrative. *Poetics, 20*, 1–26.

Greeno, J., Pearson, P., & Schoenfeld, A. (1996). *Implications for NAEP of research on learning and cognition. Report to the National Academy of Education.* Washington, DC: National Academy of Education.

Guthrie, J., Britten, T., & Barker, K. (1991). Roles of document structure, cognitive strategy, and awareness in searching for information. *Reading Research Quarterly, 26*, 300–324.

Haas, C., & Flower, L (1988). Rhetorical reading strategies and the construction of meaning, *College Composition and Communication, 39*, 167–183.

Haastrup, K. (1987). Using thinking aloud and retrospection to uncover learners' lexical inferencing procedures. In C. Faerch & G. Kasper (Eds.), *Introspection in second language research* (pp. 197–212). Philadelphia: Multilingual Matters, Ltd.

Hall, R., Kibler, D., Wenger, E., & Truxaw, C. (1989). Exploring the episodic structure of algebra story problem solving. *Cognition and Instruction, 6*, 223–283.

Hare, V. (1981). Readers' problems identification and problem solving strategies for high- and low-knowledge articles. *Journal of Reading Behavior, 13*, 359–365.

Hartmann, D. (1995). Eight readers reading: The intertextual links of proficient readers reading multiple passages. *Reading Research Quarterly, 30*, 520–561.

Huey, E. (1908). *The psychology and pedagogy of reading.* Cambridge, MA: MIT Press.

James, W. (1890). *The principles of psychology.* New York: Holt.

Johnston, P., & Afflerbach, P. (1985). The process of constructing main ideas from text. *Cognition and Instruction, 2*, 207–232.

Just, M., & Carpenter, P. (1980). A theory of reading: From eye fixations to comprehension. *Psychological Review, 87*, 329–354.

Kavale, K., & Schreiner, R. (1979). The reading process of above average and average readers: A comparison of the use of reasoning strategies in responding to standardized comprehension measures. *Reading Research Quarterly, 15*, 102–128.

Kintgen, E. (1983). *The perception of poetry.* Bloomington: Indiana University Press.

Kucan, L., & Beck, I. (1997). Thinking aloud and reading comprehension research: Inquiry, instruction, and social interaction. *Review of Educational Research, 67*, 271–299

Langer, J. (1990). The process of understanding: Reading for literary and informative purposes. *Research in the Teaching of English, 24* , 229–260.

Leinhardt, G., & Young, K. (1996). Two texts, three readers: Distance and expertise in reading history. *Cognition and Instruction, 14*, 441–486.

Loxterman, J., Beck, I., & McKeown, M. (1994). The effects of thinking aloud during reading on students' comprehension of more or less coherent text. *Reading Research Quarterly, 29*, 353–368.

Lundeberg, M. (1987). Metacognitive aspects of reading comprehension: Studying understanding in legal case analysis. *Reading Research Quarterly, 22*, 407–432.

Lytle, S. L (1982). *Exploring comprehension style: A study of twelfth-grade readers' transactions with texts.* Doctoral dissertation, University of Pennsylvania. (University Microfilms No. 82-27292)

Magliano, J., & Graesser, A. (1993). A three-pronged method for studying inference generation in literary text. *Poetics, 20*, 193–232.

Marbe, K. (1964). *Experimentell-psychologische: Untersuchungen uber das Urteil.* Reprinted and translated in J. Mandler & G. Mandler (Eds.). (1964). *Thinking: From association to gestalt* (pp. 143–148). New York: Wiley. (Original work published 1901)

McCallister, J. (1930). Reading difficulties in studying content subjects. *Elementary School Journal, 31*, 191–201.

Miller, K., & Stigler, J. (1991). Meanings of skill: Effects of abacus expertise on number representation. *Cognition and Instruction, 8*, 29–67.

Neutelings, R., & Maat, H. (1997). Investigating the processes of reading-to-assess among Dutch legislators. *Journal of Literacy Research, 29*, 47–71.

Newell, A., & Simon, H. (1972). *Human problem solving.* Englewood Cliffs, NJ: Prentice Hall.

Nisbett, R., & Wilson, T. (1977). Telling more than we can know: Verbal reports on mental processes. *Psychological Review, 84*, 231–259.

Norris, S. (1990). Effect of eliciting verbal reports of thinking on critical thinking test performance. *Journal of Educational Measurement, 27*, 41–58.

Norris, S. (1992). A demonstration of the use of verbal reports of thinking in multiple-choice critical thinking test design. *Alberta Journal of Educational Research, 38*, 153–176.

Nuthall, G., & Alton-Lee, A. (1995). Assessing classroom learning: How students use their knowledge and experience to answer classroom achievement text questions in science and social studies. *American Educational Research Journal, 32*, 185–223.

Olshavsky, J. (1976–1977). Reading as problem solving: An investigation of strategies. *Reading Research Quarterly, 12*, 654–674.

Olson, G., Mack, R., & Duffy, S. (1981). Cognitive aspects of genre. *Poetics, 10*, 283–315.

Palincsar, A., & Brown, A. (1984). Reciprocal teaching of comprehension-fostering and monitoring activities. *Cognition and Instruction, 1*, 117–175.

Paris, S., Lipson, M., & Wixson, K. (1983). Becoming a strategic reader. *Contemporary Educational Psychology, 8*, 293–316.

Pearson, P., & Fielding, L. (1991). Comprehension instruction. In R. Barr, M. L. Kamil, P. B. Mosenthal, & P. D. Pearson (Eds.), *Handbook of reading research* (Vol. II, pp. 815–860). New York: Longman.

Peskin, J. (1998). Constructing meaning when reading poetry: An expert-novice study. *Cognition and Instruction, 16*, 235–263.

Peterson, P., Swing, S., Braverman, M., & Buss, R. (1982). Students' aptitudes and their reports of cognitive processes during instruction. *Journal of Educational Psychology, 74*, 535–547.

Phillips, L. (1988). Young readers' inference strategies in reading comprehension. *Cognition and Instruction, 5*, 193–222.

Piekarz, J. (1954). *Individual responses in interpretive responses in reading.* Unpublished doctoral dissertation, University of Chicago.

Pirolli, P., & Recker, M. (1994). Learning strategies and transfer in the domain of programming. *Cognition and Instruction, 12*, 235–275.

Polya, G. (1954a). *Mathematics and plausible reasoning (a) Induction and analogy in mathematics.* Princeton, NJ: Princeton University Press.

Polya, G. (1954b). *Patterns of plausible inference.* Princeton, NJ: Princeton University Press.

Pressley, M., & Afflerbach, P. (1995). *Verbal protocols of reading: The nature of constructively responsive reading.* Hillsdale, NJ: Lawrence Erlbaum Associates.

Pressley, M., Harris, K., & Marks, M. (1992). But good strategy instructors are constructivists!! *Educational Psychology Review, 4,* 1–32.

Pritchard, R. (1990a). The evolution of introspective methodology and its implications for studying the reading process. *Reading Psychology: An International Quarterly, 11,* 1–13.

Pritchard, R. (1990b). The effects of cultural schemata on reading processing strategies. *Reading Research Quarterly, 25,* 273–295.

Ransom, J. (1979). *The new criticism.* Westport, CT: Greenwood Publishing.

Reinking, D. (1992). Differences between electronic and printed texts: An agenda for research. *Journal of Educational Multimedia and Hypermedia, 1,* 11–24.

Rich, A. (1974). *The dream of a common language.* New York: Norton.

Rogers, T. (1991). Students as literary critics: The interpretive experiences, beliefs, and processes of ninth-grade students. *Journal of Reading Behavior, 23,* 391–423.

Rosenblatt, L. (1978). *The reader, the text, the poem: The transactional theory of the literary work.* Carbondale, IL: Southern Illinois University Press.

Schellings, G., & Van Hout Walters, B. (1995). Main points in an instructional text, as identified by students and their teachers. *Reading Research Quarterly, 30,* 742–756.

Schmalhofer, F., & Boschert, S. (1988). Differences in verbalization during knowledge acquisition from texts and discovery learning from example situations. *Text, 8,* 369–393.

Schoenfeld, A. (1983). Beyond the purely cognitive: Belief systems, social cognitions and metacognitions as driving forces in intellectual performance. *Cognitive Science, 1,* 329–363.

Schwegler, R., & Shamoon, L. (1991). Meaning attribution in ambiguous texts in sociology. In C. Bazerman & J. Paradis (Eds.), *Textual dynamics of the professions* (pp. 216–233). Madison: University of Wisconsin Press.

Shearer, B., Coballes-Vega, C., & Lundeberg, M. (1993, December). *How do teachers who are professionally active select, read, and use professional journals?* Paper presented at the annual meeting of the National Reading Conference, Charleston, SC.

Simon, D., & Simon, H. (1978). Individual differences in solving physics problems. In R. Siegler (Ed.), *Children's thinking: What develops?* (pp. 325–348). Hillsdale, NJ: Lawrence Erlbaum Associates.

Slotta, J., Chi, M., & Joram, E. (1995). Assessing students' misclassifications of physics concepts: An ontological basis for conceptual change. *Cognition and Instruction, 12,* 373–400.

Smagorisnsky, P. (1998). Thinking and speech and protocol analysis. *Mind, Culture, and Activity, 5,* 157–177.

Smith, M. (1990). Knowledge structures and the nature of expertise in classical genetics. *Cognition and Instruction, 7,* 287–302.

Squire, J. (1964). *The responses of adolescents while reading four short stories.* Champaign, IL: National Council of Teachers of English.

Titchener, E. (1912a). Prolegomena to a study of introspection. *American Journal of Psychology, 23,* 427–448.

Titchener, E. (1912b). The schema of introspection. *American Journal of Psychology, 23,* 485–508.

Trabasso, T., & Magliano, J. (1996). How do children understand what they read and what can we do to help them? In M. Graves, P. van den Broek, & B. Taylor (Eds.), *The first r: A right of all children* (pp. 160–188). New York: Teachers College Press.

van den Broek, P., Fletcher, C., & Risden, K. (1993). Investigations of inferential processes in reading: A theoretical and methodological integration. *Discourse Processes, 16,* 169–180.

van Dijk, T., & Kintsch, W. (1983). *Strategies of discourse comprehension.* New York: Academic Press.

VanSledright, B., & Afflerbach, P. (2000). "But the pale faces knew it not": Using revisionist history texts to challenge traditional views of America's past. *Theory and Research in Social Education, 28,* 411–444.

Vygotsky, L. (1978). *Mind in society: The development of higher psychological processes.* Cambridge, MA: Harvard University Press.

Wade, S., Trathen, W., & Schraw, G. (1990). An analysis of spontaneous study strategies. *Reading Research Quarterly, 25,* 147–166.

Waern, Y. (1988). Thoughts on text in context: Applying the think-aloud method to text processing. *Text, 8,* 327–350.

Watson, J. (1913). Psychology as the behaviorist views it. *Psychological Review, 20,* 158–177.

Watson, J. (1920). Is thinking merely the action of language mechanisms? *British Journal of Psychology, 11,* 87–104.

Werner, H., & Kaplan, E. (1950). Development of word meaning through verbal context: An experimental study. *Journal of Psychology, 29,* 251–257.

Wertsch, J. (1991). *Voices of the mind: A sociocultural approach to mediated action.* Cambridge, MA: Harvard University Press.

Wimsatt, W., & Beardsley, M. (1954). *The verbal icon.* Lexington: University of Kentucky Press.

Wineburg, S. (1991). On the reading of historical texts: Notes on the breach between school and academy. *American Educational Research Journal, 28,* 495–520.

Wineburg, S. (1998). Reading Abraham Lincoln: An expert/expert study in the interpretation of historical texts. *Cognitive Science, 22,* 319–346.

Wyatt, D., Pressley, M., El-Dinary, P., Stein, S., Evans, P., & Brown, R. (1993). Reading behaviors of domain experts processing professional articles that are important to them: The critical role of worth and credibility monitoring. *Learning and Individual Differences, 5,* 49–72.

Young, K., & Leinhardt, G. (1998). Writing from primary documents: A way of knowing history. *Written Communication, 15,* 25–68.

CHAPTER 8

A Case for Single-Subject Experiments in Literacy Research

Susan B. Neuman
Temple University

Sandra McCormick
The Ohio State University

From the mid 1800s through the present, there have been cycles of interest in research methods used to explore literacy issues. For example, questions examining the efficacy of various literacy interventions have traditionally employed experimental group research designs, whereas questions focusing on process characteristics, the "hows" and "whys" of literacy research, have looked more toward qualitative methodologies. Noticeably absent from the research literature, however, have been studies based on a single subject, or $N = 1$ research designs. The purpose of this chapter, therefore, is to examine the utility of single-subject experimental design for literacy research. We begin by briefly describing its history and logic, then turn to its theoretical and practical advantages. We end by delineating both potential problems and possible solutions for future investigations pertaining to literacy development.

Single-subject design is an experimental technique where one subject or a small number of subjects is studied intensively. Unlike much traditional group-data analysis, these designs allow for the study of response changes in single individuals. Thus, although there may be any number of subjects in an investigation, the designation *single-subject* means that each subject's behaviors and outcomes are analyzed individually, not averaged with other members of an experimental or control group. In this respect, the method has something in common with case-study research. Unlike much case-study research, however, single-subject experimental studies allow the researcher to describe cause-and-effect relationships between independent and dependent variables.

In most cases, single-subject experimental studies are conducted in the context in which the behavior is practiced (i.e., the classroom), rather than in contrived laboratory settings. Here, the emphasis is on examining the *functional relationship* between an independent variable (the intervention) and a dependent variable (the outcome measure) for a particular individual. Typically, the dependent variable (or variables) focuses on behaviors that are measurable and practically important for student success (i.e., increase in number of inferential questions correctly identified). Consequently, whether or not the intervention is inferred to be successful is based on its educational (or social) relevance and importance rather than on statistically significant standards.

Single-subject experimental design has evolved over the last decades in response to a need to systematically examine the effects of instruction on student behavior. In the 1950s and 1960s, a number of investigators (Baer, Wolf, & Risley, 1968; Bellack & Chassan, 1964; Shapiro & Ravenette, 1959) in several subfields of psychology, such as psychotherapy, experimental personality research, psychopathology, and psychoanalysis, increasingly expressed concern about the lack of an approach to study behavior changes that was individualized and intensive, yet controlled. Although case study methodologies were extensively used, and regarded as useful for in-depth and personalized clinical work in these disciplines, researchers also wanted an experimental technology that could describe the functional relationships between interventions and outcomes. Although recognizing the merits of between-subject experimental studies to serve the latter aim, questions were raised concerning the incongruities seen in averaged group data with actual behaviors observed in individual clients participating in large-group studies. The result of these concerns were efforts that led to the evolution of single-subject experimental research.

Several investigators have been innovators and pacesetters in crafting the basic tenets and procedures of this research paradigm. Although as early as 1947 Thorne had suggested certain guidelines for single-case experiments, these had little impact until Shapiro and Ravenette (1959) presented a design model that formed the basis for a present, widely used analysis system in single-subject experimental research, the A-B-A-B design. The essential components of this design were a no-treatment phase (A) and a treatment (B), followed by the withdrawal of the treatment (A), and the reintroduction of treatment (B), the basic logic being that performance under baseline conditions predicts future performance if the treatment were not introduced. Shapiro (1961, 1966) also is credited with other important initial drives in developing the called-for methodology, such as definition, manipulation, and repeated administration of independent variables—with single cases. Sidman's now classic book, published in 1960, outlined other research designs appropriate for response analysis with single individuals, including the multi-element design. He also confronted the issue of generality in $N = 1$ studies, delineating several methods for replication of single-subject experiments within and across individuals for establishment of general hypotheses.

Shortly thereafter, and from a different disciplinary perspective, Campbell and Stanley (1963) suggested equivalent time-series designs for use in psychological and educational research, also a suitable means for experimental investigation of individual behaviors, and also involving basic principles of the A-B-A-B design. Bellack and Chassan's (1964) pharmacological work further advanced the A-B-A-B design prototype, and Chassan (1960, 1967) suggested appropriate statistics for extending single-subject analyses (for an update, see Kamil, 1995; Kratochwill & Levin, 1992). In 1968, Baer, Wolf, and Risley's introduction of the multiple-baseline design widened the analysis systems available for examining research questions with single individuals within an experimental framework. As this methodology has evolved over the last several decades, the literature has become replete with variants of the basic research designs, as well as principles for conducting robust studies and interpreting analyses.

THE LOGIC OF SINGLE-SUBJECT EXPERIMENTAL RESEARCH

Essentially, all single-subject experimental designs are considered to rest on a baseline logic. That is, the behavior of each subject during no-treatment conditions, or baseline, is compared with the subject's behavior during treatment conditions. It is assumed that performance under baseline predicts what would typically occur if the treatment were not introduced. In this respect, single-subject experimental research shares the same underlying assumption of group experimentation.

Although there are many variations in designs, several characteristics are central to all single-subject experimental research studies (see McCormick, 1995, for more detail). The first and foremost characteristic is *individual data analysis* (also called *personalized data analysis*). Because individual differences can be obscured when data are averaged across a group and reported as group mean, individual data analysis is undertaken because it is believed that the understanding of human variability is critical to the solution of specific problems. Thus, instead of attempting to control for variability through randomization and statistical procedures, the purpose of single-subject design strategy is to uncover and carefully examine variability.

A second characteristic is *direct manipulation of independent variables*; that is, here, the focus is on altering conditions, rather than on describing existing conditions. Therefore, a third earmark of single-subject experimental studies is the implementation of *planned and monitored interventions*. For example, it is standard procedure to systematically check the consistency with which the intervention is implemented to ensure that it is conducted as planned throughout the study. Based on frequent monitoring, data on the integrity of the independent variable, along with reliability coefficients for the dependent variable, are typically included in all data descriptions.

Differing from many well-established research models, single-subject experimental research does not rely on a single pretest to document pre-intervention behaviors. Instead, there is *data collection over several sessions to establish a baseline* to account for day-to-day variability in human responses. Furthermore, an important overriding practice is the *repeated, and frequent, measurement of variables during intervention*; again because of the possibility of day-to-day response variability, a single posttest at the end of an intervention is not considered a sufficient measure of behavior change. These intervention data are compared with a participant's own baseline responses. Comparison of every participant's own baseline data with their own specific responses during intervention is referred to as "using each subject as his or her own control." Once the intervention begins, there usually is *manipulation of only one independent variable at a time*. This is to provide assurance that the particular variable being studied is implicated in any changes of behavior that might occur. Throughout, *standardized measurement conditions* are maintained; the dependent variable is consistent across all phases of the study. Independent observers are often used to conduct checks throughout the study to ensure reliability of the observations or other data.

Most single-subject experimental studies include *maintenance assessments*, and *measure transfer of effects*. Although literacy researchers have been encouraged to include measures to assess maintenance of effects in research contextualized within other experimental paradigms, frequently this is not done. In contrast, it is a rare single-subject experiment that does not assess maintenance of the behavior after a relatively extended time has elapsed following termination of the study. Moreover, it is customary to evaluate reliability of both the dependent variable and the independent variable (i.e., providing measures of treatment integrity, as well as standard reliability coefficients).

With its emphasis on experimental control, single-subject research is considered to be strong with respect to internal validity because of the continuous measurement of responses over time, the use of subjects as their own controls, and the dual reliability assessments (Campbell & Stanley, 1963). Thus, single-subject research is known to use control procedures instead of control groups (McCormick, 1995). On the other hand, the issue of external validity—that is, the question of how generality can be established when the numbers of subjects are small (as also has been the case with qualitative studies)—is addressed through repeating the study to determine if an experimentally produced effect will occur another two, three, or more times. To establish external validity, single-subject researchers may undertake replications of the same experiment with other subjects, and/or replications in other settings. As Wixson has suggested (1993), "many replications of small studies may inform us as well as one large study that attempts to control so many factors that we have little 'ecology validity'" (p. 3; see Palincsar & Parecki, 1995, for a more detailed discussion).

Concerns for social validity (Tawney & Gast, 1984), as well, are often addressed in single-subject design research. That is, if a major change occurs as a result of an intervention, is it meaningful to the learner, and educationally significant? Social validity might address: What is the magnitude of the effect of improving one's ability to answer inferential questions, or to be able to assess one's writing? Does it impact classroom participation? Grades? Locus of control? Wolf (1978), for example, argued for the inclusion of subjective measures in studies to examine the student's view of the goals, procedures, and effects of an intervention. Given these concerns, more studies are beginning to include self-assessment measures, or debriefing interviews to determine student's perception of the benefits (and perhaps, costs) of an instructional intervention.

SELECTED TYPES OF DESIGNS

All of these procedures are carried out within certain designs that are specific to single-subject research. The most commonly used are three of those conceptualized during the early years of development of single-case experimental methodology, although over time these designs and their appropriate uses have been refined. These are the A-B-A-B reversal design, the alternating-treatments design (originally termed the multielement design), and the multiple-baseline design. The A-B-A-B reversal design (see Fig. 13.1) allows measurement of a baseline condition (condition A), the introduction of an intervention (condition B), return to the baseline condition (i.e., return to condition A), and reintroduction of the intervention (i.e., return to condition B). This design is based on the premise that if desired responses increase with the introduction of the intervention, diminish again with return to the baseline condition (i.e., temporary removal of the intervention), and increase once more with reinstatement of the intervention, this attests to the strength of that intervention. Had a study been terminated after the first A and B conditions only, threats to internal validity, such as maturational factors, would weaken conclusions about the effectiveness of the program being investigated. As can be seen for the hypothetical study represented by Fig. 13.1, an intervention involving use of word sorts to increase attention to orthographic features of words on spelling lists appears to be effective for Bob and Amy, but not for Rob. Because data have been maintained separately for these students, individual decisions can be made about their programs.

The multielement design, introduced almost four decades ago, is currently more commonly called the *alternating-treatments design* (Neuman, 1995). In 1979 Barlow and Hayes suggested the latter name as being more descriptive of its functions. With use of this analysis model, several interventions (most typically three) are randomly alternated for each subject, enabling the researcher to draw conclusions about which yields the most useful modifications in performance. Fig. 13.2 demonstrates use of this design with three participants. As can be noted in the hypothetical investigation, use of discussion through cooperative groups (condition 1) and through paired learning (condition 2) shows equally positive effects on Judy's understanding of cause-and-effect relationships, with both of these interventions leading to greater success than independent work (condition 3) in dealing with such questions. As can be seen in the figure, Anne, too, has improved achievement with these two interventions; however, for Anne cooperative group work clearly has the larger impact of the two. On the other hand, none of the arrangements appear to better than any other for Dan. Individual examination of the data portrays variability in student needs.

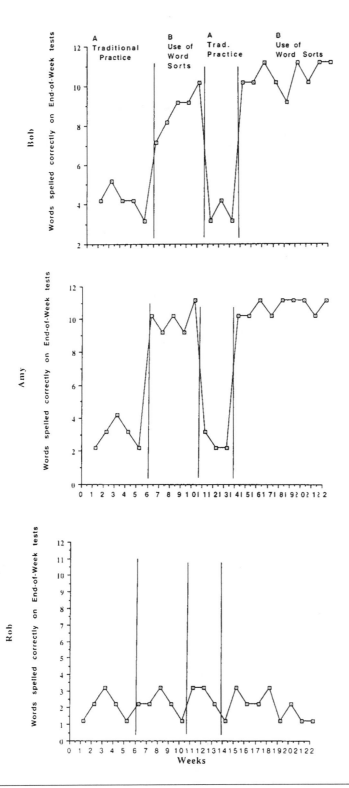

FIG. 8.1. Hypothetical example of a study employing an A–B–A–B design.

109

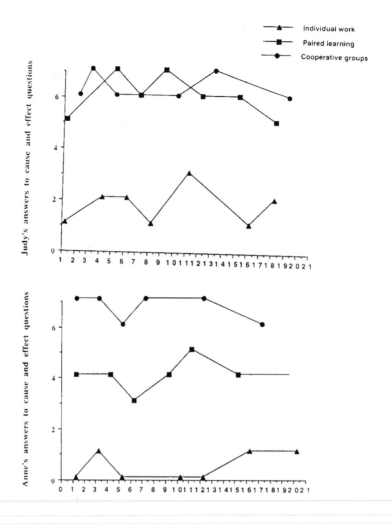

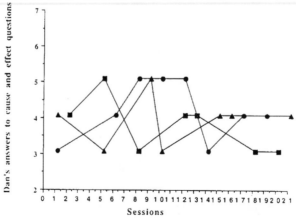

FIG. 8.2. Hypothetical example of use of an alternating treatments design with three subjects.

The third extensively used design is the *multiple-baseline design*. With this means of analysis, evaluations can be made across several subjects, several behaviors, or several settings. An example of the logic of the multiple-baseline design can be seen as applied to three subjects in Fig. 13.3. This example hypothetically examines the effect of use of study guides during independent reading of expository text. After baseline measurement, an intervention is initially introduced to one subject, but not to the others. Because a positive change in responses is seen with Diane, and is absent with those not yet receiving the intervention, this provides one confirmation of its effectiveness. Next, the intervention is applied with Jim. The change in response level for this subject, and again, its absence with Elaine, who is still in the baseline condition (i.e., not yet receiving the intervention), provides a replication of this confirmation. And, finally, when Elaine also demonstrates responsiveness to the intervention, an affirmation of its constructiveness is provided. The same logic is exercised when examining several interventions with a single individual, or one behavior across several settings.

As this discussion illustrates, it is critical for researchers to be in contact with their data to insure that students are truly benefiting from an intervention. Consequently, data are analyzed in these designs through visual analysis. Although statistical analyses of data are possible, visual analysis is the most frequent data analytic strategy. There are several reasons for analyzing the data in graphic form. First, it is a dynamic process; it provides continuous and concrete evidence of the impact of specific targeted instruction. Decisions about the efficacy of instruction for an individual can be determined; one can shorten or lengthen the intervention on the basis of whether the approach continues to be effective. Second, one can examine the effectiveness of the intervention across different types of learners, leading to better instruction designed for individual learners. For example, one approach may be most effective with one learner, but not with another, who might benefit from a different approach. And third, the visual analysis of data is a more conservative estimate of impact than statistical analysis (particularly with large sample sizes). Generally, if you can see it (i.e., changes in a target behavior), you can believe it. If the patterns show substantial differences as a result of an intervention, the findings are likely to be robust and reliable.

More comprehensive discussions of single-subject experimental designs and the analysis of graphic data are available in a number of texts (e.g., Barlow & Hersen, 1984; Cooper, Heron, & Heward, 1987; Johnston & Pennypacker, 1993; Kazdin, 1982; Kratochwill & Levin, 1992; Neuman & McCormick, 1995). For those interested in conducting well-controlled intervention research, these texts offer a rich resource of information on expanded descriptions of tenets, designs, and ways to conduct single-subject experimental studies.

WHY USE SINGLE-SUBJECT EXPERIMENTAL DESIGNS IN LITERACY RESEARCH?

Traditionally, single-subject design research has been most widely used to examine interventions in psychology-related fields and special education. More recently, however, these designs have attracted the attention of literacy researchers. For example, studies have been reported on a wide range of topics including the effects writing processes, story grammar instruction, spelling, study skills, story mapping, word identification strategies, sociodramatic play and language performance, methods of teacher cueing, context use, self-correction behaviors, comprehension, family literacy, reciprocal teaching, and oral reading (e.g., Bianco & McCormick, 1989; Danoff, Harris, & Graham, 1993; Gurney, Gersten, Dimino, & Carnine, 1990; Guza & McLaughlin, 1987; Idol & Croll, 1987; Lenz & Hughes, 1990; Levy, Wolfgang, & Koorland, 1992; McCormick & Cooper, 1991; Mudre & McCormick, 1989; Neuman & Gallagher, 1994; Newby,

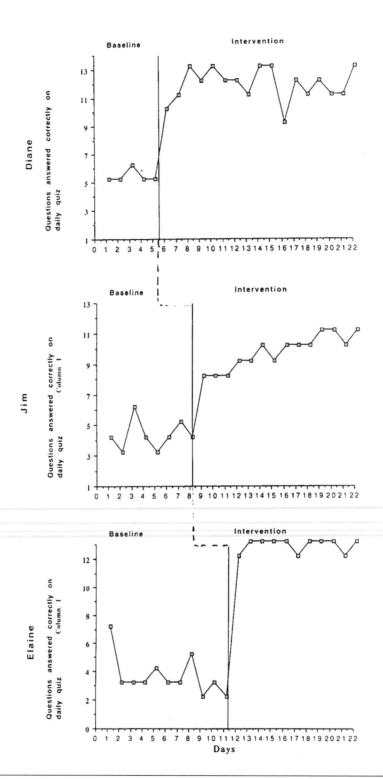

FIG. 8.3. Hypothetical study employing a multiple-baseline across-subject design.

Caldwell, & Recht, 1989; Palincsar & Brown, 1984; Rose & Beattie, 1986; Schumaker, Deshler, Alley, Warner, & Denton, 1982).

Why has single-subject experimental design become increasingly attractive to those of us studying literacy development? First, these designs have been constructed to investigate specific interventions and their effects in great detail. Carefully designing the measurement strategy, with each variable studied at length to determine its effects, allows researchers to systematically determine whether or not a particular intervention (or a part of an overall intervention) is most effective and for whom, since individual subjects may respond differently. As data from these studies accumulate, factors that do and do not influence reading can be addressed, bringing the profession closer to an understanding of how written language is learned for many students across ages. Eventually, it may even be possible to describe characteristics of learners for which specific interventions might be most effective. In this respect, single-subject experimental design can provide literacy researchers with a mechanism for examining the theoretical nature of reading.

Second, single-subject designs have many ecological factors that make them especially useful to literacy researchers. The alternating-treatments design for example, is both an experimentally sound and an efficient method to measure a particular student, or groups of students' performance on a target behavior in classrooms. Following a brief baseline, treatments are alternated randomly, and are continued until one treatment proves to be more effective than the others (or until it is clear than no method is superior to another). During the entire experiment, the learner's performance for each treatment is plotted on a graph, and the effects of the treatments can easily be discerned through visual analysis. These procedures control for many of the intervening threats to the internal validity of a study, such as differential selection of subjects as well as history effects. Yet, unlike many experimental studies where control conditions are required, these procedures are highly compatible with classroom instruction. They can be conducted in the context of instruction, can be targeted to individual learners and their needs, and can provide answers to critical instructional questions in a relatively short time. Further, procedurally, single-subject research is compatible with the aims and ecological variables of teacher research in classrooms (see, e.g., Braithwaite, 1995).

The third, and perhaps the most critical, reason for using single-subject design is the growing complexity of research issues in literacy. Where once a particular research method might have been sufficient to address a research issue, today's questions about literacy interventions often require combinations of designs. There are a number of studies, for example, that use standard group designs along with single-subject design, providing both power in terms of potential generalizability yet specificity in determining whether or not the intervention may be appropriate for different types of learners (see, e.g., Neuman & Gallagher, 1994; Palincsar & Brown, 1984). As systems for inquiry continue to advance, some researchers have suggested the advantages of combining single-subject designs with qualitative research (e.g., Bisesi & Raphael, 1995), as well as linkages to sophisticated statistical, nonparametric, and meta-analytic procedures (see Kamil, 1995; Kratochwill & Levin, 1992). Encompassing features of quantitative research and qualitative research, these combinations of methods help researchers not only to examine whether or not an intervention was successful, but why, how, and for whom.

TECHNICAL ADVANTAGES OF SINGLE-SUBJECT DESIGNS
FOR LITERACY RESEARCH

There are a number of technical advantages for using single-subject methodology to explore a range of questions in literacy today. These include, but are certainly not limited to the following advantages.

Identifying Functional Relationships.   Functional relationships mean that the researcher or teacher has confidence (based on empirical verification) that the behavioral change is due to the intervention and not for other likely reasons (Tawney & Gast, 1984). Single-subject designs add a sophisticated methodology for establishing functional relationships by control over variability in behavior—a central goal of research design (Campbell & Stanley, 1963). Because the intervention (or phases of intervention) is introduced while other variables are held constant, one can isolate a particular phase to determine if it is responsible for changing behavior. This kind of a controlled experiment, therefore, not only can demonstrate that power of an intervention, but also what particular phase was most influential in determining change. For example, in their study of teenage mothers' interactions with their children, Neuman and Gallagher (1994) found that one of three phases—"contingent responsivity," a mother's ability to respond to her child's language request—was particularly influential in increasing the child's active engagement in storybook reading and play. Similarly, in a study designed to improve students' ability to assess their own writing, Marteski (1998) found that two of three phases of intervention (content and mechanics, but not sentence construction), were most responsible for students' writing improvement. Without such experimental control, therefore, we might make the mistake of attributing an improvement in behavior to a total intervention, when in reality the improvement occurred in a particular part of it. Single-subject experimental designs can help investigators avoid such errors.

Exploration of Intersubject Variability.   Another technical advantage of using single-subject designs is the capability to examine variability among subjects. It is long been recognized that children typically defined as "struggling readers" are hardly homogeneous. As teachers can clearly attest, there are differences in degree of difficulty and kind. However, variability among students or their sensitivity to particular types of instruction is rarely examined. Further, the results of intervention studies are based typically on statistically significant improvements for groups, even though some in the group might respond favorably to an intervention, whereas others may not benefit at all.

Single-subject designs circumvent this problem (or if used in combination with other designs, may respond to these concerns). That is, single-subject designs examine a functional relationship between an independent and dependent variable in a single subject, and replicate the experiment for a second, third and fourth time with other subjects. In Marteski's study (1998), for example, replications were conducted with below-average, average, and above-average learners. In each case, the results of self-assessment of content and analysis of writing mechanics showed improvement in writing, indicating that the intervention was effective for all three types of learners. In other cases, however, when variability is observed across replications, the researcher can seek out sources of variability among subjects. Examining the effects of a taped words treatment on reading proficiency, for example, Shapiro and McCurdy (1989) found that the intervention was effective for four of five students, suggesting a limitation for using the strategy more broadly. When such variability is found, the researcher might adjust the intervention and measure it against its previous effectiveness with other subjects, leading to a modified intervention. This type of flexibility may add a critical dimension to our analysis to examine literacy interventions among difference types of struggling readers that is difficult to accomplish in group experimental designs.

Exploration of Intrasubject Variability.   Essentially, single-subject designs involve time-series analyses of repeated measures for each individual subject (McReynolds & Thompson, 1986). Consequently, it allows us to understand the natural variability that occurs for individual students. For example, perhaps a simple intervention like asking students to reread the text before answering questions is highly effective in improving reading comprehension scores immediately. Yet over several weeks, the intervention becomes ineffective for one learner, but not for another. This might suggest that the once-useful strategy for the first student has become overautomaticized, curtailing its usefulness, whereas for another, it becomes more powerful over time.

This variability, readily observed with single-subject design, would not likely be noticed in group experimental designs. Most experimental designs involve only two measurement periods (before and after), and the data that are gathered are averaged across subjects. In contrast, because measurement is ongoing, and analyzed individually, instructional decisions regarding whether or not a particular intervention is effective are dependent on its educational utility, and not on a preconceived time period of how long the intervention should be administered.

Environment for Conducting Studies and Relation to Practice.   Single-subject research studies are best examined in the context in which the behavioral changes are likely to take place. For example, the researcher who is attempting to determine if prompting a child to use a metacognitive strategy, like predicting, might improve the child's comprehension would likely conduct the study in the classroom context, and in the course of guided reading activity rather than in a laboratory study with specialized text. Changes in the child's ability, therefore, would be directly related to the skills and strategies needed to accomplish successful reading in the classroom. Thus, single-subject studies potentially diminish two age-old problems in research: (a) translating research findings into practical settings, and (b) involving children in activity that may take time away from classroom instruction. Rather, single-subject research can be conducted during ongoing instruction, and can use materials for recording and scoring that need not be elaborate. Further, such ongoing assessment has been recommended as a strategy to help teachers better tailor instruction to meet children's individual needs.

PROBLEMS AND POTENTIAL SOLUTIONS IN USING SINGLE-SUBJECT DESIGNS IN LITERACY RESEARCH

Although single-subject design has many advantages for literacy research, there are some limitations. These include methodological problems in the research design and demonstration of experimental control, analysis and reliability of data, and generalization of results.

Research Design and Experimental Control

Experimental control, a key feature of single-subject research, is demonstrated by systematically and repeatedly establishing that changes in behavior covary with changes in an intervention. Consequently, interventions must have discriminatory power from other techniques in the classroom. For example, a special intervention that uses a particular spelling technique must be clearly differentiable from other writing activities that occur on a day-to-day basis, so that any changes in behavior may be attributable to the independent variable rather than to many other activities in the classroom. This suggests that the intervention must be potentially powerful enough to demonstrate reasonably immediate effects. For example, it would not be wise to examine the effects of sustained silent reading (SSR) versus strategic instruction on the percent of time spent reading because it may take multiple sessions before the investigator might observe real changes in the dependent variable on the basis of the treatment.

Further, literacy researchers must be concerned about carryover effect, which may limit the kinds of questions that can be answered using single-subject design research. Consider, for example, the case of contrasting the effects on comprehension recall of a guided visualization strategy with a verbal think-aloud approach during reading. Even with counterbalancing treatments, it may be obvious to the researcher that after several sessions, the guided visualization strategy is being used to organize how the individual might verbally think aloud. In this case, one treatment may ostensibly influence how the other treatment is being used.

These concerns suggest that the researcher who uses these designs carefully select independent variables to avoid contaminating the intervention with another or with ongoing instruction. This may be difficult in studies in which learned behaviors are specifically transferable to other behaviors. Thus, the kinds of questions that can be addressed must be suited to experimental control procedures. Some examples are:

- Effects of oral versus silent reading on reading fluency.
- The impact of a self-assessment strategy on a child's ability to examine strengths and weaknesses of writing.
- Effects of key word method on oral reading.

Analysis and Reliability of Data

Single-subject researchers must be able to provide an operational definition that is precise, exclusive, and clear, for each dependent variable. Because standardized assessments are often not used, reliability of dependent measures is crucial in these studies. Reliability requires that the definition of a dependent variable is targeted and specific to insure appropriate and concise coding of what may constitute a response. Ambiguity cannot exist.

Particularly in the area of literacy research, this may mean that an analysis of one dependent variable is not enough to make a case for an effective intervention. Reading is a construct. Thus, studies that attempt to influence a specific behavior such as comprehension, for example, might include multiple, dependent variables like prediction, recall, and inference that are independent from one another, and could be reliably measured by two or more independent observers. To insure that there is no overlap, however, it is critical to include definitions of variables, and methods used for establishing reliability in all studies, enhancing the confidence of the study results, as well as insuring the possibility of replication.

Generality of Results

Generalizing from a single study, whether it be a group or single-subject design, can be highly problematic. Even in the case of the traditional group experimental design where sampling strategies involve random assignment, findings may have limited generality to any particular individual within the population. Thus, concerns raised about generalizability of single-subject research studies may actually share much in common with other experimental approaches as well.

In practice, some single-subject researchers (see, e.g., Axelrod, 1983) argue that as an applied field, generalizability is not of crucial importance, because the goal is to improve effective teaching for individual students. Others, however, argue for direct, and systematic replications for establishing generalizability (see Palincsar & Parecki, 1995). Direct replication, most often used, involves repeating the intervention with new but similar subjects. To enhance generalization beyond direct replication to individuals who are dissimilar to those included in the original study, however, involves systematic replications. Here, we might involve students that are qualitatively different from those in the original study or in earlier replications, in different settings. This type of replication allows us to answer the question of generality simultaneously across settings and subjects.

The ability to generalize in single-subject research is directly related to the number of replications performed and to the specificity of methodology in the original study. Therefore, authors should be encouraged to incorporate many different replications, as well as to replicate earlier studies.

CONCLUSIONS

Since the 1960s, single-subject experimental research has migrated into a number of fields, including social work, medicine, and education. Articles reporting investigations have appeared in numerous social science journals, with its use seen in both basic and applied research. Still, this research analysis system has not been broadly embraced by the literacy field. There are, however, a number of reasons for considering incorporating single-subject experimental research into the methodological repertoires of literacy investigators because of (a) the efficacy of the methodology, (b) its close ties to practical applications, and (c) the consistency of the approach with current conceptualization about literacy learning and literacy study.

Single-subject experimental research is a sophisticated methodology that, alone or in combination with other methodologies, may address complex literacy issues. It is a research design grounded in scientific logic that can be used for investigation of a wide range of experimental questions. These designs allow us to empirically demonstrate causal relations, responding to the impact that a specific intervention may have on changes in behavior. When used appropriately, single-subject design may provide investigators with an additional methodological tool that is capable of generating new theory and practical application for literacy research.

REFERENCES

Baer, D. M., Wolf, M. M., & Risley, T. (1968). Current dimensions of applied behavior analysis. *Journal of Applied Behavior Analysis, 1*, 91–97.

Barlow, D. H., & Hayes, S. C. (1979). Alternating treatments design: One strategy for comparing the effects of two treatments in a single behavior. *Journal of Applied Behavior Analysis, 12*, 199–210.

Barlow, D. H., & Hersen, M. (1984). *Single case experimental designs* (2nd ed.). New York: Pergamon.

Bellack, L., & Chassan, J. B. (1964). An approach to the evaluation of drug effects during psychotherapy: A double-blind study of a single case. *Journal of Nervous and Mental Disease, 139*, 20–30.

Bianco, L., & McCormick, S. (1989). Analysis of effects of a reading study skill program for high school learning-disabled students. *Journal of Educational Research, 82*, 282–288.

Bisesi, T. L., & Raphael, T. E. (1995). Combining single-subject designs with qualitative research. In S. B. Neuman & S. McCormick (Eds.), *Single-subject experimental research: Applications for literacy* (pp. 104–119). Newark, DE: International Reading Association.

Braithwaite, J. A. (1995). Teachers using single-subject designs in the classroom. In S. B. Neuman & S. McCormick (Eds.), *Single-subject experimental research: Applications for literacy* (pp. 120–136). Newark, DE: International Reading Association.

Campbell, D. T., & Stanley, J. C. (1963). *Experimental and quasi-experimental designs for research.* Chicago: Rand-McNally.

Chassan, J. B. (1960). Statistical inference and the single case in clinical design. *Psychiatry, 23*, 173–184.

Chassan, J. B. (1967). *Research designs in clinical psychology and psychiatry.* New York: Appleton-Century-Crofts.

Cooper, J. O., Heron, T. E., & Heward, W. L. (1987). *Applied behavior analysis.* New York: Macmillan.

Danoff, B., Harris, K. R., & Graham, S. (1993). Incorporating strategy instruction within the writing process in the regular classroom: Effects on the writing of students with and without learning disabilities. *Journal of Reading Behavior, 25*, 295–322.

Gurney, D., Gersten, R., Dimino, J., & Carnine, D. (1990). Story grammar: Effective literature instruction for high school students with learning disabilities. *Journal of Learning Disabilities, 6*, 335–342, 348.

Guza, D. S., & McLaughlin, T. F. (1987). A comparison of daily and weekly testing on student spelling performance. *Journal of Educational Research, 80*, 373–376.

Idol, L., & Croll, V. J. (1987). Story-mapping training as a means of improving reading comprehension. *Learning Disability Quarterly, 10,* 214–229.

Johnston, J. M., & Pennypacker, H. S. (1993). *Strategies and tactics of behavioral research* (2nd ed.). Hillsdale, NJ: Lawrence Erlbaum Associates.

Kamil, M. L. (1995). Statistical analyses procedures for single-subject designs. In S. B. Neuman & S. McCormick (Eds.), *Single-subject experimental research: Applications for literacy* (pp. 84–103). Newark, DE: International Reading Association.

Kazdin, A. E. (1982). *Single-case research designs: Methods for clinical and applied settings.* New York: Oxford University Press.

Kratochwill, T. R., & Levin, J. R. (Eds.). (1992). *Single-case research designs and analysis: New directions for psychology and education.* Hillsdale, NJ: Lawrence Erlbaum Associates.

Kucera, J., & Axelrod, S. (1995). Multiple-baseline designs. In S. B. Neuman & S. McCormick (Eds.), *Single-subject experimental research: Applications for literacy* (pp. 47–63). Newark, DE: International Reading Association.

Lenz, B. K., & Hughes, C. A. (1990). A word identification strategy for adolescents with learning disabilities. *Journal of Learning Disabilities, 23,* 149–158, 160.

Levy, A., Wolfgang, C. H., & Koorland, M. A. (1992). Sociodramatic play as a method for enhancing the language performance of kindergarten age students. *Early Childhood Research Quarterly, 7,* 245–262.

Lipson, M. Y., & Wixson, K. K. (1986). Reading disability research: An interactionist perspective. *Review of Educational Research, 56,* 111–136.

Marteski, F. (1998). *Developing student ability to self assess.* Doctoral dissertation, Temple University, Philadelphia, PA.

McCormick, S. (1995). What is single-subject experimental research? In S. B. Neuman & S. McCormick (Eds.), *Single-subject experimental research* (pp. 1–31). Newark, DE: International Reading Association.

McCormick, S., & Cooper, J. O. (1991). Can SQ3R facilitate secondary learning disabled students' literal comprehension of expository text? *Reading Psychology, 12,* 239–271.

McReynolds, L., & Thompson, C. (1986). Flexibility of single-subject experimental designs. *Journal of Speech and Hearing Disorders, 51,* 194–203.

Mudre, L. H., & McCormick, S. (1989). Effects of meaning-focused cues on underachieving readers' context use, self-corrections, and literal comprehension. *Reading Research Quarterly, 24,* 89–113.

Neuman, S. B. (1995). Alternating-treatments designs. In S. B. Neuman & S. McCormick (Eds.), *Single-subject experimental research: Applications for literacy* (pp. 64–83). Newark, DE: International Reading Association.

Neuman, S. B., & Gallagher, P. (1994). Joining together in literacy learning: Teenage mothers and children. *Reading Research Quarterly, 29,* 383–401.

Neuman, S. B., & McCormick, S. (1995). *Single-subject experimental research: Applications for literacy.* Newark, DE: International Reading Association.

Newby, R. F., Caldwell, J., & Recht, D. (1989). Improving the reading comprehension of children with dysphonetic and dyseidetic dyslexia using story grammar. *Journal of Learning Disabilities, 22,* 373–379.

Palincsar, A. S., & Brown, A. L. (1984). Reciprocal teaching of comprehension-fostering and comprehension-monitoring activities. *Cognition & Instruction, 1,* 117–175.

Palincsar, A. S., & Parecki, A. D. (1995). Important issues related to single-subject experimental research. In S. B. Neuman & S. McCormick (Eds.), *Single-subject experimental research: Applications for literacy* (pp. 137–150). Newark, DE: International Reading Association.

Rose, T. L., & Beattie, J. R. (1986). Relative effects of teacher-directed and taped previewing on oral reading. *Learning Disability Quarterly, 7,* 39–44.

Schumaker, J. B., Deshler, D. D., Alley, G. R., Warner, M. M., & Denton, P. H. (1982). Multipass: A learning strategy for improving reading comprehension. *Learning Disability Quarterly, 5,* 295–311.

Shapiro, E. S., & McCurdy, B. R. (1989). Effects of a taped words treatment on reading proficiency. *Exceptional Children, 55,* 321–325.

Shapiro, M. B. (1961). The single case in fundamental clinical psychological research. *British Journal of Medical Psychology, 34,* 255–263.

Shapiro, M. B. (1966). The single case in clinical-psychological research. *Journal of General Psychology, 74,* 3–23.

Shapiro, M. B., & Ravenette, A. T. (1959). A preliminary experiment of paranoid delusions. *Journal of Mental Science, 105,* 295–312.

Sidman, M. (1960). *Tactics of scientific research: Evaluating scientific data in psychology.* New York: Basic Books.

Tawney, J., & Gast, D. (1984). *Single-subject research in special education.* Columbus, OH: Charles Merrill.

Thorne, F. C. (1947). The clinical method in science. *American Psychologist, 2,* 161–166.

Watson, J. B., & Rayner, R. (1920). Conditioned emotional reactions. *Journal of Experimental Psychology, 3,* 1–14.

Wixson, K. (1993, November). *A review of literacy studies using single-subject design.* Paper presented at the National Reading Conference, Austin, TX.

Wolcott, H. F. (1973). *The man in the principal's office: An ethnography.* Prospect Heights, IL: Waveland Press.

Wolf, M. (1978). Social validity: The case for subjective measurement or how applied behavior analysis is finding its heart. *Journal of Applied Behavior Analysis, 11,* 203–214.

Yaden, D. B. (1995). Reversal designs. In S. B. Neuman & S. McCormick (Eds.), *Single-subject experimental research: Applications for literacy* (pp. 32–46). Newark, DE: International Reading Association.

CHAPTER 9

Discourse and Sociocultural Studies in Reading

James Paul Gee
University of Wisconsin at Madison

This chapter develops an integrated perspective on language, literacy, and the human mind, a perspective that holds important implications for the nature of reading, both cognitively and socioculturally. I start with a brief discussion of the converging areas of study that constitute the background for discourse-based and sociocultural studies of language and literacy. Then, I turn to a particular view of the mind as social, cultural, and embedded in the world. This view of mind implies that meaning is always situated in specific sociocultural practices and experiences. After a discussion of how this notion of *situated meaning* applies to reading, I turn to a discussion of *cultural models*, that is, the often tacit and taken-for-granted, socioculturally specific "theories" through which people organize and understand their situated experiences of the world and of texts. I then discuss how humans enact different identities in distinct forms of spoken and written language conveying distinctive situated meanings and cultural models. I close with a brief discussion of some implications for literacy research and practice.

CONVERGING AREAS

One of the most important recent developments in the study of language and literacy is the way in which a variety of formerly discrete areas are beginning to converge around some central themes. These themes tend to undermine long-standing dichotomies in reading research: for example, dichotomies between cognition and context, skills and meaning, formal structures and communicative functions, and the individual and the social. Some of the converging areas I have in mind, beyond current work in reading research itself (for overviews on reading theory and practice, see, e.g., Adams, 1990; Reutzel & Cooter, 1996), are briefly discussed next:

Ethnomethodology and conversational analysis, with related work in *interactional sociolinguistics* (Duranti & Goodwin, 1992; Goffman, 1981; Goodwin, 1990; Mehan, 1979; Ochs, Schegloff, & Thompson, 1996; Schiffrin, 1994, chap. 4), has argued that social and institutional order is the product of the moment-by-moment intricacies of social and verbal interaction that produce and reproduce that order. "Knowing" is a matter of "knowing how to proceed" ("go on") in specific social interactions. Related work in discursive psychology (Billig, 1987; Edwards & Potter, 1992; Harre & Gillet, 1994; Harre & Stearns, 1995; Shotter, 1993) stressed the ways in which "mental" states (things like remembering, emotion, interpreting, and intending) are not just "in the head," but strategically constructed and negotiated in interaction.

The ethnography of speaking (Gumperz, 1982a, 1982b; Gumperz & Levinson, 1996; Hymes, 1974, 1996) has argued that language in use does not convey general and decontextualized meanings. Rather, participants in interaction use various lexical, structural, and prosodic "cues," in speech or writing, to infer just what context (or part of a context) is relevant and how this context gives words meanings specific to it. The form and meaning of these "contextualization cues" differ across different cultures, even among people from different social groups speaking the same language.

Sociohistorical psychology, following Vygotsky and later Bakhtin (Bakhtin, 1986; Cole, 1996; Engestrom, 1987, 1990; Scribner & Cole, 1981; Vygotsky, 1978, 1987; Wertsch, 1985, 1991, 1997), has argued that the human mind is "furnished" through a process of "internalizing" or "appropriating" images, patterns, and words from the social activities in which one has participated. Further, thinking is not "private," but almost always mediated by cultural tools, that is, artifacts, symbols, tools, technologies, and forms of language that have been historically and culturally shaped to carry out certain functions and carry certain meanings (cultural tools have certain "affordances," although people can transform them through using them in new settings).

Closely related work on *situated cognition* (Hutchins, 1995; Lave, 1988, 1996; Lave & Wenger, 1991; Rogoff, 1990; Rogoff & Lave, 1984; Tharp & Gallimore, 1988), also with an allegiance to Vygotsky, has argued that knowledge and intelligence reside not solely in heads, but rather are distributed across the social practices (including language practices) and the various tools, technologies, and semiotic systems that a given "community of practice" uses in order to carry out its characteristic activities (e.g., part of a physicist's knowledge is embedded and distributed across that person's colleagues, social practices, tools, equipment, and texts). Knowing is a matter of being able to participate centrally in practice, and learning is a matter of changing patterns of participation (with concomitant changes in identity).

Cultural models theory (D'Andrade, 1995; D'Andrade & Strauss, 1992; Holland & Quinn, 1987; Shore, 1996; Strauss & Quinn, 1998), a social version of schema theory, has argued that people make sense of their experiences by applying largely tacit "theories" or "cultural models" to them. Cultural models, which need not be complete or logically consistent, are simplified and prototypical arguments, images, "storylines," or metaphorical elaborations, shared within a culture or social group, that explain why and how things happen as they do and what they mean. These "theories" (which are embedded not just in heads, but in social practices, texts, and other media) guide action, inform judgments of self and others, and shape ways of talking and writing.

Cognitive linguistics (Lakoff, 1987; Lakoff & Johnson, 1980; Ungerer & Schmid, 1996) argues that all human languages are organized in terms of intricate, complex, intersecting, and overlapping systems of metaphors (and related figurative devices). These metaphors shape, in different ways in different cultures, how we interpret our experience and how we think about ourselves and the material, social, and cultural world. For example, in English we often think and talk about argument in ways shaped by how we talk about warfare ("I *defended* my argument and *destroyed* his case at the same time") or talk about minds as if they were enclosed spaces ("He just couldn't get it *into* his head").

The new science and technology studies (Bloor, 1991; Collins, 1992; Collins & Pinch, 1993; Latour, 1987, 1991; Latour & Woolgar, 1986; Mulkay, 1991; Pickering, 1992, 1995; Shapin, 1994; Shapin & Schaffer, 1985) have argued that scientific knowledge is rooted in scientists' day-to-day social practices and distributed across (and stored within) those practices and the characteristic spaces, tools, texts, symbols, and technologies that scientists use. Scientists' day-to-day practices are far more historically, technologically, socially, and culturally conditioned than appears from the "write-up" of their results in books and journals. Scientists' knowledge is a matter of "coordinating" and "getting coordinated by" (in mind and body) colleagues, objects, nature, texts, technologies, symbols, language, and social and instrumental practices.

Modern composition theory (Bazerman, 1989; Berkenkotter & Huckin, 1995; Bizzell, 1992; Faigley, 1992; Myers, 1990; Swales, 1990, 1998) has stressed the ways in which knowledge and meaning are situated within the characteristic talking, writing, acting, and interacting genres (patterns) of disciplines and other specialized domains. These (historically changing) genres create both the conditions for and the limits to what can be said and done in the discipline at a given time and place.

Sociocultural literacy studies *("the new literacy studies":* Barton & Hamilton 1998; Cazden, 1988; Cook-Gumperz, 1986; Gee, 1996; Heath, 1983; Kress, 1985; Scollon & Scollon, 1981; Street, 1984, 1995) have stressed that there are multiple literacies (many different ways of writing and reading connected to ways of speaking and listening), each embedded in specific sociocultural practices and each connected to a distinctive and "political" set of norms, values, and beliefs about language, literacy, and identity (*political* here means that things like power, status, and other social goods are at stake).

Work on *connectionism* (Churchland, 1995; Clark 1989, 1993, 1997; Elman et al., 1996; Gee, 1992; Karmiloff-Smith, 1992; Winograd & Flores, 1989) in cognitive science has argued that humans do not primarily think and act on the basis of mental representations that are general rules or logical propositions. Rather, thinking and acting are a matter of using, and adapting to current circumstances, stored patterns or images of our past experiences. These patterns or images are shaped (edited) by the social, cultural, and personal contexts of those experiences.

Modern sociology (Beck, Giddens, & Lash, 1994; Giddens, 1984, 1987) has stressed the ways in which human thinking, acting, and interaction are simultaneously structured by institutional forces and, in turn, give a specific order (structure, shape) to institutions such that it is impossible to say which comes first, institutions or the human social practices that continually enact and reproduce (and transform) them. Modern sociology has also stressed, as well, the ways in which this reciprocal exchange between human interaction and human institutions is being transformed by global economic and demographic changes such that the nature of time, space, human relationships, and communities is being radically transformed.

Finally, a good deal of so-called *poststructuralist* and *postmodernist* work (e.g., Bakhtin, 1986; Bourdieu, 1979/1984; Fairclough, 1992; Foucault, 1973, 1977), much of it earlier than the movements just discussed, has centered around the notion of *discourses*. Discourses are characteristic (socially and culturally formed, but historically changing) ways of talking and writing about, as well as acting with and toward, people and things (ways that are circulated and sustained within various texts, artifacts, images, social practices, and institutions, as well as in moment-to-moment social interactions) such that certain perspectives and states of affairs come to be taken as "normal" or "natural" and others come to be taken as "deviant" or "marginal" (e.g., what counts as a "normal" prisoner, hospital patient, or student, or a "normal" prison, hospital, or school, at a given time and place).

THE SOCIAL MIND

There are two ways in which the mind is *social*, two ways in which it "leaks" outside the head and into the world. Both have important consequences for reading research and practice. The first way is rooted in the nature of the mind itself. When confronted with data (experience), the human mind is not so much a *rule follower* as a powerful *pattern recognizer* (Clark, 1993, 1997; Gee, 1992). However, given that the world is full of potentially meaningful patterns, and the human mind is adept at finding patterns, something must guide the learner in selecting which patterns to focus on (Elman, 1993; Elman et al., 1996: chap. 6; Gee, 1994). This "guiding something" is the site at which the role of the teacher and "more expert peers," as well as of the curriculum itself, is being redefined in many contemporary reform-based pedagogies (Greeno, 1997).

The second way in which the mind is social is that human thinking is often distributed across other people and various symbols, tools, objects, and technologies. In navigating a large ship, for example, each sailor's cognition is attached to the knowledge of others (who have different sorts of interlocking expertise) and to the "cognition" built into charts, instruments, and technologies. Knowledge is distributed throughout the "system" (Hutchins, 1995). It is not fully coherent or useful if viewed from the perspective of any one decontextualized part of the system. Readers and written texts can often usefully be seen as parts of larger systems, often composed of other people and other sorts of language, symbols, and tools, across which "cognition" is distributed (both in terms of knowledge and values). Such a distributed view of knowledge is at the base of current reform-based classroom "learning communities" (Brown & Campione, 1994; Brown, Collins, & Dugid, 1989).

To say that the mind is a "pattern recognizer" is to say first and foremost that it operates primarily with (flexibly transformable) *patterns* extracted from experience, not with highly general or decontextualized *rules* (Churchland, 1995; Margolis, 1987). It is crucial to note, however, that the patterns most important to human thinking and action follow a sort of "Goldilocks Principle": They are not too general and not too specific. They are *mid-level generalizations* between these two extremes (Barsalou, 1992).

Think about recognizing faces. If you see your friend when she is sick as a different person than when she is well, your knowledge is too specific. If, on the other hand, you see all your female friends as the same, your knowledge is too general. The level at which knowledge is most useful for practice is the level at which you see your friend's many appearances as one person, although different from other people like her. So, too, there is little you can do in physics, if you can only recognize specific refraction patterns: Your knowledge is too specific. There is also little you can effectively do, beyond passing school tests, if all you can do is recite the general theory of electromagnetism: Your knowledge is too general.

Really effective knowledge, then, is being able to recognize, work on, transform, and talk about mid-level generalizations such as, to continue the physics example, "light as a bundle of light waves of different wave lengths combinable in certain specific ways" or "light as particles (photons) with various special properties in specific circumstances" or "light as a beam that can be directed in specific ways for various specific purposes (e.g., lasers)" or "light as colors that mix in certain specific ways with certain specific results." Note the mix of the general and the specific in these patterns.

And it is not just in technical areas like physics that mid-level generalizations are crucial. In everyday life as well, they are the basis of thinking for practice. For example, the word (concept) *coffee* is primarily meaningful as a set of mid-level generalizations that simultaneously define and are triggered by experience: dark-liquid-in-a-certain-type-of-cup; beans-in-a-certain-type-of-bag; grains-in-a-certain-sort-of-tin; berries-on-a-certain-type-of-tree; flavoring-in-certain-type-of-food (Clark, 1989).

Let me call such mid-level generalizations *situated meanings* (later I call them *world-building situated meanings* to distinguish them from other sorts of situated meanings, because they are concerned with *content*). What I have said so far about situated meanings can, however, be misleading. Situated meanings are not static, and they are not definitions (though they are the primary way in which words have meanings in use). Rather, they are flexibly transformable patterns that come out of experience and, in turn, construct experience as meaningful in certain ways and not others. They are always, in fact, adapted (contextualized) to experience in practice (activity).

To see the dynamic nature of situated meanings, imagine the situated meaning (mid-level generalization) you have for a *bedroom* (Clark, 1989; Rumelhart, McClelland, & PDP Research Group, 1986). You conjure up an image that connects various objects and features in a typical bedroom, relative, of course, to your sociocultural experience of bedrooms and homes. Now I tell you to imagine that the bedroom has a refrigerator in it. At once you transform your situated meaning for a bedroom, keeping parts of it, deleting parts of it, and adding, perhaps, things like a desk and a college student.

You can even make up (assemble) situated meanings de novo. For example, say that I tell you to form a meaning for the phrase (concept) *things you would save first in a fire* (Barsalou, 1991). You have no trouble putting together a pattern—again based on your sociocultural experiences—of things like children, pets, important documents, expensive or irreplaceable items, and so forth. You have just invented a mid-level generalization suitable for action, a new concept, one we could even assign a word to, but a concept tied intimately to your sociocultural experiences in the world.

The moral is this: Thinking and using language is an active matter of assembling the situated meanings that you need for action in the world (Barsalou, 1992; Bruner, 1996; Clark, 1996). This assembly is always relative to your socioculturally defined experiences in the world and, more or less, routinized ("normed") by the sociocultural groups to which you belong and with whom you share practices (Gee, 1992). The assembly processes for *coffee* (in "everyday life") and *light* (in physics) are fairly routinized, but even here the situated meanings are adapted each time to the specific contexts they are used in and are open to transformations from new experiences. The situated meanings behind words (concepts) like *democracy, honesty, literacy,* or *masculine* are, of course, less routinized.

SITUATED MEANINGS IN READING

The theoretical notion of situated meanings is a dynamic (connectionist-inspired) and contextualized version of *schemas* (D'Andrade, 1995), a notion that has, for many years now, played a major role in reading research, theory, and practice (Anderson & Pearson, 1984; Rumelhart, 1980). The idea of situated meanings is highly consequential when applied not just to social practices generally, but to the specific social practices in which written texts play a major role. Let me give two examples. The first is relevant to the current worldwide controversy over *genre* in theory and pedagogical practice (Cope & Kalantzis, 1993; Hasan & Williams, 1996).

The names of genres—just like the word *light*—have a spurious generality. We do not operate (effectively) at the (overly) general level of *report, explanation, argument, essay, narrative,* and so forth. Rather, we operate at the "next level down," so to speak (a level at which we have no simple labels). For example, in certain academic fields, things like *an essay review, a theoretical piece, a research-based journal article,* and *an overview of the literature (a review article)* are the situated meanings of genre labels. The "real" genres we work with exist between overly general labels like *article* or *essay* and specific concrete instantiations of writing. Furthermore, genres, as situated meanings, must be flexibly fit to and transformed by the actual contexts in which they are used (remember the bedroom example earlier).

The same is true of the writing and reading that children do at all levels of schooling. Children (like all writers and readers) operate at the next level down from things like *narrative in general* or *reports in general*. They need to operate with mid-level instantiations of types-of-narratives-(or reports)-for-types-of-contexts-for-types-of-purposes, whether these have "official" labels or not. They need to be exposed to multiple examples of these, examples that display the sorts of variations that occur even within a "type" for the purposes of "best fit" to context and purpose (remember our *bedroom* example, again). Children need, as well, overt guidance to focus on the features of language and context that help them recognize and produce the "right" situated meanings (mid-level patterns)—that is, those shared by the community of practice to which they are being "apprenticed."

My second example comes from a study by Lowry Hemphill (1992) investigating how high school students from different socioeconomic backgrounds read various canonical works of literature. In the case I consider here, the students were reading Robert Frost's poem "Acquainted With the Night." One girl, whom I call Maria, responded to the line *I have passed by the watchman on his beat* as follows:

> I think he's trying to say that though he [has] like seen the sadder situations. And the watchman meaning I would think a cop was on his daily routine. The watchman still couldn't stop the situation that was happening. Which was probably something bad. Or you know dishonest. But he still was able to see what was going on.

And then to the line *And dropped my eyes unwillingly to explain*:

> Oh well this line's making me think that well the watchman caught him. And he was ashamed of what he was doing. And he didn't want to explain his reasons for his own actions to the watchman. Cause he was so ashamed.

Another girl, whom I call Mary, responded to her reading of the poem, in an essay, as follows (I cite only parts of the essay):

> Figuratively, Frost is describing his life....
>
> In the third stanza, he says "I have stood still...." Maybe he has stopped during his walk of life and heard people with different paths or lives calling him but he later finds they were not calling him after all.
>
> There is a slight undertone of death in the last two or three lines. The clock symbolizing the time he has left. The clock telling him that he can't die yet however much he may want to.
>
> ... the reader, if he looks closely can see past the words on the paper and into Robert Frost's soul.

In reading, we recognize situated meanings (mid-level generalizations/patterns/inferences) that lie between the "literal" specifics of the text and general themes that organize the text as a whole. These situated meanings actually mediate between these two levels. In the Frost poem, Maria uses (recognizes) situated meanings like "Something bad is happening and an authority figure can't stop it," "One avoids authority figures if and when one has done something bad," "An authority figure catches one doing something bad and one is ashamed." Mary uses (recognizes) situated meanings like "Choosing among different paths through a landscape is like making different decisions in one's life" or "Time passing as shown by things like clocks is like the passing of time in a life as one ages."

Maria and Mary have seen different patterns in Frost's poem, in terms of which they situate its meanings. We see later, too, that the girls are reading out of different "theories" of reading and different "theories" of literature. These "theories" are constructed out of the different sorts of situated meanings the girls find and, in turn, these theories lead them to find these situated meanings in the text.

CULTURAL MODELS

Confronted with situated meanings, it is natural to ask why words (concepts), like *light* or *coffee*, seem to us, in fact, to have much more general meanings. Part of the answer is simply the fact that a single word exists, and we are misled by this to think that a single, general meaning exists. But another and more important part of the answer is that words are tied to "cultural models," "storylines," or "theories" that "belong" to socioculturally defined groups of people (Bruner, 1996; D'Andrade & Strauss, 1992; Holland & Quinn, 1987; Strauss & Quinn, 1998). These cultural models, storylines, or theories "explain" (relative to the standards of the sociocultural group) why the features in the mid-level patterns "hang together" in the way they do (Gee, 1994). Furthermore, these cultural models, storylines, or theories are usually not stored in any one person's head, but are distributed across the different sorts of "expertise" and viewpoints found in the sociocultural group (Shore, 1996).

The storyline connected to *coffee* for some of us is something like: Berries are picked and then prepared as beans or grain to be made later into a drink, as well as into flavorings for other foods. Different types of coffee, drunk in different ways, have different social and cultural implications, for example, in terms of status. This is about all of the storyline I know—the rest of it (I trust) is distributed elsewhere in the society should I need it. The storyline for *light* in physics is a formal theory, a theory distributed across physicists of different sorts, as well as across written texts and instruments (and it is quite different from the cultural model of light that many people use in their everyday lives).

Cultural models, storylines, and theories organize the thinking and work of sociocultural groups (or "communities of practice"). They "rationalize" the situated meanings and practices that people in those groups use. They are part (but only part) of what defines the group in the first place.

Consider Maria and Mary again. They operate with different cultural models (theories) of what it is to read Frost's text, models tied to the allegiances they have (or are forming) to specific "communities of practice" (Cranny-Francis, 1996; Martin, 1996; Wenger, 1999). Maria appears to operate with a cultural model of reading (at least in this situation) that finds significance in relating the words of the text to situated meanings (patterns) that she finds in her "everyday" life, keeping in mind that what counts as "everyday life" differs for different sociocultural groups of people. In her world, if people are out late at night and avoiding contact with authority figures, they are, in all likelihood, in trouble. Her cultural model of reading seems also to stress social contacts and relationships between people. Maria reads from her own experience to the words and back again to her social experience.

Mary appears to operate with a cultural model of reading (in this situation) that finds significance in treating concrete details and actions as "correlates" for more universal emotions and themes. Patterns in the world (e.g., paths through landscapes, clocks telling time) are correlated with emotions or themes. Mary's "theory of reading," of course, was quite explicitly delineated by people like T. S. Eliot and William Carlos Williams, among other canonical (Anglo) modernists (Perkins, 1976). Hemphill (1992) found that students like Maria fared less well than students like Mary in English classes, although, in fact, both ways of reading (one out of narrative schemas and the other out of figurative schemas) have been celebrated in the reading literature (Reutzel & Cooter, 1996).

The pedagogical bite of all this discussion about situated meanings and cultural models is this: Any efficacious pedagogy must be a judicious mixture of *immersion* in a community of practice (Lave, 1996) and *overt focusing* and scaffolding from "masters" or "more advanced peers" (Vygotsky, 1987) who focus learners on the most fruitful sorts of patterns in their experience ("fruitful" for developing the cultural models that are used by the community of practice to which the learner is being "apprenticed"). Just what constitutes a "judicious mixture," in different settings, is a cutting-edge topic for research (Cazden, 1992). Fights over "rich immersion (e.g., whole language) as against "overt instruction" (e.g., phonics) are, as dichotomies, irrelevant and meaningless (other than politically).

WHO AND WHAT: FURTHER SITUATED MEANINGS

So far I have argued that language is given meaning-in-use through its association with situated meanings, cultural models, and the sociocultural groups that socialize learners into these. But there are two other sorts of situated meanings that language always involves just as much as the "world-building" ones we have discussed thus far.

In addition to "world-building situated meanings" (content), any utterance communicates what I call a *who* and a *what* (Wieder & Pratt, 1990; see also Edwards & Potter, 1992; Harre & Gillett, 1994; Shotter, 1993). What I mean by a *who* is a socially situated place (position) from which the utterance is "authorized" and issued (and these are not always the same). With written texts, this *who* may or may not be a person or, at least, a single person (it may, for instance, be an institution). What I mean by a *what* is a socially situated activity or practice that the utterance helps (with other nonlanguage "stuff") to constitute.

To understand the meaning of any piece of language, written or oral, then, we must grasp the situated world-building, *who*, and *what* meanings the language communicates. In turn, we "grasp" these situated meanings (if we do) because we have participated in worldly and sociocultural experiences from which they emerge and which they, in turn, define and transform (Duranti & Goodwin, 1992; Gumperz & Levinson, 1996; Hanks, 1995; Scribner & Cole, 1981; Wertsch, 1991).

Let me give a specific example. Biologists and other scientists write differently in professional journals than they do in popular science magazines, and these different ways of writing construct different worlds, accomplish different activities (social practices), and display different identities. It is in understanding these that we come to understand the texts. Consider, then, the two extracts that follow, the first from a professional journal, the second from a popular science magazine, both written by the same biologist on the same topic (examples from Myers, 1990):

> Experiments show that *Heliconius* butterflies are less likely to oviposit on host plants that possess eggs or egg-like structures. These egg-mimics are an unambiguous example of a plant trait evolved in response to a host-restricted group of insect herbivores. (professional journal, p. 150)

> *Heliconius* butterflies lay their eggs on *Passiflora* vines. In defense the vines seem to have evolved fake eggs that make it look to the butterflies as if eggs have already been laid on them. (popular science, p. 150)

The first extract, from a professional scientific journal, is about the conceptual structure of a specific theory within the scientific discipline of biology. The subject of the initial sentence is *experiments*, a methodological tool in natural science. The subject of the next sentence is *these egg-mimics*: Note how plant parts are named, not in terms of the plant itself, but, rather, in terms of the role they play in a particular *theory* of natural selection and evolution, namely, "coevolution" of predator and prey (i.e., the theory that predator and prey evolve together by shaping each other). Note also, in this regard, the earlier *host plants* in the preceding sentence, rather than the "vines" of the popular passage.

In the second sentence, the butterflies are referred to as *a host-restricted group of insect herbivores*, which points simultaneously to an aspect of scientific methodology (like *experiments* did) and to the logic of a theory (like *egg-mimics* did). Any scientist arguing for the theory of coevolution faces the difficulty of demonstrating a causal connection between a particular plant characteristic and a particular predator when most plants have so many different sorts of animals attacking them. A central methodological technique to overcome this problem is to study plant groups (like *Passiflora* vines) that are preyed on by only one or a few predators (in this case, *Heliconius* butterflies). *Host-restricted group of insect herbivores* then refers both to the relationship between plant and insect that is at the heart of the theory of coevolution and to the methodological technique of picking plants and insects that are restricted to each other so as to "control" for other sorts of interactions.

The first passage is concerned with scientific methodology and a particular theoretical perspective on evolution. On the other hand, the second extract, from a popular science magazine, is not about methodology and theory, but about *animals* in *nature*. The butterflies are the subject of the first sentence and the vine is the subject of the second. Further, the butterflies and the vine are labeled as such, not in terms of their role in a particular theory.

The second passage is a story about the struggles of insects and plants that are transparently open to the trained gaze of the scientist. Further, the plant and insect become "intentional" actors in the drama: the plants act in their own "defense" and things "look" a certain way to the insects; they are "deceived" by appearances as humans sometimes are.

These two examples replicate in the present what, in fact, is a historical difference. In the history of biology, the scientist's relationship with nature gradually changed from telling stories about direct observations (seeing) of nature to carrying out complex experiments to test complex theories (Bazerman, 1989) and manage uncertainty (Myers, 1990). This change was caused, in part, by the fact that mounting "observations" of nature led scientists not to consensus but to growing disagreements as to how to describe and explain such observations (Shapin & Schaffer, 1985). "Seeing" became more and more mediated by theory and technology. This problem led, in turn, to the need to convince the public that such uncertainty did not damage the scientist's claim to be able to "see" and know the world in some relatively direct way, a job now carried out by much "popular science" writing.

This example tells us two things: First, texts (and language generally) are always connected to different *worlds* (here the "nature-as-lab" vs. "nature as open to the gaze"), different *whos* (here the experimenter/theoretician vs. the careful observer of nature), and different *whats* (the professional contribution to science and the popularization of it). Second, such worlds ("content"), *whos*, and *whats* are licensed by specific socially and historically shaped practices representing the *values* and *interests* of distinctive groups of people. To be able to read (and write) such worlds, *whos*, and *whats* requires one to understand such practices with their concomitant values and interests. If we can use the term *politics* to mean any place where social interests and social goods are at stake, then all reading (and writing) is political in a quite straightforward sense (Fairclough, 1995; Gee, 1996).

In texts (and, indeed, in all social activity) particular patterns of world-building, *whos*, and *whats* become recognizable as betokening a particular sociocultural group or *community of practice*. People (as speakers/listeners and as writers/readers) coordinate their words, deeds, values, and feelings with those of other people, as well as with the "affordances" of various spaces, objects, symbols, tools, and technologies, to create a kind of socioculturally meaningful "dance" (Latour, 1991). A particular coordination becomes the "dance" of certain types of (but not all) biologists or gang members or "greens" or elementary school students or students of history or teachers or Native Americans or executives or lawyers, and so on and so forth through a nearly endless list.

I have elsewhere (Gee, 1992, 1996, 1999) called these socioculturally meaningful "dances" (recognizable coordinations of people, places, objects, tools, technologies, and ways of speaking, listening, writing, reading, feeling, valuing, believing, etc.) *Discourses* (with a capital D; *discourse* with a little d just stands for language in use). In terms of our earlier example, thanks to the workings of history, "popular science" is a somewhat different "dance" (though with some, but not all, of the same people, places, and tools) than "professional science."

For those interested in reading and writing, it is important to note, as well, that the very form of language is always an important part of Discourses. The form of the language in the professional passage about butterflies above differs in a systematic way from the form of the language in the popular passage: for example, abstract versus concrete subjects (e.g., *experiments* vs. *butterflies*), technical versus nontechnical terms (e.g., *oviposit* vs. *lay*), complex noun phrases versus simple noun phrase (e.g., *host-restricted group of insect herbivores* vs. Heliconius *butterflies*), nominalizations versus nonderived noun phrases (e.g., *egg-mimics* vs. *fake eggs*), copulative verbs versus more contentful verbs (e.g., *are* vs. *lay*), and so forth.

These formal differences, rather then being random, "hang together" (or "co-relate") with each other to form a pattern that instantiates a particular *function*, that is, the communication of specific sorts of worlds, *whos*, and *whats*. For historical, social, linguistic, and cognitive reasons, a given co-related set of forms (like the partial list for "professional science" given earlier), is apt for this function, and this function is "married" to this set of forms (Halliday & Martin, 1993; Kress, 1996; Kress & van Leeuwen, 1996, pp. 5–12; Olson, 1996). To appreciate this "aptness" and this "marriage" is the heart and soul of acquiring the "code" in reading and writing, at all levels, from phonics to genre to Discourse (Adams, 1990).

IMPLICATIONS

A Discourse-based, situated, and sociocultural view of literacy demands that we see reading (and writing and speaking) as not one thing, but many: many different socioculturally situated reading (writing, speaking) practices. It demands that we see meaning in the world and in texts as situated in learners' experiences, experiences that, if they are to be useful, must give rise to mid-level situated meanings through which learners can recognize and act on the world in specific ways. At the same time, these experiences must be normed and scaffolded by "masters" and "more advanced peers" within a Discourse, and such norming and scaffolding must lead "apprentices" to build the "right" sorts of situated meanings based on shared experiences and shared cultural models. Minus the presence of masters of the Discourse, such norming and scaffolding is impossible. Such "sharing" is always, of course, ripe with ideological and power effects, and, it leads us always to ask of any school-based Discourse: In what sense is this Discourse *authentic*, that is, how and where does it relate to Discourses outside school (e.g., science, work, communities)? In the end, *to read* is to be able to actively assemble situated meanings in one or more specific "literate" Discourses. There is no "reading in general," at least none that leads to thought and action in the world.

REFERENCES

Adams, M. J. (1990). *Learning to read: Thinking and learning about print.* Cambridge, MA: MIT Press.
Anderson, R. C., & Pearson, P. D. (1984). A schema-theoretic view of basic processes in reading. In P. D. Pearson (Ed.), *Handbook of reading research*, (pp. 255–291). New York: Longman.
Bakhtin, M. M. (1986). Speech genres and other essays. Austin: University of Texas.

Barsalou, L. W. (1991). Deriving categories to achieve goals. In G. H. Bower (Ed.), *The psychology of learning and motivation: Advances in research and theory* (Vol. 27, pp. 1–64). New York: Academic Press.

Barsalou, L. W. (1992). *Cognitive psychology: An overview for cognitive scientists.* Hillsdale, NJ: Lawrence Erlbaum Associates.

Barton, D., & Hamilton, M. (1998). *Local literacies: Reading and writing in one community.* London: Routledge.

Bazerman, C. (1989). *Shaping written knowledge.* Madison: University of Wisconsin Press.

Beck, U., Giddens, A., & Lash, S. (1994). *Reflexive modernization: Politics, traditions and aesthetics in the modern social order.* Stanford, CA: Stanford University Press.

Berkenkotter, C., & Huckin, T. N. (Eds.). (1995). *Genre knowledge in disciplinary communication.* Hillsdale, NJ: Lawrence Erlbaum Associates.

Billig, M. (1987). *Arguing and thinking: A rhetorical approach to social psychology.* Cambridge: Cambridge University Press.

Bizzell, P. (1992). *Academic discourse and critical consciousness.* Pittsburgh: University of Pittsburgh Press.

Bloor, D. (1991). *Knowledge and social imagery* (2nd ed.). Chicago: University of Chicago Press.

Bourdieu, P. (1984). *Distinction: A social critique of the judgement of taste.* Cambridge, MA: Harvard University Press. (Original work published 1979)

Brown, A. L., & Campione, J. C. (1994). Guided discovery in a community of learners. In K. McGilly (Ed.), *Classroom lessons: Integrating cognitive theory and classroom practice* (pp. 229–270). Cambridge, MA: MIT Press.

Brown, A. L., Collins, A., & Dugid, P. (1989). Situated cognition and the culture of learning. *Educational Researcher, 18,* 32–42.

Bruner, J. (1996). Frames for thinking: Ways of making meaning. In D. Olson & N. Torrance (Eds.). *Modes of thought: Explorations in culture and cognition* (pp. 93–105). Cambridge: Cambridge University Press.

Cazden, C. (1988). *Classroom discourse: The language of teaching and learning.* Portsmouth, NH: Heinemann.

Cazden, C. (1992). *Whole language plus: Essays on literacy in the United States and New Zealand.* New York: Teachers College Press.

Churchland, P. M. (1995). *The engine of reason, the seat of the soul.* Cambridge, MA: MIT Press.

Clark, A. (1989). *Microcognition: Philosophy, cognitive science, and parallel distributed processing.* Cambridge, MA: MIT Press.

Clark, A. (1993). *Associative engines: Connectionism, concepts, and representational change.* Cambridge: Cambridge University Press.

Clark, A. (1997). *Being there: Putting brain, body, and world together again.* Cambridge, MA: MIT Press.

Clark, H. H. (1996). *Using language.* Cambridge: Cambridge University Press.

Cole, M. (1996). *Culture in mind.* Cambridge, MA: Harvard University Press.

Collins, H., & Pinch, T. (1993). *The golem: What everyone should know about science.* Cambridge: Cambridge University Press.

Collins, H. M. (1992). *Changing order: Replication and induction in scientific practice* (2nd ed.). Chicago: University of Chicago Press.

Cook-Gumperz, J. (Ed.). (1986). *The social construction of literacy.* Cambridge: Cambridge University Press.

Cope, B., & Kalantzis, M. (Eds.). (1993). *The powers of literacy: A genre approach to teaching writing.* Pittsburgh: University of Pittsburgh Press.

Cranny-Francis, A. (1996). Technology and/or weapon: The discipline of reading in the secondary English classroom. In R. Hasan & G. Williams (Eds.), *Literacy in society* (pp. 172–190). London: Longman.

D'Andrade, R. (1995). *The development of cognitive anthropology.* Cambridge: Cambridge University Press.

D'Andrade, R., & Strauss, C. (Eds.). (1992). *Human motives and cultural models.* Cambridge: Cambridge University Press.

Duranti, A., & Goodwin, C. (Eds.). (1992). *Rethinking context: Language as an interactive phenomenon.* Cambridge: Cambridge University Press.

Edwards, D., & Potter, J. (1992). *Discursive psychology.* London: Sage.

Elman, J. L. (1993). Learning and development in neural networks: The importance of starting small. *Cognition, 48,* 71–99.

Elman, J. L., Bates, E. A., Johnson, M. H., Karmiloff-Smith, A., Parisi, D., & Plunkett, K. (1996). *Rethinking innateness: A connectionist perspective on development.* Cambridge, MA: MIT Press.

Engestrom, Y. (1987). *Learning by expanding: An activity-theoretical approach to developmental research.* Helsinki: Orienta-Konsultit.

Engestrom, Y. (1990). *Learning, working and imagining: Twelve studies in activity theory.* Helsinki: Orienta-Konsultit.

Faigley, L. (1992). *Fragments of rationality: Postmodernity and the subject of composition.* Pittsburgh: University of Pittsburgh Press.

Fairclough, N. (1992). *Discourse and social change.* Cambridge: Polity Press.

Fairclough, N. (1995). *Critical discourse analysis.* London: Longman.

Foucault, M. (1973). *The birth of the clinic: An archaeology of medical perception.* New York: Vintage.

Foucault, M. (1977). *Discipline and punish: The birth of the prison.* New York: Pantheon.

Gee, J. P. (1992). *The social mind: Language, ideology, and social practice.* New York: Bergin & Garvey.

Gee, J. P. (1994). First language acquisition as a guide for theories of learning and pedagogy. *Linguistics and Education, 6,* 331–354.

Gee, J. P. (1996). *Social linguistics and literacies: Ideology in Discourses* (2nd ed.). London: Taylor & Francis.

Gee, J. P. (1999). *An introduction to discourse analysis: Theory and method.* London: Routledge.

Giddens, A. (1984). *The constitution of society: Outline of the theory of structuration.* Cambridge: Polity Press.

Giddens, A. (1987). *Social theory and modern sociology.* Stanford, CA: Stanford University Press.

Goffman, I. (1981). *Forms of talk.* Philadelphia: University of Pennsylvania Press.

Goodwin, M. H. (1990). *He-said-she-said: Talk as social organization among black children.* Bloomington: Indiana University Press.

Greeno, J. G. (1997). Response: On claims that answer the wrong questions, *Educational Researcher, 26,* 5–17.

Gumperz, J. J. (1982a). *Discourse strategies.* Cambridge: Cambridge University Press.

Gumperz, J. J. (Ed.). (1982b). *Language and social identity.* Cambridge: Cambridge University Press.

Gumperz, J. J., & Levinson, S. C. (Eds.). (1996). *Rethinking linguistic relativity.* Cambridge: Cambridge University Press.

Halliday, M. A. K., & Martin, J. R. (1993). *Writing science: Literacy and discursive power.* Pittsburgh: University of Pittsburgh Press.

Hanks, W. F. (1995). *Language and communicative practices.* Bolder, CO: Westview Press.

Harre, R., & Gillett, G. (1994). *The discursive mind.* Thousand Oaks, CA: Sage.

Harre, R., & Stearns, P. (Eds.). (1995). *Discursive psychology in practice.* London: Sage.

Hasan, R., & Williams, G. (Eds.). (1996). *Literacy in society.* London: Longman.

Heath, S. B. (1983). *Ways with words: Language, life and work in communities and classrooms.* Cambridge: Cambridge University Press.

Hemphill L. (1992, September). *Codeswitching and literary response.* Paper presented at the conference on literacy and identity, Carlisle, MA: Carlisle Education Center.

Holland, D., & Quinn, N. (Eds.). (1987). *Cultural models in language and thought.* Cambridge: Cambridge University Press.

Hutchins, E. (1995). *Cognition in the wild.* Cambridge, MA: MIT Press.

Hymes, D. (1974). *Foundations in sociolinguistics: An ethnographic approach.* Philadelphia: University of Pennsylvania Press.

Hymes, D. (1996). *Ethnography, linguistics, narrative inequality: Towards an understanding of voice.* London: Taylor & Francis.

Karmiloff-Smith, A. (1992). *Beyond modularity: A developmental perspective on cognitive science.* Cambridge, MA: MIT Press.

Kress, G. (1985). *Linguistic processes in sociocultural practice.* Oxford: Oxford University Press.

Kress, G. (1996). *Before writing: Rethinking paths into literacy.* London: Routledge.

Kress, G., & van Leeuwen, T. (1996). *Reading images: The grammar of visual design.* London: Routledge.

Lakoff, G. (1987). *Women, fire, and dangerous things.* Chicago: University of Chicago Press.

Lakoff, G., & Johnson, M. (1980). *Metaphors we live by.* Chicago: University of Chicago Press.

Latour, B. (1987). *Science in action.* Cambridge, MA: Harvard University Press.

Latour, B. (1991). *We have never been modern.* Cambridge, MA: Harvard University Press.

Latour, B., & Woolgar, S. (1979). *Laboratory life.* London: Sage.

Lave, J. (1988). *Cognition in practice.* Cambridge: Cambridge University Press.

Lave, J. (1996). Teaching, as learning, in practice. *Mind, Culture, and Activity, 3,* 149–164.

Lave, J., & Wenger, E. (1991). *Situated learning: Legitimate peripheral participation.* Cambridge: Cambridge University Press.

Margolis, H. (1987). *Patterns, thinking, and cognition: A theory of judgment.* Chicago: University of Chicago Press.

Martin, J. R. (1996). Evaluating disruption: Symbolizing theme in junior secondary narrative. In R. Hasan & G. Williams (Eds.), *Literacy in society* (pp. 124–171). London: Longman.

Mehan, H. (1979). *Learning lessons.* Cambridge, MA: Harvard University Press.

Mulkay, M. (1991). *Sociology of science: A sociological pilgrimage.* Bloomington: Indiana University Press.

Myers, G. (1990). *Writing biology: Texts in the social construction of scientific knowledge.* Madison: University of Wisconsin Press.

Ochs, E., Schegloff, E. A., & Thompson, S. A. (Eds.). (1996). *Interaction and grammar.* Cambridge: Cambridge University Press.

Olson, D. (1996). Literate mentalities: Literacy, consciousness of language, and modes of thought. In D. Olson & N. Torrance (Eds.), *Modes of thought: Explorations in culture and cognition* (pp. 141–151). Cambridge: Cambridge University Press.

Perkins, D. (1976). *A history of modern poetry: From the 1880s to the high modernist mode.* Cambridge, MA: Harvard University Press.

Pickering, A. (Ed.). (1992). *Science as practice and culture.* Chicago: University of Chicago Press.

Pickering, A. (1995). *The mangle of practice: Time, agency, and science.* Chicago: University of Chicago Press.

Reutzel, D. R., & Cooter, R. B., Jr., (1996). *Teaching children to read: From basals to books* (2nd ed.). Englewood Cliffs, NJ: Prentice Hall.

Rogoff, B. (1990). *Apprenticeship in thinking: Cognitive development in social context.* New York: Oxford University Press.

Rogoff, B., & Lave, J. (Eds.). (1984). *Everyday cognition: Its development in social context.* Cambridge, MA: Harvard University Press.

Rumelhart, D. E. (1980). Schemata: The building blocks of cognition. In R. Spiro, B. Bruce, & W. Brewer (Eds.), *Theoretical issues in reading comprehension* (pp. 33–58). Hillsdale, NJ: Lawrence Erlbaum Associates.

Rumelhart, D. E., McClelland, J. L., & PDP Research Group (1986). *Parallel distributed processing: Explorations in the microstructure of cognition (Vol. 1): Foundations.* Cambridge, MA: MIT Press.

Schiffrin, D. (1994). *Approaches to discourse.* Chicago: University of Chicago Press.

Scollon, R., & Scollon, S. B. K. (1981). *Narrative, literacy, and face in interethnic communication.* Norwood, NJ: Ablex.

Scribner, S., & Cole, M. (1981). *The psychology of literacy.* Cambridge, MA: Harvard University Press.

Shapin, S. (1994). *A social history of truth: Civility and scient in seventeenth-century England.* Chicago: University of Chicago Press.

Shapin, S., & Schaffer, S. (1985). *Leviathan and the air-pump: Hobbes, Boyle and the experimental life.* Princeton, NJ: Princeton University Press.

Shore, B. (1996). *Culture in mind: Cognition, culture, and the problem of meaning.* New York: Oxford University Press.

Shotter, J. (1993). *Cultural politics of everyday life.* Toronto: University of Toronto Press.

Strauss, C., & Quinn, N. (1998). *A cognitive theory of cultural meaning.* Cambridge: Cambridge University Press.

Street, B. (1984). *Literacy in theory and practice.* Cambridge: Cambridge University Press.

Street, B. (1995). *Social literacies: Critical approaches to literacy development, ethnography, and education.* London: Longman.

Swales, J. M. (1990). *Genre analysis: English in academic and research settings.* Cambridge: Cambridge University Press.

Swales, J. M. (1998). Textography: Toward a contextualization of written academic discourse. *Research on Language and Social Interaction, 31,* 109–121.

Tharp, R., & Gallimore, R. (1988). *Rousing minds to life: Teaching, learning, and schooling in social context.* Cambridge: Cambridge University Press.

Ungerer, F., & Schmid, H.-J. (1996). *An introduction to cognitive linguistics.* London: Longman.

Vygotsky, L. S. (1978). *Mind in society: The development of higher psychological processes.* Cambridge, MA: Harvard University Press.

Vygotsky, L. S. (1987). *The collected works of L. S. Vygotsky (Vol. 1): Problems of general psychology. Including the volume Thinking and speech.* (R. W. Rieber & A. S. Carton, Eds.). New York: Plenum Press.

Wenger, E. (1999). *Communities of practice: Learning, meaning, and identity.* Cambridge: Cambridge University Press.

Wertsch, J. V. (1985). *Vygotsky and the social formation of mind.* Cambridge, MA: Harvard University Press.

Wertsch, J. V. (1991). *Voices of the mind: A sociocultural approach to mediated action.* Cambridge, MA: Harvard University Press.

Wertsch, J. V. (1997). *Mind as action.* Oxford: Oxford University Press.

Wieder, D. L., & Pratt, S. (1990). On being a recognizable Indian among Indians. In D. Carbaugh (Ed.), *Cultural communication and intercultural contact* (pp. 45–64). Hillsdale, NJ: Lawrence Erlbaum Associates.

Winograd, T., & Flores, F. (1989). *Understanding computers and cognition.* Reading, MA: Addison-Wesley.

CHAPTER 10

Research Synthesis: Making Sense of the Accumulation of Knowledge in Reading

Timothy Shanahan
University of Illinois at Chicago

Research synthesis has a long and distinguished history in reading research, although formal methods for conducting such inquiry have been formulated only recently. Perhaps no research paradigm is perceived to be as immediately applicable to policy and practice, nor is as widely misunderstood, as synthesis research. This chapter provides a brief history of synthesis research in reading, and a sketch of some of its basic methodological techniques and interpretive issues.

The term *research synthesis*, as well as its synonyms *integrative review, research integration,* and *literature review,* refer to those methods of inquiry used to derive generalizations from the collective findings of a body of existing studies. A fundamental notion of scientific inquiry is that knowledge accumulates. No single investigation is sufficient for creating a full understanding of any complex phenomena, and we thus need systematic ways for constructing insights and understandings from the findings of a multiplicity of studies. Synthesis methodology allows for a systematic and replicable analysis of extant research studies. By pooling the results of a collection of investigations, we can draw more reliable conclusions, resolve discrepancies and contradictions, and become more fully cognizant of the contexts that influence the phenomena of interest. Research synthesis is an essential part to knowledge building within the research process, and it is fundamental to the idea of applying research to issues of practice and policy.

Literature reviews tend to be of two very different types, and the confusion of these often leads to misunderstandings. The first type of review serves as an adjunct to empirical studies, such as the background sections of published research or the second chapters of doctoral and master's theses. Thesis reviews tend to be more comprehensive than the background sections of published studies, but their purposes are the same. These reviews place the author's investigation within the context of relevant findings and methods, and the reviews are subordinate to the empirical studies that they accompany. This kind of review helps make the case for a study or method, but rarely relies on systematic methods or concludes with independent research findings.

A second type of literature review sets out to test hypotheses or to formulate new generalizations for policy, practice, or research. It is these reviews that are the focus of this chapter. Such reviews are published in research journals devoted solely to research synthesis, such as *Review of Educational Research, Psychological Bulletin,* and *Review of Research in Education,* or in various research handbooks and encyclopedias of educational research including the *Handbooks of Reading Research, Handbook of Research on Teaching Literacy Through Communicative and Visual Arts* (Flood, Heath, & Lapp, 1997), and the *Handbook of Research on Teaching the English Language Arts* (Flood, Jensen, Lapp, & Squire, 1991). They also might appear as books, or in research journals that publish a wider variety of studies, such as *Reading Research Quarterly.* Such reviews are best thought of as independent research efforts, and are not simply rhetorical adjuncts to new empirical efforts. These reviews are research studies in that they systematically collect, analyze, and evaluate data in order to determine answers to the researchers' questions. The data that must be collected and analyzed for synthesis research consists of the universe of relevant studies that have already been conducted. Research syntheses, as independent research studies, are held to the same evaluative standards used with other forms of research.

Another important distinction should be made, this one between qualitative and quantitative research reviews. Quantitative reviews pool data from the original or primary studies and statistically analyze the effects of contextual factors and confounds on the dependent measures of interest. Because of their reliance on rigorously documented and standardized procedures, quantitative reviews are replicable. Conversely, qualitative or narrative reviews provide a more intuitive description and analysis of research findings, and are more dependent on researchers' judgment and insight than on a well-defined collection of analytic techniques. Throughout the history of the study of reading, research integration has been a qualitative pursuit. At their best, narrative reviews have been perceptive and useful, but such efforts are being supplanted or supplemented by more organized and explicitly defined quantitative techniques such as meta-analysis, as well as by more rigorous qualitative approaches. Quantitative or meta-analytic approaches are less likely than narrative reviews to miss subtle, but key, relationships (Cooper, Door, & Bettencourt, 1995; Cooper & Rosenthal, 1980). The term *integrative* review is probably more often applied to quantitative than qualitative reviews, but this is not consistent, probably because both types of review are ultimately integrative in nature. Many of the more recent research integration efforts published in reading have tended to use quantitative analysis or some combination of quantitative and qualitative techniques.

HISTORY OF RESEARCH SYNTHESIS IN READING

Empirical research studies in reading date back to the 1870s with the eye movement investigations of Javal (1879), mental measurements studies of Cattell (1886), and studies of reading disability (Morgan, 1896). By 1908, enough information had accumulated so that Edmund Burke Huey found it useful to review the studies. There were so few up to that time (fewer than 40) that Huey was able to carry out a nearly comprehensive analysis of existing research (Huey, 1908/1968).

By the 1920s, William S. Gray began to guide the future accumulation of research studies in reading with the first publication of *Summary of Investigations Relating to Reading* (1925). This work, not much more than an annotated list of 436 studies, first appeared as a monograph issued by the University of Chicago Press. Subsequently, it was released annually by the *Elementary School Journal* (1926–1932), the *Journal of Educational Research* (1933–1960), the *Reading Teacher* (1961–1964), *Reading Research Quarterly* (1965–1979), and finally as a monograph again, this time from the International Reading Association (1980–1997). The later summaries were compiled by Helen M. Robinson and Samuel Weintraub, and they included information on approximately 1,000 new reports on reading each year. The summaries were of great significance to research synthesis as they made accessible the findings of a diverse collection of works relevant to reading, including those drawn from physiology and psychology, sociology, and education. The usefulness of the Gray collection was eventually superceded by the advent, beginning in 1966, of the Educational Resources Information Clearinghouse (*ERIC*), an index of articles, books, and unpublished papers on a wide variety of educational topics. Once *ERIC*, along with several other indexing services, were computerized, allowing greater and more systematic access to the accumulation of research, subscriptions to the *Summary of Investigations Relating to Reading* dwindled, and it was eventually brought to an end.

Gray also published several literature reviews himself. Like Huey before him, Gray's summaries attempted to make sense of the entire scope of research on reading, rather than emphasizing a particular topic or issue. These works—for example, his landmark review "Reading" that appeared in the *Encyclopedia of Educational Research* (1941/1984)—were more like compendia or summaries of disparate studies than critical integrative analyses. Still, as Guthrie (p. vii) wrote in the preface to the republication of that review, "Gray anticipated the trend for research synthesis as a basis of research generalization."

Also significant in the history of reading instruction were the several volumes of reviews prepared by the National Society for the Study of Education (NSSE). The NSSE yearbooks, particularly volumes 20 (Whipple, 1921), 24 (Whipple, 1925), 36 (Gray, 1937), 47 (Henry, 1948), 48 (Henry, 1949), 60 (Henry, 1961), and 67 (Robinson, 1968), were widely distributed and were influential of practice and research in reading. The syntheses published in these volumes were often cited in the teacher preparation textbooks and journals of the time, and guided contemporary research efforts. A later volume on reading instruction (Purves & Niles, 1984) seems to have been less influential, probably due to the availability of other syntheses. NSSE also published literacy-relevant reviews on the teaching of English (Brown, 1906), composition (Hudelson, 1923), adult reading (Henry, 1956), the teaching of English (Squire, 1977), linguistics (Marckwardt, 1970), writing (Petrosky & Bartholomae, 1986), and reading-writing relationships (Nelson & Calfee, 1998).

The early reliance on syntheses of research in education is interesting. The 24th volume of the NSSE yearbooks is a case in point. It was prepared not by NSSE, but by a National Committee on Reading that emerged from a 1922 meeting of school superintendents. The synthesis was to provide "recommendations concerning debatable issues in the field of reading, based on experimental evidence, as far as possible, and on expert opinion when evidence was lacking" (Whipple, 1925, p. v). Not only did this report provide 12 specific research-based recommendations for instruction, but it raised 38 research questions that it indicated to be "in urgent need of investigation." The 47th NSSE yearbook was undertaken, similarly, in response to a letter from William S. Gray that "suggested that changing conceptions of the role of reading … indicate the need of a yearbook providing an authoritative interpretation of the significance of new knowledge and of emerging problems in the area" (Henry, 1949, p. v). These efforts, especially that of 1922, appear to prefigure the recent synthesis panels formed by the National Research Council (Snow, Burns, & Griffin, 1998) and the U.S. Congress (http://www.nationalreadingpanel.org).

To a great extent, the *Handbooks of Reading Research* (Barr, Kamil, Mosenthal, & Pearson, 1991; Pearson, Barr, Kamil, & Mosenthal, 1984), of which this chapter is an entry in volume 3, have replaced the NSSE yearbooks as a widely used source of "authoritative interpretation" of research on reading. After examining the substantial accumulation of research studies in reading, Robert Dykstra (1984, p. xix), in his forward to the first volume of the *Handbook*, wrote, "What has been lacking, however, is a comprehensive analysis and interpretation of this rich cumulative data base. The *Handbook of Reading Research* fills this void admirably."

One final source of useful research syntheses in reading should be noted. The National Reading Conference selects a researcher to conduct and report a topical review of research at its annual meeting. These reviews have considered metacognition, reading–writing connections, social organization of reading instruction, and a number of other issues and have been published annually in the *NRC Yearbook* since 1989.

Since the earliest reviews by Huey and Gray, many research reviews in reading have been published. These syntheses have been more focused, integrative, and analytic than those earlier inventories. Nevertheless, as in other fields (Dunkin, 1996), the value of existing literature reviews has sometimes been undercut by subjective and biased procedures. It is due to the recognition of such limitations that synthesists are increasingly adopting more systematic procedures. This is not to say that no worthwhile syntheses preceded the recent formulation of such methods. Table 15.1 provides a summary list of 25 particularly influential literature reviews in reading. To compile

TABLE 10.1
Twenty-Five Influential Research Syntheses in Literacy

Adams, M. J. (1990). *Beginning to read*. Cambridge, MA: MIT Press.

Anderson, R. (1996). Research foundations to support wide reading. In V. Greaney (Ed.), *Promoting reading in developing countries* (pp. 55–77). Newark, DE: International Reading Association.

Anderson, R., Hiebert, E. Scott, J. A., & Wilkinson, I. A. G. (1985). *Becoming a nation of readers: The report of the Commission on Reading*. Washington, DC: National Institute of Education.

Barr, R. (1997). Reading teacher education. *Handbook of research on teaching* (4th ed.). Washington, DC: American Educational Research Association.

Carver, R. (1990). *Reading rate*. San Diego, CA: Academic Press.

Chall, J. S. (1967). *Learning to read: The great debate*. New York: McGraw-Hill.

Clay, M. (1991). *Becoming literate: The construction of inner control*. Portsmouth, NH: Heinemann.

Corder, R. (1971). *The information base for reading: A critical review of the information base for current assumptions regarding the status of instruction and achievement in reading in the United States*. Berkeley, CA: ETS. (ED 054 922)

Curtis, M. E. (1997). Teaching reading to children, adolescents, and adults: Similarities and differences. In L. R. Putnam (Ed.), *Readings in language and literacy: Essays in honor of Jeanne S. Chall* (pp. 37–54). Cambridge, MA: Brookline Books.

Davis, F. B. (1971). *The literature of research in reading with emphasis on models*. New Brunswick, NJ: Rutgers University Press.

Hiebert, E., & Raphael, T. (1996). In D. C. Berliner & R. C. Calfee (Eds.), *Handbook of educational psychology* (pp. 550–602). New York: Macmillan.

Hillocks, G., Jr. (1987). *Research on written composition*. Urbana, IL: National Conference on Research in English.

Hoetker, J., & Ahlbrand, W. P., Jr. (1969). The persistence of recitation. *American Educational Research Journal, 6, 145–167.*

Klare, G. M. (1963). *The measurement of readability*. Ames: Iowa State University Press.

(Continues)

TABLE 10.1 (Continued)

Lysynchuk, L. M., Pressley, M., d'Ailly, H., Smith, M., & Cake, H. (1989). A methodological analysis of experimental studies of comprehension strategy instruction. *Reading Research Quarterly, 24,* 458–470.

Moore, D. (1996). Contexts for literacy in secondary schools. In D. J. Leu, C. K. Kinzer, & K. A. Hinchman (Eds.), *Literacies for the 21st century: Research and practice. Forty-fifth Yearbook of the National Reading Conference* (pp. 15–46). Chicago: National Reading Conference.

Rosenshine, B., & Meister, C. (1994). Reciprocal teaching: A review of the research. *Review of Educational Research, 64,* 479–530.

Shanahan, T., & Barr, R. (1995). Reading Recovery: An independent evaluation of the effects of an early instructional intervention for at-risk learners. *Reading Research Quarterly, 30,* 958–997.

Singer, H., & Ruddell, R. (1976). *Theoretical models and processes of reading* (2nd ed.). Newark, DE: International Reading Association. (The 1st, 3rd, and 4th editions were also frequently cited).

Stahl, S. A., & Miller, P. D. (1989). Whole language and language experience approaches for beginning reading: A quantitative research synthesis. *Review of Educational Research, 59,* 87–116.

Stanovich, K. E. (1986). Matthew effects in reading: Some consequences of individual differences in the development of reading fluency. *Reading Research Quarterly, 21,* 360–406.

Sticht, T. G., Beck, L. J., & Hauke, R. N. (1974). *Auding and reading: A developmental model.* Alexandria, VA: Human Resources Research Organization.

Vellutino, F. R. (1979). *Dyslexia: Theory and research.* Cambridge, MA: MIT Press.

Wade, S. (1983). A synthesis of the research for improving reading in the social studies. *Review of Educational Research, 53,* 461–497.

Wagner, R. K., & Torgesen, J. K. (1987). The nature of phonology: Processing. *Psychological Bulletin, 101,* 192–212.

these, I invited the members of the Reading Hall of Fame to nominate reviews that they thought to be particularly excellent or significant in the history of reading. From these nominations, I culled a representative list, omitting the many mentions of the NSSE yearbooks and *Handbooks of Reading Research.* Another listing of 41 exemplary literature reviews in reading has been developed on the basis of citation frequency (Guthrie, Seifert, & Mosberg, 1983). The use of formal, systematic methods of review and analysis should increase the probability of producing syntheses that are this useful.

CONDUCTING SYNTHESIS RESEARCH

The fundamental idea behind modern research synthesis is that the review should rise above authoritative opinion. That is, synthesis research strives for clear selection standards in the identification of relevant research, explicit criteria for judgments, operational definitions, and replicability of methods. Research syntheses, in other words, should be conducted and reported in the fashion of other empirical studies as they are empirical studies in their own right. The need for unbiased approaches is possibly even more important with synthesis studies, as it has been found that scholars use or cite them at substantially higher rates than they do other empirical works (Garfield, 1989). It has also been found that reading research syntheses accomplish higher citation rates than other reviews of educational research (Guthrie et al., 1983).

The following four sections provide a brief synopsis of the fundamental procedures and issues of conducting a literature synthesis with regard to identification and selection of studies; description and classification of study characteristics; analysis of the findings of the primary studies; and reporting the results. For a more complete treatment of all of these topics, as well as several other related issues, readers are encouraged to turn to *The Handbook of Research Synthesis* (Cooper & Hedges, 1994) and *Meta-Analysis in Social Research* (Glass, McGaw, & Smith, 1981).

Identification and Selection of Studies

The validity or trustworthiness of any study is highly dependent on the soundness of the procedures used to construct the data. When a researcher collects too little data to allow reasonable generalizations, or collects data in a manner that biases the results, we have little trouble rejecting the findings of the work. Synthesis studies should be held to the same standards of research practice, although evidence suggests that this often has not been the case (Cooper, 1995; Dunkin, 1996; Jackson, 1980; Sohn, 1995). The "data" collected and analyzed in research synthesis are the characteristics and findings of the studies being synthesized, and from these data, generalizations to the population of all studies of that phenomenon are made. Integrative reviews that fail to consider key studies or that systematically bias the outcomes toward particular results will mislead practice and policy decisions.

Fortunately, over the past two decades, a number of search strategies and tools have emerged that can increase the systematicity, thoroughness, and replicability of literature reviews, and the use of these strategies is on the increase (White, 1994). These approaches can be summarized under the categories of formulating questions, identifying key terms, conducting a systematic search, and selecting studies for analysis.

Formulating Questions.   Light and Pillemer (1984) stressed the importance of formulating research questions that have sufficient precision to structure the search and to guide the eventual synthesis of results. The researcher must initially decide whether the questions are to be general (What do we know about phonemic awareness?), or specific (What is the average effect of teaching comprehension strategies on reading achievement?). If the questions are to be general, then it is essential that a wide net be cast initially, to ensure the identification of appropriate materials; it seems particularly advisable to search both within and across disciplines. Green (1992), for instance, described how researchers in pursuit of information about "communicative competence" found relevant studies within four disciplines: anthropology/ethnography of communication, child language/psycholinguistics, social psychology, and sociology. At times, even with more specific and constraining questions, a researcher might profitably draw information from more than one discipline, although the specificity of the questions is likely to reduce the need for this to some extent.

The specificity of the original questions will depend on what the researcher already knows, but as the process proceeds the nature of the questions will often change, depending on what information is in the literature. Researchers may begin with fairly global or general questions about a phenomenon, but as they proceed through the literature, they will often uncover more specific questions. This seems especially likely when a graduate student is conducting an initial review on a topic, or when a more experienced scholar is branching out into a new area of interest. For example, in a synthesis on Reading Recovery (Shanahan & Barr, 1995), we began with questions about program effectiveness, but added questions about the differences in that program between New Zealand and the United States. We also became sensitive to the issues of program cost that had been raised in a number of papers, and developed questions on this aspect of the program as well.

Rarely does a scholar write a review in an area in which he or she has not already developed substantial knowledge and even conducted his or her own empirical work. Some exceptions to this are invited reviews or the reviews conducted by graduate students. However, even in the more typical case in which the scholar has substantial prior knowledge, it is wise for the researcher to go beyond his or her own individual perspective by considering the state of knowledge in the field as described in extant authoritative summations. This aids the refinement of the synthesis questions, and can be essential in the next stages of the search, particularly in identifying key terms that will allow for a systematic search. As White (1994) aptly stated, "The point is not to track down every paper that is somehow related to the topic.... The point is *to avoid missing a useful paper that lies outside one's regular channel purview,* thereby ensuring that one's habitual channels of communication will not bias the results of studies obtained by the search" (p. 44). It is reasonable to use what one knows, but our research approaches help us to get beyond our own narrow perspectives.

Reading is particularly fortunate as a scholarly field in that it has a rich collection of authoritative summations that can be used as a jumping-off point for literature reviews. Some key resources are *The Handbooks of Reading Research, The Literacy Dictionary* (Harris & Hodges, 1995), *The Encyclopedia of English Studies and Language Arts* (Purves, 1994), and the *Handbook of Research on Teaching the English Language Arts* (Flood et al., 1991). There are various encyclopedias and handbooks of research in the areas of curriculum, education, teaching, and teacher education that also contain review chapters on reading. The researcher should also seek out previous reviews that have been written on the topic of interest. Jackson (1980) highlighted the importance of building on existing reviews, and was critical of how often integrative reviews neglect such information. I recently wrote a review on tutoring in reading, and was surprised to find that 11 published reviews already existed on this topic, many from the field of special education—a literature that I do not examine regularly (Shanahan, 1998). There were also reviews on reading tutoring that predated my own interest in the topic, as well as those that focused on tutoring of other subjects that I found to be helpful. The availability of these syntheses saved me a lot of time, and helped focus the questions that I set out to answer.

Identifying Key Terms.   Some search strategies, such as looking through the journals to which you subscribe, do not require the identification of key terms. The researchers, in such a case, know what they want and can adjust the boundaries of the search to include whatever they choose. Unfortunately, such haphazard approaches will be biased and unreplicable. Truly systematic approaches, on the other hand, require that the researcher identify key terms—terms that other researchers could use—to find the relevant work. The identification and use of key terms within reading education is, at this time, still more art than science, as consistency of use and match of terms with constructs are not as precise as in some fields of study. Are *phonemic awareness* and *phonological awareness* the same? What about *auditory discrimination*? Does *critical reading* include *inferencing*, or is that a separate construct? What is the term that is used to describe classroom organizations in which students stay with one teacher over multiple years?

The value of examining previous reviews and other summative materials has already been considered. Additionally, there are various indices for identifying key terms in research. The most useful of these sources for those in reading are likely to be the *Thesaurus of ERIC Descriptors, Thesaurus of Psychological Index,* and *Thesaurus of Sociological Indexing.* These not only help to identify subject terms that are used to organize the information contained in the computerized databases, but they also show relationships among terms and provide historical information about the use of terms. For example, the *ERIC* system did not begin to use the term *reading–writing relationships* until 1982. To identify studies of the integration of reading and writing completed prior to that time will require different search terms or strategies. Finally, it is useful to identify two or three studies early on that are exactly what you seek. These can be found through prior knowledge, access to the "invisible college" (i.e., an informal network of researchers doing work on a particular topic), informal analysis of journals, or by conducting a preliminary computer search. Once these locator studies have been identified, locate them in the indexing sources to find out what key terms were used to place them within the information systems; the use of these terms should sharpen the search strategy.

The use of these indexing terms to conduct subject searches can be problematic, however. The system of indexing is fallible, highly dependent on the judgment of a reference librarian who might not adequately understand the contents of a given study or the study author who might lack a complete grasp of potential indexing terms. Given this limitation, subject searching alone will fail to uncover many potentially valuable studies. To guard against this, the researcher can conduct *keyword searches* or natural language searches, in which all studies are identified that use particular terms in the title or abstract or even in the entire document, no matter how the document itself is indexed in the system. These procedures overcome the noted indexing problems and increase comprehensiveness, but they give up a great deal of precision and add to the cost of the synthesis in terms of researcher time.

Most computerized information systems, such as *PsycINFO* or *ERIC,* are capable of carrying out Boolean searches. This means that the researcher can use terms such as *or, and,* and *not* to identify intersections and unions among various research terms and to thereby refine the search. So, for example, if researchers want to identify all studies of either *word analysis* or *phonics,* they would search for: *word analysis OR phonics.* The use of *or* in this context will find all studies indexed under either term, but it will only find a single instance of the doubles, a real time saver for the researcher. Or, if the search descriptors were *reading comprehension AND vocabulary,* the search would result only in those studies that had used both of these terms, and would omit any study that focused only on reading comprehension or only on vocabulary. Increasingly, various search tools provide electronic interfaces that can make these Boolean searches easier and more transparent. A search of *word analysis,* for example, in the *Ovid* system will result in a listing of related terms that the researcher can check off if they are to be added to the search. The current list for *word analysis* includes *reading instruction, oral reading, phonemes,* and *phonics,* and allows me to choose to search for *word analysis* as a keyword rather than a subject. In this case, I neither have to know all of the related terms already nor is it necessary for me to type in a bunch of *or* terms between the choices.

However, at least for now, it is essential that the researcher understand the logic of Boolean searches, as current search aids are still pretty primitive. A researcher might be interested in only examining studies of *word analysis* that have been conducted with particular age or grade levels or types of populations; these delimiters will not come up automatically in the newer systems, but still can be used to narrow down the population of potential studies. Terms such as *preschool, teacher education, adolescents,* and *immigrants* can be used to refine our search even though none of these are obviously related to *word analysis* or hundreds of other topics in reading. The use of this approach can also help a researcher to overcome the limitations of the *ERIC* system, which does not focus entirely on research. *ERIC* often includes curriculum guides and other materials that are not the result of empirical study. When searching *ERIC* for research studies, it can be helpful to use the word *research* or *reading research* as a subject to limit the numbers of nonrelevant items identified. This strategy cannot profitably be used with other major indexes, as those tend to include few items that are not empirical studies.

Conducting a Systematic Search.   "Every past study does not have an equal chance of being retrieved by the reviewer" (Light & Pillemer, 1984, p. 295). Systematic search techniques can help to prevent the bias caused by unequal access to various studies. Given the goal of accurately representing the research, it is essential that the synthesis analyze a representative collection of pertinent studies. As has been noted, representativeness is even more important than comprehensiveness, although obviously the more comprehensive a search, the less possibility there is that it could be nonrepresentative (Jackson, 1980). Still, it is possible to miss key information, even with a thorough search. Kamil and colleagues (Kamil & Intrator, 1999; Kamil & Lane, 1998) in studying the technology and reading literature found that many relevant studies had been omitted systematically by the electronic search tools. A large number of the studies on this topic had appeared in newer journals not yet represented in the databases, and these tools also omitted recent publications as it takes time for indexing. They used hand searching to supplement their electronic search to compensate for such omissions.

The lack of any clear way to specify a complete population of studies has plagued, and will continue to plague, synthesis research. As Jackson (1980, p. 444) indicated, "There is no way of ascertaining whether a set of *located* studies is representative of the full set of *existing* studies on the topic." There are many reasons for this. In an applied field like reading, it can be difficult to know which disciplines to search within, although even when confined to a single discipline there will be no complete list of all of the published works, not to mention the unpublished ones. *ERIC* includes contents from approximately 700 journals, but even this listing omits several relevant research journals.

A more serious concern, and one that has received much attention, is the so-called *file drawer problem* (Rosenthal, 1979). Not every piece of research is published, and unpublished studies have been found to be systematically different than published ones. Generally, published studies are of somewhat higher quality, but they also have a greater tendency toward statistical significance. That this is a form of bias is pointedly illustrated by Greenwald (1975), who found that about 50% of researchers would submit their work for publication if they found statistically significant results, but only about 6% would do so if the results were nonsignificant. A comparison of published studies with unpublished doctoral dissertations found a substantially greater tendency (a difference of about one-third standard deviation) for journal articles to report significant differences (Glass et al., 1981). Thus, it is not surprising that some experts would reason that "the likelihood of the Type I error [the error of concluding significant differences when no such differences exist] is inestimably greater in the case of the literature review than in the case of the empirical study" (Sohn, 1995, p. 109).

Because of this bias toward significance, it is usually advisable to synthesize more than published research. Because the *ERIC* system includes unpublished technical reports and conference papers—including documents produced by the various national centers for research on reading, writing, and adult literacy—it can be a good source for expanding the search pool. *PsycINFO* is also a useful resource in this regard as it includes non-English-language studies and unpublished doctoral dissertations. The latter are best examined through *Dissertation Abstracts International*, which includes a broad collection of dissertation studies from fields such as engineering, natural sciences, and divinity, each of which, surprisingly, includes reading studies. The inclusion of a more representative sample of studies, including those with findings of nonsignificant differences, will lead to sounder conclusions and more specific understandings of the relationships under examination. However, when only published studies are to be reviewed, it is essential that the researcher explicitly note the bias inherent in the sampling procedure as a potential limitation of the synthesis.

White (1994) described five major modes of searching: searches in subject searchers, footnote chasing, consultation, browsing or hand searching, and citation searches. Each of these strategies has wide use (Cooper, 1995), and each presents particular problems for the researcher trying to avoid bias. Given the differences in the various approaches, a combination of strategies will be most powerful. Combined approaches are more likely to lead to a more comprehensive and representative population of research studies.

The use of various subject searchers, especially electronic ones, is particularly powerful. A large number of journal entries and other documents have been indexed since 1966, and *ERIC, PsycINFO, Wilson Social Science Abstracts*, and similar databases have made it possible for the researcher to sort through tens of thousands of documents in a matter of minutes. As of June 1999, *ERIC* listed 134,538 documents on reading, writing, and literacy, and *PsycINFO* included an overlapping set of 43,222 (different entry points—CD-ROM, various Internet connections to the electronic systems—can result in different numbers of references). Often a researcher relies on only a single searcher. This can be a mistake. Even though there is redundancy among the searchers, each retrieves a different pattern of data. This variation is partly due to the fact that each database references a different list of sources. However, differences also result because of variations in terminology or precision of terminology usage. In any event, searches in different databases lead to different results. For instance, the term *reciprocal teaching* results in 134 documents in *ERIC*, and 88 in *PsycINFO; expository writing* leads to 1,322 hits in *ERIC* and 53 in *PsycINFO;* and *readability* results in 2,517 and 713 hits, respectively. It is not just that the numbers of documents differ either, as the overlap among these searches varies and is sometimes quite low (Glass et al., 1981). Other searchers tend to have even less overlap, and their use can lead to the location of items that might be missed with a single searcher.

But what of "fugitive," or hard to find, literature? As has been noted, *ERIC* includes unpublished work, and *Dissertations Abstracts International* is a good source for doctoral dissertations. Other sources can help identify research presented at conferences. The *Cambridge Scientific Abstracts* provides listings of conference program presentations since 1973, and the *Index to Social Sciences and Humanities Proceedings* is a guide to published conference proceedings (this latter source provides an indexed listing of the studies published in *National Reading Conference Yearbook*, but it does not include papers presented at the International Reading Association or American Educational Research Association as neither publishes proceedings). When conference papers of this type are found it is usually necessary to contact the scholars who produced the work to obtain a copy. Studies—even published ones—that predate the development of computerized search tools are becoming a form of fugitive literature. The *Educational Index,* a noncomputerized database, is available for searching educational research by topic or author as far back as 1929. Finally, research published in book or chapter form should not be neglected either, so a Library of Congress search of books will be helpful at least in some cases. Other sources for finding fugitive literature are detailed in Rosenthal (1994).

Once a computerized search has been conducted, and the relevant studies have been found, what White (1994) has labeled "footnote chasing" becomes possible. A researcher should comb the references in these studies to identify additional sources. This allows the researcher to uncover a variety of citation networks, extends the search back in time, and helps locate unpublished materials. A researcher can carry such a search back as many "generations" as seems to have value. Cooper (1982) claims that such tracking has a tendency to favor the identification of published work, and that it is used infrequently by researchers (Cooper, 1995) despite its effectiveness.

Researchers develop networks of contact among various parts of the scholarly community. The reliance on these networks can help identify work that might be unobtainable in any other way, but it can also be a source of bias. Novice researchers are more likely to use computerized databases and, consequently, their syntheses tend to be more comprehensive, whereas senior scholars rely more extensively on the narrower information drawn from their networks of colleagues (Cooper, 1995). It is not that senior researchers should avoid using the "invisible college," only that they should do so in less biased and more replicable ways. The search strategies already noted should result in the identification of relevant research articles and the names of key researchers. It is useful to consult with these key researchers, to obtain copies of their unpublished materials and to request any related bibliographies that they may have developed. Although making such contacts can be forbidding to the novice, researchers usually comply with such requests (Garvey & Griffith, 1979).

Studies can also be found by browsing journals and books. Researchers do this with the journals that they subscribe to or read regularly. Green and Hall (1984) recommend a more systematic browsing that requires going through the "best" journals, year by year, page by page, to find relevant materials. There is always a certain amount of lag time between publication and inclusion of a study in the various indexes, so browsing can identify especially recent materials that might be neglected if only a computerized index were used. Browsing is reasonable, however, only when there is a chance "to find a relatively high concentration of things one is looking for" (Wilson, 1992, p. 51). For instance, in one review, we examined the reference lists of all articles and chapters in the most highly cited journals and books in reading and writing, including all of the journals published by major professional organizations (Shanahan & Kamil, 1994). Such an approach can expand the comprehensiveness of the search, and can be repeated by other researchers. The examination of books that have been grouped together by the Library of Congress can similarly help identify relevant materials (White, 1994).

Finally, citation searches are useful under certain circumstances. Although researchers rarely examine the *Social Science Citation Index (SSCI)* in their integrative searches (Cooper, 1995), these can pull in a vast array of material. Unlike the footnote or reference tracking approaches noted earlier in which the researcher traces the reference lists for previous studies, here the researcher works in the opposite direction. If I know, for instance, that someone has conducted an earlier study, *SSCI* allows me to seek articles and chapters conducted since that time that have cited this study. Citation searches only work when there is a primary research study to begin from. Citation searches tend to end up with a lot of "noise"—that is, they identify many irrelevant items as various researchers might cite an article for different purposes. Such searches are most helpful when you can only identify one or two key studies, or when you have reason to believe that the other search strategies will fail to identify key work.

Selecting Studies for Inclusion.   Not all of the studies that are identified will necessarily be included in the final synthesis. Arguments about inclusion usually turn on two issues: quality and relevance (Wortman, 1994). The quality issue concerns whether studies can suffer from flaws so fundamental that their inclusion in a synthesis will mislead more than enlighten. Slavin (1986) argues for "best evidence syntheses" in which only studies of high quality are included to ensure valid conclusions. By this method the researcher systematically sets aside results obtained from badly flawed studies, and draws conclusions based on only the best evidence. This seems reasonable, unless the selection procedures systematically excludes results that run counter to the synthesist's perspective.

Glass has probably been the most vocal proponent of including all identified studies in a review: "To make these decisions *a priori* may inject arbitrariness and bias into the conclusions" (Glass et al., 1981, p. 67). Glass is not unaware of the problems posed by the differential quality of various studies. However, he believes that the most serious problems in past literature reviews have been due to bias, and such qualitative judgment is an easy way to introduce such bias. The researcher who claims to have selected only the best studies might be, surreptitiously or unconsciously, choosing those conducted from a particular perspective or with a particular outcome. Instead of making unstudied judgments of this type, Glass proposes that such limitations be coded and treated as measurable sources of variation in study outcomes. Rather than throwing out particular studies due to their limitations, we should try to use these studies to figure out if an intervention appears to do better when the treatment is kept brief or when there was no pretest. Methods for such analysis are described in the next section of this chapter.

An examination of recent reviews suggests that most reviewers are more selective than Glass recommends. In any event, contemporaneous reviews are more *systematically* selective than older ones. Increasingly, they include descriptions of the decision rules or procedures for selection. Usually the synthesizer establishes standards that specify essential reporting features or research procedures. If these standards are not met, then the study is excluded. Standards might require that the report include certain statistics (i.e., numbers of participants, lengths of treatment, means and standard deviations), or that certain research characteristics be apparent (i.e., pre- and posttest measures, control group, random assignment). As long as care is taken not to use such procedures to omit studies with discrepant results, these approaches seem quite reasonable. In my analysis of studies of tutoring in reading (Shanahan, 1998), I wanted to focus only on studies that reported group means and standard deviations. The tutoring literature includes many studies that used single-subject designs, however, and they report outcomes differently than what I had envisioned analyzing. Under these circumstances, it was essential that I analyze these studies separately to determine whether they had a different pattern of results. I could not omit these studies until I had determined that both types of research were in agreement about the effectiveness of tutoring. If they disagreed, then I would have needed to report the discrepancy and try to explain it. I should not just define the difference away through my selection criteria, however.

Light and Pillemer (1984) suggested that another valid approach to the selection of appropriate studies is to use a panel of experts to make the selection. This has been common in medical synthesis or for integrative studies conducted by the General Accounting Office, and it is now beginning to appear in syntheses of reading (Snow et al., 1998). Such an approach seems sound, if it accomplishes a reliable result from a panel that accurately reflects the various competing perspectives. The idea of using more than a single selector of studies, and providing some numerical estimate of interevaluator agreement, would go a long way to protecting the findings against arbitrariness (Wanous, Sullivan, & Malinak, 1989). Whatever approach is taken, it is important that clear selection criteria be used, and that these be established prior to the examination of the data (Light & Pillemer, 1984).

Given the techniques that have been recommended here, a word of caution should be noted. When seeking literature in multiple places, the researcher will often find multiple studies by the same author. Care must be taken when selecting from these, to ensure that the same data are not being counted again and again (Dunkin, 1996). Such double counting increases the influence of these data in a manner that reduces the validity of the report. When there is a question about the separability of data from different analyses, the author of the original reports should be contacted.

A final note on the selection of studies has to do with the relevance criteria. Everyone agrees that only relevant studies should be reviewed. Unfortunately, educational research is undermined by its reliance on an imprecise lexicon. What is comprehension? How do you distinguish emergent literacy and beginning reading? No matter how certain your answers to such questions, be assured that at least some of your colleagues will differ in their use of these terms. This is especially true with regard to operational definitions of abstract terms; for instance, can we combine the results of reading comprehension studies that measure improvements on cloze tests and summarization, or are these different? Because of this, it is possible for researchers to disagree about the relevance of certain types of studies.

Qualitative researchers (Green, 1992; Masterman, 1970) have developed rigorous analytic procedures that are useful for determining the similarities and differences in the use of lexical terms. By carefully noting each use or operationalization of a term by a given researcher, and by conducting a semantic feature analysis of these usages, it is possible to determine whether various measures or definitions reflect the same underlying ideas. Such charts or maps can then be used in the selection process itself, or in the coding processes that are next described. The use of such procedures within meta-analytic syntheses would go a long way to meeting the criticisms that such approaches often combine apples and oranges.

Description and Classification of Study Characteristics

Meta-analysis, "the statistical analysis of the summary findings of many empirical studies" (Glass et al., 1981, p. 21), is the most thorough and systematic of integrative review techniques in its consideration of the influence of study characteristics on outcomes. However, it is fair to say that all literature reviews provide at least some consideration of the influence of such factors, although they tend to do so more subjectively. No matter what approach is used to analyze the data, the researcher should develop a rigorous system for describing and classifying the characteristics of studies under review so that relationships among key variables can be determined.

"A well-designed coding scheme is more likely if the synthesizer knows both the research domain and research integration methods, because this knowledge provides the basis for making critical choices" (Stock, 1994, p. 126). Stock recommends the use of seven categories for classifying study features: *report identification* (e.g., author, country, year, source of publication, coder of study); *setting* (e.g., scope of sampling, involvement of special populations, climate characteristics, subject matter); *subjects* (e.g., demographics, cognitive abilities); *methodology* (e.g., subject assignment, source of data, treatment of missing data); *treatment* (e.g., theoretical orientation, components of the treatment, nature of control groups, duration of treatment, check of fidelity); *process* (e.g., confidence of coding, how missing information is handled); and *effect size* (e.g., outcome measures, sample size). This scheme includes three types of information: variables that are substantively related to the phenomena of interest, variables related to how the phenomena have been studied, and variables that reveal the procedures and judgments of the synthesizer. The researcher should decide on a key set of coding variables, and summarize each study as it is read and analyzed. Wortman (1994) provided an example of a partial coding form that might be the basis for such work.

Coding is a time-consuming aspect of synthesis, and it can pose threats to validity (Orwin, 1994). Complications often arise because studies can be deficient in their reporting as they may omit key information needed by the synthesizer. It is also possible that the way information is reported in a study fails to match well with the coding scheme. Studies, for instance, will sometimes only report aggregate results, even though it would be possible to parcel the variance across various groupings, or they may provide such breakdowns with no aggregate results; either approach can be problematic depending on the synthesis strategy. When the data have been separated by the primary researcher, judgments must be made whether to treat each outcome as a separate study, to take an average of the outcomes, or to select a single representative indicator from each (Lipsey, 1994).

Coding errors are also possible, even when the primary research is well reported; studies are complex and it is easy to miss things. Several ways to reduce coding errors have been proposed. Researchers should, when there are questions about the primary studies, contact the original investigators or turn to external sources for filling in missing information (Orwin, 1994). There are detailed statistical procedures for making missing data decisions (Piggot, 1994). More than one coder should be employed so that independent coding can take place, and interrater agreement can be evaluated (Wanous et al., 1989). Orwin (1994) described how to train coders, pilot the coding protocol, assess reliability, and provide confidence estimates on the various judgments inherent in coding. Nevertheless, this remains one of the less studied, and least understood, aspects of research synthesis.

Analysis of the Findings

Traditional narrative literature reviews tend to rely on subjective determinations of the effects or so-called "box score" or "vote counting" methods, in which the researcher simply counts the number or proportion of studies that arrived at a particular result. These approaches have been criticized because of their failure to take account of the strengths of the effects found in the primary studies, and their inability to account for differences in numbers of participating subjects. Nonparametric analyses of the numbers of studies reporting statistical differences, such as sign tests, suffer from the same weaknesses, and do not actually offer greater precision of analysis.

Methods have been proposed for overcoming these problems, and aggregating the statistical significance across studies (Becker, 1994; Rosenthal, 1978). Each of these methods suffers from various interpretive problems, and none has achieved wide use in reading research.

The preferred method for synthesizing research findings is to calculate effect sizes based on the numbers of participants and the sizes of relationships or differences evident in the primary studies. The effect size statistic was originally formulated for combining the results from experimental studies. Thus, an effect size is the standardized mean difference between experimental and control groups, divided by within-group standard deviation, or $ES = (X_E - X_C)/s_x$. There are now methods for estimating effect sizes from studies using factorial designs, studies without control groups, studies with dichotomous variables, correlational data, and significance tests (Glass et al., 1981; Rosenthal, 1994).

The benefit of the various effect size statistics is that they permit unbiased estimates of the differences and relationships found in the primary studies, and allow these to be compared and combined across studies. Effect size estimates have proven valuable for their ability to identify subtle differences ignored or missed by narrative approaches. Effect sizes are reasonably easy to interpret, too. In an experimental study, a positive effect size indicates that the experimental treatment is successful, whereas a negative effect would mean that the control group had been superior. An effect size of 1.0 means that the treatment led to a 1 standard deviation improvement in outcome. For example, Stahl and Fairbanks (1986) found that the impact on reading comprehension of vocabulary instruction had an effect size of .30. "This indicates that students at the 50th percentile of the instructed groups scored as well as children at the 62nd percentile of the control groups on the global reading comprehension measures" (p. 94).

However, effect sizes have different meanings at different points of the sampling distribution. For example, a treatment with a 1.0 effect size would be expected to move average students, those initially at the 50th percentile, up to the 85th percentile, but it would only be expected to take those who began at the 3rd percentile up to the 16th. This is because standard deviation units vary in size. For the purposes of comparison, a 1 standard deviation difference in terms of elementary reading scores on a standardized test would typically be comparable to a 1-year gain in reading. So if a treatment that lasted for 3 months were associated with an effect size of 1.0, we could assume the students who received this treatment raised their scores about one standard deviation (from whatever point they began) or made about a 1-year gain in reading ability.

Although the statistical interpretation of effect sizes is generally rather simple, they can easily be misunderstood when they have been derived from very different studies.

For instance, I found similar effect sizes for various types of tutoring, including tutoring provided by highly trained teachers, tutoring provided by adult volunteers with minimum training, and peer tutoring arrangements where elementary students taught each other (Shanahan, 1998). The similar effect sizes could be misinterpreted as meaning that the use of highly trained teachers is a waste of resources, as even elementary school students are as effective. However, in the tutoring studies that I examined, highly trained teachers were used only when those being tutored were in need of long-term educational support because of their extensive deficiencies in reading, and peer tutoring was usually used with normal learners for brief periods of time. The effects were roughly equal, but the conditions under which they were derived require different interpretations.

Another problem with effect sizes is that they can offer a sense of greater precision or accuracy than they actually possess (Cook & Leviton, 1980). This is not much a problem if the researcher has identified a comprehensive or nearly comprehensive collection of studies, if the studies are truly representative of relevant research (meaning that error will be randomized), or if sources of bias are identified and analyzed. However, if this kind of care has not been taken, then effect size calculations can make the findings appear to be more scientific than they deserve.

In traditional reviews, synthesizers would hope to find a collection of studies with reasonably homogeneous findings. They would strive to select studies with similar outcomes, although this would introduce error and arbitrariness. In contrast, meta-analysis depends on variation (Light & Pillemer, 1984). By using the varied effect sizes calculated for each of the primary studies as the dependent measure, it becomes possible for the researcher, subjectively or through multiple regression analysis, to parcel out the variance. This allows the researcher to examine reasons for the differences in effect sizes. It becomes possible to search for publication bias (do studies in special education journals attribute greater effectiveness to phonics instruction than do those in reading journals?), to determine whether population estimates change over time (are recent studies more or less likely to find significant improvement from study skills programs than older studies?), or to connect variation with a variety of substantive independent variables.

Effect size is only useful for making sense of quantitative results, of course, and it is not applicable with most case studies, ethnographies, or single-subject designs. As these more qualitative approaches seem to be on the increase in reading research, this is a serious limitation. It is important that the synthesizer find ways to summarize both kinds of information. Light and Pillemer (1984) give many reasons why qualitative research should be used to help explain, interpret, and amplify the statistical or quantitative results. Qualitative information allows for the documentation of process differences. It can help with interpretation when critical outcomes or conditions are difficult to measure quantitatively, when there are multiple levels of impact, and when subtle differences exist between conditions that have received the same label. Qualitative information can help to qualify consistent findings, and to help in the interpretation of inconsistent ones.

Reporting the Results

Various reporting criteria have been proposed for research synthesis (Becker, 1991; Bem, 1995; Ellis, 1991; Jackson, 1980). Bem pointed out that reviews are difficult to write, because they can turn into "mind-numbing lists of citations and findings that resemble a phone book—impressive cast, lots of numbers, but not much plot" (p. 172). Most editorial problems with research syntheses appear to focus on clarity, and the various guidelines suggest several ways to enhance clarity of purpose, problem definition, arguments, and conclusions. For example, they recommend that authors not allow subpoints or the analysis of needless literatures to overwhelm the major findings of the synthesis, and they highlight the importance of providing clear-cut conclusions.

Bem (1995) went on to suggest that although there is no one way to organize a review, conceptual clarity is most likely when the synthesis adopts a plan built around a guiding theory, a set of competing models, or a particular point of view. This is in marked contrast to advice that traditional empirical study format (introduction, method, results, implications) be used with synthesis research (Cooper, 1982). Examples of both conceptual and traditional empirical organizational strategies are evident in the reading research literature, and both can be effective.

Unlike style issues, there is no disagreement among research synthesizers about the need for explicitness in reporting the variety of judgements underlying the study. "A widely held precept in all the sciences is that reports of research ought to include enough information about the study that the reader can critically examine the evidence. This precept should probably also apply to integrative reviews, since such reviews are a form of research" (Jackson, 1980, p. 456).

Research syntheses should clearly specify the search strategies used. This means that the review should include statements that specify all sources used (including which computerized databases), all subject headings and other descriptors including a specification of how these were used singly and in combination, and selection principles (Dunkin, 1996). Unexplained selectivity undermines the validity of the synthesis; studies that fall within the scope of the review can only be excluded when the reviewer explains or justifies the exclusion. This kind of detailed explanation of decisions and judgments allows others to identify systematic bias that might be influencing the conclusions of the synthesis, and it provides the basis for future replication and extension. It is essential that a list of the studies reviewed be included in the report.

In terms of summarizing the primary studies, there is a need for balance between the demands of clarity and interesting reporting on the one hand, and the demand for scientific thoroughness and explicitness on the other. Rather than providing narrative summaries of all studies included, it is usually best to provide essential coding and reference information in tabular form. Key studies can then be used to illustrate the major findings of the synthesis.

CONCLUSIONS

Ultimately, no matter what methodological choices are made, synthesis research is about arriving at valid descriptions of or generalizations about the accumulation of knowledge. Thus, the synthesis researcher is engaged in the enterprise of determining the nature of intellectual progress in the field (Mosenthal & Kamil, 1991). Synthesis, more than any other empirical approach, tends to convey the sense that it is arriving at some immutable and complete conception of truth because of its rhetorical power in describing what we have found out collectively and what still needs to be understood. However, like any empirical method, its purchase on "truth" is tied directly to the theoretical perspectives and methodological approaches used to generate its findings.

REFERENCES

Barr, R., Kamil, M. L., Mosenthal, P., & Pearson, P. D. (Eds.). (1991). *Handbook of reading research* (Vol. 2). New York: Longman.

Becker, B. J. (1994). Combining significance levels. In H. Cooper & L. V. Hedges (Eds.), *The handbook of research synthesis* (pp. 215–230). New York: Russell Sage Foundation.

Becker, B. J. (1991). The quality and credibility of research reviews: What the editors say. *Personality and Social Psychology Bulletin, 17,* 267–272.

Bem, D. J. (1995). Writing a review article for *Psychological Bulletin. Psychological Bulletin, 118,* 172–177.

Brown, G. P. (1906). *On the teaching of English. Fifth Yearbook of the National Society for the Study of Education* (Part 1). Bloomington, IN: NSSE.

Cattell, J. M. (1886). The time it takes to name and see objects. *Mind, 11,* 63–65.

Cook, T. D., & Leviton, L. C. (1980). Reviewing the literature: A comparison of traditional methods with meta-analysis. *Journal of Personality, 48,* 449–472.

Cooper, H. M. (1982). Scientific guidelines for conducting integrative research reviews. *Review of Educational Research, 52,* 291–302.

Cooper, H. M. (1995). Literature searching strategies of integrative research reviews. *American Psychologist, 40,* 1267–1269.

Cooper, H. M., Door, N., & Bettencourt, B. A. (1995). Putting to rest some old notions about social science. *American Psychologist, 50,* 111–112.

Cooper, H. M., & Rosenthal, R. (1980). Statistical versus traditional procedures for summarizing research findings. *Psychological Bulletin, 87,* 442–449.

Cooper, H. M., & Hedges, L. V. (Eds.). (1994). *The handbook of research synthesis.* New York: Russell Sage Foundation.

Dunkin, M. J. (1996). Types of errors in synthesizing research in education. *Review of Educational Research, 66,* 87–97.

Dykstra, R. (1984). Foreword. In P. D. Pearson, R. Barr, M. L. Kamil, & P. Mosenthal (Eds.), *Handbook of reading research* (pp. xix–xx). New York: Longman.

Ellis, M. V. (1981). Conducting and reporting integrative research reviews: Accumulating scientific knowledge. *Counselor Education and Supervision, 30,* 225–237.

Flood, J., Heath, S. B., & Lapp, D. (1997). *Handbook of research on teaching literacy through communicative and visual arts.* New York: Macmillan.

Flood, J., Jensen, J. M., Lapp, D., & Squire, J. R. (Eds.). (1991). *Handbook of research on teaching the English language arts.* New York: Macmillan.

Garfield, E. (1989). Reviewing review literature. *Essays of an information scientist 10,* 113–122). Philadelphia: ISI Press.

Garvey, W. D., & Griffith, B. C. (1979). Scientific communication as a social system. In W. D. Garvey (Ed.), *Communication: The essence of science* (pp. 148–164). Oxford, England: Pergamon Press.

Glass, G. V., McGaw, B., & Smith, M. L. (1981). *Meta-analysis in social research.* Beverly Hills, CA: Sage.

Gray, W. S. (1925). *Summary of investigations relating to reading.* Chicago: University of Chicago Press.

Gray, W. S. (1937). *The teaching of reading.* Thirty-sixth Yearbook of the National Society for the Study of Education (Part 1). Chicago: NSSE.

Gray, W. S. (1984). *Reading* (J. T. Guthrie, Ed.). Newark, DE: International Reading Association. (Original work published 1941)

Green, B. F., & Hall, J. A. (1984). Quantitative methods for literature reviews. *Annual Review of Psychology, 35,* 37–53.

Green, J. L. (1992). Multiple perspectives: Issues and directions. In R. Beach, J. L., Green, M. L. Kamil, & T. Shanahan (Eds.), *Multidisciplinary perspectives on literacy research* (pp. 19–33). Urbana, IL: National Conference on Research in English.

Greenwald, A. G. (1975). Consequences of prejudice against the null hypothesis. *Psychological Bulletin, 82,* 10–12.

Guthrie, J. T., Seifert, M., & Mosberg, L. (1983). Research synthesis in reading: Topics, audiences, and citation rates. *Reading Research Quarterly, 19,* 16–27.

Harris, T. L., & Hodges, R. E. (1995). *The literacy dictionary.* Newark, DE: International Reading Association.

Henry, N. B. (1956). *Adult reading. Fifty-sixth yearbook of the National Society for the Study of Education* (Part 2). Chicago: NSSE.

Henry, N. B. (1961). *Development in and through reading: Sixtieth yearbook of the National Society for the Study of Education* (Part 1). Chicago: NSSE.

Henry, N. B. (1949). *Reading in the elementary school: Forty-eighth yearbook of the National Society for the Study of Education* (Part 2). Chicago: NSSE.

Henry, N. B. (1948). *Reading in the high school and college: Forty-seventh yearbook of the National Society for the Study of Education* (Part 2). Chicago: NSSE.

Hudelson, E. (1923). *English composition: Its aims, methods, and measurement: Twenty-second yearbook of the National Society for the Study of Education.* Bloomington, IL: NSSE.

Huey, E. B. (1968). *The psychology and pedagogy of reading.* Cambridge, MA: MIT Press. (Original work published 1908)

Jackson, G. B. (1980). Methods for integrative reviews. *Review of Educational Research, 50,* 438–460.

Javal, E. (1879). Essai sur la physiologie de la lecture. *Annales d'Oculsitique, 82,* 242–253.

Kamil, M. L., & Intrator, S. M. (1999). Quantitative trends in publication of research on technology and reading, writing, and literacy. *National Reading Conference Yearbook, 47,* 385–396.

Kamil, M. L., & Lane, D. M. (1998). Researching the relationship between technology and literacy: An agenda for the 21st century. In D. Reinking, M. McKenna, L. Labbo, & R. Kieffer (Eds.), *Handbook of literacy and technology: transformations in a post-typographic world* (pp. 323–342). Mahwah, NJ: Lawrence Erlbaum Associates.

Light, R. J., & Pillemer, D. B. (1984). *Summing up: The science of reviewing research.* Cambridge, MA: Harvard University Press.

Lipsey, M. W. (1994). Identifying potentially interesting variables and analysis opportunities. In H. Cooper & L. V. Hedges (Eds.), *The handbook of research synthesis* (pp. 111–124). New York: Russell Sage Foundation.

Marckwardt, A. H. (Ed.). (1970). *Linguistics in school programs. Sixty-ninth yearbook of the National Society for the Study of Education* (Part 2). Chicago: NSSE.

Masterman, M. (1970). The nature of paradigm. In I. Lakatos & A. Musgrave (Eds.), *Criticism and the growth of knowledge* (pp. 59–89). London: Cambridge University Press.

Morgan, W. P. (1896). A case of congenital word-blindness. *British Medical Journal, 2,* 1612–1614.

Mosenthal, P. B., & Kamil, M. L. (1991). Epilogue: Understanding progress in reading research. In R. Barr, M. L. Kamil, P. Mosenthal, & P. D. Pearson (Eds.), *Handbook of reading research* (Vol. 2, pp. 1013–1046). New York: Longman.

Nelson, N., & Calfee, R. (1998). *The reading-writing connection: Ninety-seventh yearbook of the National Society for the Study of Education* (Part 2). Chicago: NSSE.

Orwin, R. G. (1994). Evaluating coding decisions. In H. Cooper & L. V. Hedges (Eds.), *The handbook of research synthesis* (pp. 139–162). New York: Russell Sage Foundation.

Pearson, P. D., Barr, R., Kamil, M. L., & Mosenthal, P. (Eds.). (1984). *Handbook of reading research.* New York: Longman.

Petrosky, A. R., & Bartholomae, D. (1986). *The teaching of writing: Eighty-fifth yearbook of the National Society for the Study of Education* (Part 2). Chicago: NSSE.

Piggot, T. D. (1994). Methods for handling missing data in research synthesis. In H. Cooper & L. V. Hedges (Eds.), *The handbook of research synthesis* (pp. 163–176). New York: Russell Sage Foundation.

Purves, A. C. (1994). *Encyclopedia of English studies and language arts.* New York: Scholastic.

Purves, A. C., & Niles, O. (1984). *Becoming readers in a complex society: Eighty-third yearbook of the National Society for the Study of Education* (Part 1). Chicago: NSSE.

Robinson, H. M. (1968). *Innovation and change in reading instruction: Sixty-seventh yearbook of the National Society for the Study of Education* (Part 2). Chicago: NSSE.

Rosenthal, R. (1978). Combining results of independent studies. *Psychological Bulletin, 85,* 185–193.

Rosenthal, R. (1979). The "file drawer problem" and tolerance for null results. *Psychological Bulletin, 85,* 185–193.

Rosenthal, R. (1994). Parametric measures of effect size. In H. Cooper & L. V. Hedges (Eds.), *The handbook of research synthesis* (pp. 231–244). New York: Russell Sage Foundation.

Shanahan, T. (1998). On the effectiveness and limitations of tutoring in reading. In P. D. Pearson & A. Iran-Nejad (Eds.), *Review of Research in Education, 23,* 217–234. Washington, DC: American Educational Research Association.

Shanahan, T., & Barr, R. (1995). Reading Recovery: An independent evaluation of the effects of an early instructional intervention for at risk learners. *Reading Research Quarterly, 30,* 958–997.

Shanahan, T., & Kamil, M. L. (1994). *Academic libraries and research in the teaching of English.* Champaign, IL: Center for the Study of Reading.

Slavin, R. E. (1986). Best evidence synthesis: An alternative to meta-analytic and traditional reviews. *Educational Researcher, 15*(9), 5–11.

Snow, C. E., Burns, M. S., & Griffin, P. (1998). *Preventing reading difficulties in young children.* Washington, DC: National Academy Press.

Sohn, D. (1995). Meta-analysis as a means of discovery. *American Psychologist, 50,* 108–110.

Squire, J. R. (1977). *The teaching of English: Seventy-sixth yearbook of the National Society for the Study of Education* (Part 1). Chicago: NSSE.

Stahl, S. A., & Fairbanks, M. M. (1986). The effects of vocabulary instruction: A model-based meta-analysis. *Review of Educational Research, 56,* 72–110.

Stock, W. A. (1994). Systematic coding for research synthesis. In H. Cooper & L. V. Hedges (Eds.), *The handbook of research synthesis* (pp. 125–138). New York: Russell Sage Foundation.

Wanous, J. P., Sullivan, S. E., & Malinak, J. (1989). The role of judgment calls in meta-analysis. *Journal of Applied Psychology, 74,* 259–264.

Whipple, G. M. (1921). *Factors affecting results in silent reading, and exercises for making reading function: Twentieth yearbook of the National Society for the Study of Education* (Part 2). Bloomington, IL: NSSE.

Whipple, G. M. (1925). *Report of the National Committee on Reading: Twenty-fourth yearbook of the National Society for the Study of Education.* Bloomington, IL: NSSE.

White, H. D. (1994). Scientific communication and literature retrieval. In H. Cooper & L. V. Hedges (Eds.), *The handbook of research synthesis* (pp. 41–56). New York: Russell Sage Foundation.

Wilson, P. (1992). Searching: Strategies and evaluation. In H. D. White, M. J. Bates, & P. Wilson (Eds.), *For information specialists: Interpretations of reference and bibliographic work* (pp. 153–181). Philadelphia: ISI Press.

Wortman, P. M. (1994). Judging research quality. In H. Cooper & L. V. Hedges (Eds.), *The handbook of research synthesis* (pp. 97–110). New York: Russell Sage Foundation.

Author Index

W

Wade, S., 96, *102*, 137
Waern, Y., 89, *102*
Wagner, R. K., 137
Walker, B. J., 5, 9, 11, *19*
Walker, R. J., 42, *45*
Wallace, S., 84, *85*
Walsh, C., 72, *75*
Wanous, J. P., 144, 146, *150*
Warner, M. M., 113, *118*
Watkins, J., 29, *32*
Watson-Gegeo, K. A., 81, *86*
Watson, J., 88, *102*
Weaver, J., 5, 9, 13, 15, *20*
Weber, R., 37, 39, *45*
Weiler, K., 71, 72, *75*
Weiss, C. H., 27, *32*
Weiss, L., 93, *99*
Wells, D., 28, *31*
Wells, G., 2, *22*
Welty, E., 56, *63*
Wenger, E., 89, *101*, 120, 125, *130*, *131*
Werner, H., 88, 94, *102*
Wertsch, J. V., 93, *102*, 120, 126, *131*
Wexler, P., 69, 71, 73, *75*
Whipple, G. M., 135, *150*
White, H. D., 138, 139, 141, 142, 143, *150*
Whitehead, A. N., viii, *x*
Wieder, D. L., 126, *131*
Wigfield, A., 25, *31*, 66, *75*
Wilkinson, I. A. G., 136

Williams, G., 123, *130*
Williams, J. M., 15, *19*
Williams, L., 93, *99*
Williams, W. O., 27, *31*
Willinsky, J., 73, *75*
Willis, A. I., 26, *32*
Willis, P., 69, *75*
Wilson, P., 143, *150*
Wilson, T., 89, *101*
Wimsatt, W., 91, *102*
Wineburg, S., 91, 94, *102*, *103*
Winograd, P., 90, *100*
Winograd, T., 121, *131*
Wixson, K., 93, *101*, 108, *118*
Wolfgang, C. H., 111, *118*
Wolf, M., 108, *118*
Wolf, M. M., 53, *63*, 106, 108, *117*, *118*
Wolf, R. M., 23, *32*
Women on Words and Images, 39, *45*
Wood, K., 6, 10, 14, *22*
Woolgar, S., 120, *130*
Worthy, J., 27, *31*
Wortman, P. M., 143, 145, *150*
Wright, C. R., 27, *31*
Wyatt, D., 91, 94, *103*

Y

Yaden, D. B., 25, *32*
Young, J. P., 51, 52, *61*, *63*
Young, K., 91, *101*, *103*
Young, M. F. D., 65, *75*

Subject Index

identification and selection of, 138–145
  searching for, 140–143
Subjectivity, 53–54, 84
Subjects, 145
Substantive theory, 16

T

Talented readers, protocol analysis of, 92–93
Talk story, 49–50, 83
Teacher research, *see also* Literacy research
  definition of, 2
  methodology in, 1–22
  as new genre, 17–18
  themes and categories in, 7*t*–8*t*, 8–16, 9*t*–11*t*
Technology, new studies of, 120–121
Theory, 125–126
  and teacher research, 7*t*, 12
  undergirding, identification of, 39–40
Think-aloud protocols, nature of, 94, 96–97
Think scene, 52
Topic, identification of, 39
Transfer of effects, measurement of, 107
Treatment, 145
Truth claims, crisis of, 54–56
Truth, versus power, 72

U

Unsettling process, 7*t*, 13–14

V

Verbal reports, 87–103
  content of, 90–94
  history of, 87–90
  issues in, 94, 95*t*
Verge, viii
Verisimilitude, 55

W

What, in discourse, 126–128
Who, in discourse, 126–128
World-building situated meanings, 126–128
  definition of, 122–123
Writing
  of historical research, 42–43
  narrative approaches, 47–63
  of research synthesis, 147-148
  of teacher research, 8*t*, 15–16